More praise for
THE END OF EMPIRE

"Kelly's well-told and reliable account is the best to have come along in years, showing a judicious approach to archaeological evidence that one could wish more widely imitated."
—Michael Kulikowski, professor of history, University of Tennessee, *London Review of Books*

"Kelly has an unrivalled feel for the power game of late antiquity. His shrewd sympathy brings to life the concerns not only of Byzantine eunuchs and nomadic warlords, but also of their victims, as he steers the hapless ambassadors at the centre of his account, a brilliantly imagined Rosencrantz and Guildenstern, through times more disastrously out of joint than their philosophy could conceive."
—Neil McLynn, professor of classics, Oxford University

"A thoughtful and sophisticated account of a notoriously complicated and controversial period."
—R. I. Moore, *Times Literary Supplement*

"An imaginative account of the man who humbled the mighty Roman Empire."
—Bryan Ward-Perkins, author of *The Fall of Rome and the End of Civilisation*

"With the grace of a good storyteller, Kelly narrates the Huns' origins as nomadic peoples who eventually settled in the Great Hungarian Plain. . . . Kelly's first-rate history provides a singularly fresh look at a fractious period in the life of ancient Rome."
—*Publishers Weekly*

ALSO BY CHRISTOPHER KELLY

Ruling the Later Roman Empire
The Roman Empire: A Very Short Introduction

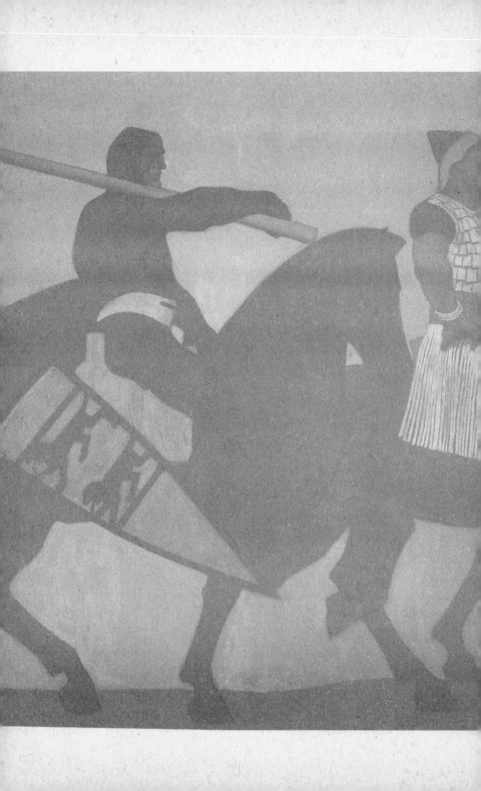

THE END OF EMPIRE

Attila the Hun and the Fall of Rome

CHRISTOPHER KELLY

W. W. NORTON & COMPANY
New York London

For information about permission to reproduce selections from this book,
write to Permissions, W. W. Norton & Company, Inc., 500 Fifth Avenue,
New York, NY 10110

For information about special discounts for bulk purchases, please contact
W. W. Norton Special Sales at specialsales@wwnorton.com or 800-233-4830

Manufacturing by RR Donnelley, Bloomsburg
Book design by Iris Weinstein
Maps by Adrian Kitzinger
Production manager: Anna Oler

Library of Congress Cataloging-in-Publication Data

Kelly, Christopher, 1964–
[Attila the Hun]
The end of empire : Attila the Hun and the fall of Rome /
Christopher Kelly. — 1st American ed.
p. cm.
Originally published: Attila the Hun : barbarian terror and
the fall of the Roman Empire. London : Bodley Head, 2008.
Includes bibliographical references and index.
ISBN 978-0-393-06196-3 (hardcover)
1. Attila, d. 453. 2. Huns—Biography. 3. Huns—History. 4. Rome—History—Empire,
284–476. I. Title.
D141.K45 2009
937'.09—dc22   2009009072

ISBN 978-0-393-33849-2 pbk.

W. W. Norton & Company, Inc.
500 Fifth Avenue, New York, N. Y. 10110
www.wwnorton.com

W. W. Norton & Company Ltd.
Castle House, 75/76 Wells Street, London W1T 3QT

1 2 3 4 5 6 7 8 9 0

FOR MY MOTHER
(1937–2009)

CONTENTS

ACKNOWLEDGMENTS

Warm thanks are due to a small—but fiercely loyal—band. For their thoughts, enthusiasm, and help I wish to particularly mention Julian Alexander, Richard Flower, Maria Guarnaschelli, Jörg Hengsen, Stuart Hill, Bettany Hughes, Gavin Kelly, Jan and Tony Leaver, Margaret Maloney, Rosamond McKitterick, Lily Richards, Will Sulkin, and Melanie Tortoroli. I am also most grateful to the Leverhulme Trust for its generous award of a Senior Research Fellowship, 2006–2008.

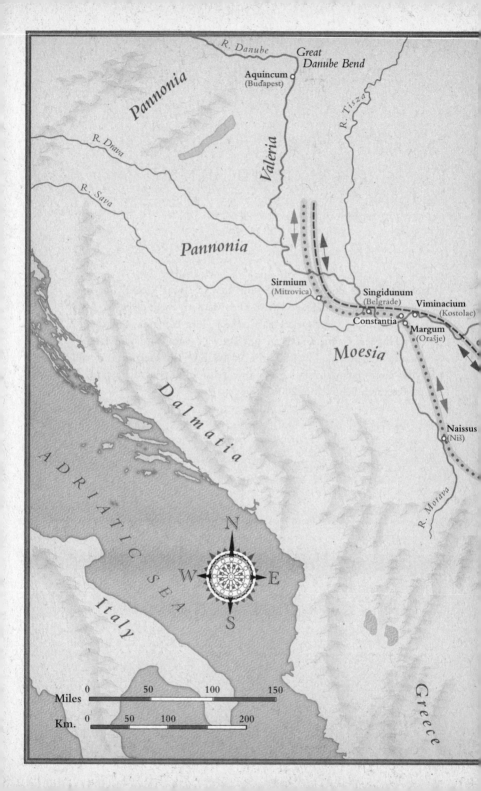

HUN CAMPAIGNS
IN THE BALKANS

•••••• The Campaign of 441–42

– – – The Campaign of 447

CARPATHIAN MOUNTAINS

R. Danube

Durostorum
(Silistra)

Ratiara
(Archar)

Novae
(Svishtov)

Marcianople

R. Utus
(R. Vit)

M o e s i a

BLACK SEA

Serdica
(Sofia)

Philippopolis
(Plovdiv)

T h r a c e

Arcadiopolis
(Lüleburgaz)

Adrianople
(Edirne)

Bosphorus

Constantinople
(Istanbul)

Heraclea
(Ereğli)

Panium

Athyras

Thessalonica
(Thessaloniki)

SEA of MARMARA

Callipolis
(Gelibolu)

Sestus
(Eceabat)

AEGEAN SEA

THE

MEDITERRANEAN

WORLD

—⚜—

*c.*450

━━━━━━ ⋯⋯⋯⋯⋯⋯ Extent of the Eastern and Western Roman Empires

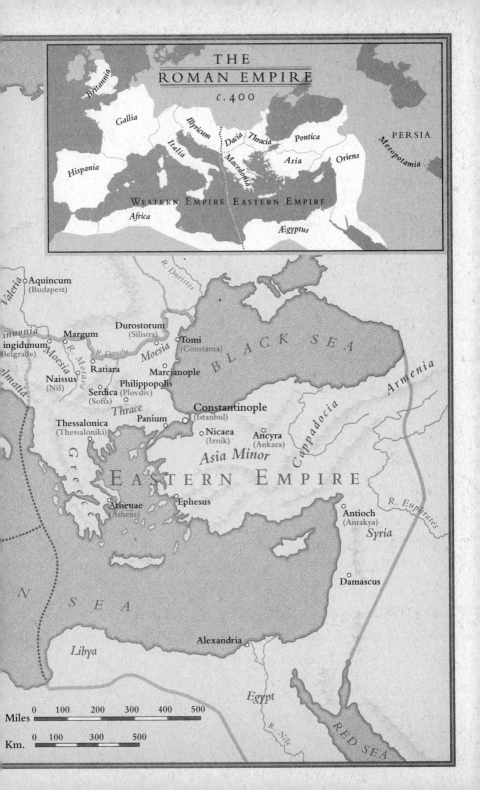

THE
ROMAN EMPIRE
c. 400

Britannia

Gallia

Illyricum

Dacia

Thracia

Pontica

PERSIA

Italia

Macedonia

Asia

Oriens

Mesopotamia

Hispania

WESTERN EMPIRE EASTERN EMPIRE

Africa

Ægyptus

Valeria

Aquincum
(Budapest)

R. Dneister

Pannonia

Margum

Durostorum
(Silistra)

Tomi
(Constanta)

BLACK SEA

ingidunum
(Belgrade)

R. Morava

R. Danube

Moesia

Moesia

Ratiara

Marcianople

Armenia

almatia

Naissus
(Niš)

Serdica
(Sofia)

Philippopolis
(Plovdiv)

Thrace

Panium

Constantinople
(Istanbul)

Cappadocia

Thessalonica
(Thessaloniki)

Nicaea
(Iznik)

Ancyra
(Ankara)

Greece

Asia Minor

EASTERN EMPIRE

Athenae
(Athens)

Ephesus

Antioch
(Antakya)

R. Euphrates

Syria

N

SEA

Damascus

Libya

Alexandria

Egypt

R. Nile

RED SEA

Miles 0   100   200   300   400   500

Km. 0   100   300   500

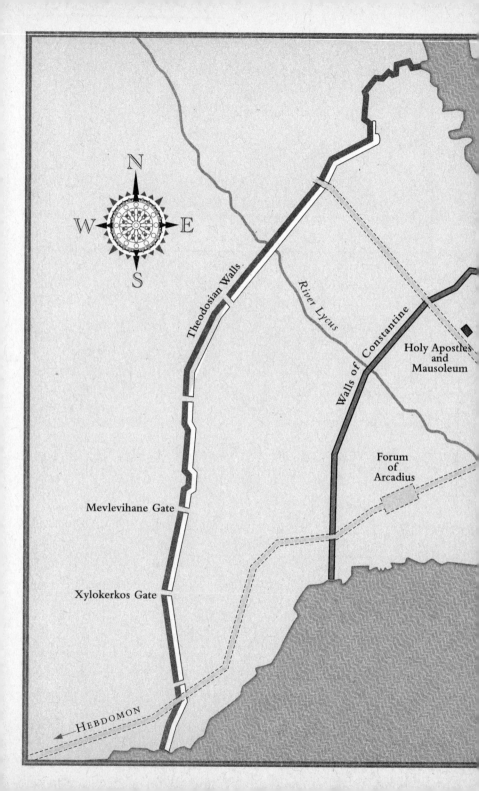

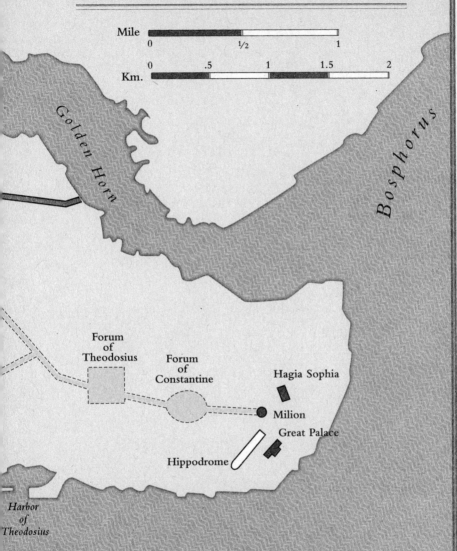

CONSTANTINOPLE

Mile

0   ½   1

0   .5   1   1.5   2

Km.

Golden Horn

Bosphorus

Forum
of
Theodosius

Forum
of
Constantine

Hagia Sophia

Milion

Great Palace

Hippodrome

*Harbor
of
Theodosius*

PROPONTIS

(Sea of Marmara)

THE END OF EMPIRE

Now what will become of us without barbarians?
Those people were some kind of solution.

—CONSTANTINE CAVAFY, *"Waiting for the Barbarians" (1898)*

THE *STRAVA* OF ATTILA THE HUN

Carefully concealed in the long grass that covered the plain, the Roman spies watched with growing fear and amazement. In the center of a cluster of tents pitched between wagons stood a splendid silken pavilion. Its open sides allowed a clear view of the body of Attila the Hun. He was short with a broad chest and a large head. Those who had seen him while alive reported that his eyes were small, his beard sparse and flecked with gray, his nose flatish, and his complexion dark. This was the powerful physique of a man who had died suddenly in his prime, a battle-hardened warrior used to fighting and to traveling for hours on horseback. This was the brilliant commander who had transformed a disorderly band of smash-and-grab nomads into a disciplined force that in the first half of the fifth century AD had marched a thousand miles across Europe from the shores of the Black Sea in Romania to the fertile fields of Champagne in France. Attila the Hun was one of the most frightening enemies ever faced by the Romans. In lightning raids his army destroyed dozens of prosperous and wealthy cities that had remained secure for centuries and even threatened Rome—the Eternal City— itself.

The Huns honored Attila in death as in life. His body, draped in rare oriental silks, glittered with magnificent jewelry, costly gifts from Roman emperors hoping to buy off an enemy whom they had repeatedly failed to defeat. On his shoulder gleamed a great golden brooch set with a single slice of onyx the size of a man's palm. Like the dark waters of the Danube glinting in the sharp summer sun, the deep purple stone flashed with the fire of burning brands held high by the horsemen riding wildly around the tent. The faces of these young men were disfigured and smeared with blood. According to the Roman historian Priscus of Panium, they had cut their long hair and slashed their cheeks "so that the greatest of all warriors should be mourned not with tears or the wailing of women but with the blood of men."

Then followed a day of grief, feasting, and funeral games: a combination of celebration and lamentation that had a long history in the ancient world. Priscus may have been reminded of the games, movingly described by Homer, that the Greek hero Achilles held for his fallen companion Patroclus before the walls of Troy. Twelve centuries after Homer, the Huns raced horses to salute the achievements of their dead leader. That night, far beyond the frontiers of the Roman empire, Attila was buried. His body was encased in three coffins: the innermost covered in gold, a second in silver, and a third in iron. The gold and silver symbolized the plunder that Attila had seized, while the harsh gray iron recalled his victories in war. The tomb was filled with the weapons of enemies defeated in battle, precious jewels, and other treasures. The servants responsible for preparing the burial were killed so that they could not reveal its location. These, too, were honorable deaths, part of the *strava*, the Hunnic for a funeral—and thanks to Priscus' account the only word of Hunnic to have survived.

What most impressed the Romans secretly watching these ceremonies was the dirge solemnly intoned by the horsemen who galloped around Attila's tent. It was a slow, deep, rhythmical chant commemorating a great leader who had established an empire for his own people and hastened the collapse of Roman rule in western Europe. No Roman could hear these words with-

out remembering the terror that Attila had inspired. No Hun
could ask for a more fitting epitaph.

> *Attila the king,*
> *Chief of the Huns,*
> *Born of his father Mundiuch,*
> *Lord of the bravest tribes.*
> *He who captured cities,*
> *He who brought fear to the Romans and their empire.*
> *Their prayers moved him;*
> *He accepted payments each year to save the rest from plunder.*
> *Attila accomplished all this through his great good fortune.*
> *He fell not by an enemy's blow,*
> *Nor by the treachery of his own followers.*
> *But he died peacefully,*
> *Happy in his joy,*
> *Without pain,*
> *His people safe.*
> *Who can call this death?*
> *When none considers that it demands vengeance?*

PART ONE

BEFORE ATTILA

CHAPTER ONE
FIRST CONTACT

No one in the Roman empire had ever heard of the Huns. It was not until the 370s, a generation before the birth of Attila, that they first fought their way into history. Then reports reached Roman troops guarding the Danube frontier of the sudden appearance of a savage people north of the Black Sea. It was not known how far they had traveled (the possibilities, ranging from Mongolia to Kazakhstan, will be explored at the end of chapter 3). The newcomers were led by fierce warriors on horseback; their families followed slowly in covered wagons. Moving west across the steppes of Asia, they brought terror and disruption to the edges of Europe.

Around the Black Sea—in modern Ukraine and Romania—the Huns encountered the Goths: first the Greuthungi (the collective label Roman observers applied to those who controlled the territory between the Don and the Dniester Rivers) and then the Tervingi (between the Dniester and the Danube). In 375 the Tervingi leader Athanaric marched north to reinforce a group of Greuthungi pushed back by the Huns' advance. The campaign was unsuccessful. Athanaric's camp on the banks of the Dniester was attacked in the night by Huns who had forded the river by moonlight. The Tervingi troops scattered, and the Huns swept onward, in the words of one Roman historian, "like an avalanche

figures 1 and 2
Emperor Valens, gold medallion from the Șimleu Silvaniei treasure.

from the mountaintops, carrying away or destroying everything in their path."

Athanaric's failure to halt the Huns was only to be expected. Six years earlier he had negotiated the end of a war with the Roman emperor Valens (see figures 1 and 2). Although they had avoided a major battle, three years of intermittent conflict had wrecked the Tervingi's farms and villages. The slow recovery weakened Athanaric's authority, and a number of high-ranking Tervingi now openly contested his right to rule. Fritigern was the most ambitious; rebuffed in his first challenge in the early 370s, he had taken refuge inside the Roman empire. His second attempt to seize power was financed by Valens. In bankrolling Fritigern the emperor hoped to engineer Athanaric's downfall and his replacement by a more cooperative regime. Roman interference in Tervingi internal affairs could not have come at a worse time. Fritigern's opposition undermined the Goths' attempts to defend their territory. He had no intention of joining Athanaric and continuing the fight, preferring to retreat rather than face the Huns. In spring 376 Fritigern and his ally Alavivus ordered their followers to head straight for the Danube. Pressing hard against the Roman frontier, eighty thousand Tervingi insisted that they had nowhere to go but into the empire. In the dramatic vision of one Roman contemporary, "a great crowd . . . standing on the opposite riverbank stretched out their hands with cries and lamentations, begging to be allowed to cross."

Valens granted their request. To refuse was too dangerous: the Danube defenses were not strong enough to hold back such large numbers, nor could reinforcements be brought up quickly. The bulk of the Roman army was six hundred miles away in Syria preparing for an expedition against the Persians farther east in Armenia. For the moment, it made no sense to resist the Tervingi and risk the collapse of a key section of the northern frontier. There were advantages, too, in accepting their offer to settle on land south of the Danube. Here the Tervingi could act as a buffer against any future threats (from the Huns or other Goths), and their young men could be drafted into the Roman army or employed as mercenaries. Fritigern and Alavivus were certainly aware that Valens was unwilling to offer resettlement to all asylum seekers. A group of Greuthungi, also fleeing from the chaos caused by the Huns, was denied permission to enter the empire. They were left to fend for themselves as best they could.

For several days and nights, the Tervingi were ferried across the Danube at one of its narrowest points, near the garrison town of Durostorum, sixty miles west of the Black Sea. This was a dangerous operation made more difficult by the fast-flowing river, still swollen by spring rains. Many Tervingi, frustrated by the slow progress and distrustful of Roman military supervision, ventured across in canoes made from hollowed-out logs; the most desperate decided to swim. Some were drowned when overcrowded rafts capsized. Darkness brought only greater confusion: the shouts of terrified families separated in the crush to board the boats, the wash of dead bodies against the banks, and the harsh orders barked by unsympathetic soldiers. The situation was beyond Lupicinus, the Roman commander on the frontier. Without warning, he was faced with eighty thousand refugees crammed together in a makeshift camp. The overflowing latrine trenches threatened an outbreak of disease; the stench drifted into nearby Durostorum. Half-starved Goths crowded around the grain wagons, whose infrequent deliveries were made under heavy guard. Some paid huge sums for food on the black market. Others were able to buy dog meat only by selling their children as slaves. The going rate was said to be one child for each dog. Many of those loyal to Fritigern and Alavivus must have wondered whether they should have followed them into the Roman empire; perhaps it would have been better to have stayed behind to support Athanaric and fight the Huns.

In early 377, seven months after the Danube crossing, the internment camp was in danger of slipping out of Roman control. Lupicinus ordered the Tervingi to be moved fifty miles south to Marcianople, a substantial walled town recently strengthened as the base for Valens' three-year campaign against these same Goths. Lupicinus also decided to deal with Fritigern and Alavivus. He invited them to dinner, but permitted only their bodyguard to enter Marcianople. The unrest in the crowd of Tervingi surging angrily against the barred gates of the city was aggravated by hunger and doubts about the safety of their leaders. Their fears were well founded: Fritigern and Alavivus had walked straight into a Roman trap. During dinner Lupicinus had Alavivus and his escort killed; but Fritigern escaped. Lupicinus was later to claim that he had released Fritigern once he had promised to calm the Tervingi now rioting outside the walls. That was probably a lie: a calculated attempt by a second-rate officer to justify a botched operation that should have eliminated both of its targets.

Letting Fritigern get away was not Lupicinus' only blunder. The soldiers escorting the Tervingi on their forced march to Marcianople had been drawn from garrisons along the Danube. In their absence, a large number of Greuthungi crossed the frontier unopposed. These were the same Goths who earlier had been denied permission to enter the empire. In a serious breach of border security, another eighty thousand men, women, and children made it safely into Roman territory. The Greuthungi immediately moved south to join the Tervingi outside Marcianople. The combined force wiped out the troops sent by Lupicinus to put down the rebellion that followed Alavivus' murder and Fritigern's escape. With this defeat went any hope that the Goths might be settled peacefully. The Romans were now at war and with a hostile force that had already entered the empire. Initial attempts to restrict the Goths to territory close to the Danube met with little success. In a bold and imaginative move, Fritigern reinforced his army by inviting a contingent of Huns (perhaps one or two thousand men) to join the Goths as mercenaries. There could be no starker indication of the Roman failure to manage the crisis. In the fight for survival, some of the Tervingi's most feared enemies had now become their allies.

In crossing the Danube, the Goths and their Hun reinforcements confronted an empire that had changed significantly in the four hundred years since the first Roman emperor, Augustus. The consequences of that transformation were most marked at the beginning of the fourth century. Following the conversion of Constantine—the first emperor to embrace Christianity—the church benefited from state support and lavish funding. Christianity was now an imperial concern. Pious emperors claimed a close and privileged relationship with Christ. In art both were shown dressed in royal purple robes. It is unsurprising then that Valens insisted the Tervingi convert to Christianity before they were permitted to enter the empire. This proviso reflected not only the emperor's strong personal convictions but also a genuine belief that the Goths would be more easily integrated if they followed the new faith of the Romans.

Constantine's religious revolution was matched by a radical political reformation. In the two centuries after Augustus, the security of the empire had been guaranteed by an elaborate network of walls, ditches, and forts. Hadrian's Wall in England is only the most westerly fragment of a defensive system that stretched along the Rhine and the Danube as far as the Black Sea. This extensive cordon was an effective solution to the problem of policing the frontiers. That said, the concentration of military assets along the edges of the empire depended on the absence of civil war and any major external threat that might require the rapid transfer of troops from one frontier to another. From the middle of the third century, such stability could no longer be guaranteed. The causes of the increased pressure along the northern frontier are difficult to trace. It may reflect social changes among those peoples living beyond the Rhine–Danube—the direct result of nearly three centuries of contact with the militarized frontier provinces of the empire. Or it may have been simple opportunism as the Roman need to counter an increasingly aggressive Persia drained manpower and resources to the eastern front. In the 270s, a century before the Tervingi fled the Huns, weakened Danube defenses allowed Gothic war bands to raid cities in the Balkans. In the same decade, the Persians pushed as far west as Antioch, in Syria, and even captured a Roman emperor in battle. Only civil war between rival claimants to the Persian throne had prevented the collapse of the eastern frontier.

The Roman empire survived, but at the cost of its unity. The pressing demands of border security exposed the problems of coordinating and deploying military resources across the Mediterranean world. Against modern expectations, communication times were painfully slow and highly variable. Hadrian's Wall and Antioch were 2,400 miles apart. It could take anywhere between 25 and 135 days after an emperor's death in Italy for officials in Egypt to start dating documents in his successor's name. Seaborne news traveled fastest in the early spring and summer, and slowest in the winter, when navigation was often hazardous and sometimes impossible. Given these constraints, an emperor on cam-

paign against Persia was simply too far away—or too dependent
on the loyalty of others—to ensure effective control of Spain or
Britain. Despite attempts by some emperors to prevent the frac-
turing of their authority, by the mid–fourth century the empire
was split between the East (the Balkans, Turkey, the Middle East,
and Egypt) and the West (Italy, France, Spain, Britain, and North
Africa). On some issues the two Roman emperors continued to
cooperate. Laws in both halves of the empire were issued jointly
in their names. There remained a strong dynastic connection. In
the 370s Valens ruled the East, and his nephew Gratian the West.
Even so, across the next century the two Roman empires drifted
apart, a process of separation forcibly accelerated by the military
and economic costs of dealing with the Goths and the Huns.

Strikingly, too, in this new Christian world, Rome was no
longer the capital of the Roman empire, not even of the West.
In the final decades of the fourth century, the western imperial
court moved to Milan and then Ravenna, in northeastern Italy.
Rome was redundant, a crumbling museum to the glories of
an imperial past. Its public spaces were crowded with temples,
statues, and triumphal arches celebrating the achievements of
centuries of generals and emperors who had not fought under
the banner of Christ. The East was ruled from a purpose-built
city on the Bosphorus, now modern Istanbul. This new, model
capital was named after its founder: Constantinople, "the city
of Constantine." (Whatever Constantine had learned from his
conversion to Christianity, it certainly wasn't modesty.) On its
landward side, the city was protected by a massive wall; at its
center was a large, oval forum surrounded by an imposing colon-
nade. A broad avenue, flanked by marble porticoes, connected the
forum to the Great Palace, whose halls, courtyards, and gardens
were fortified, walled, and secluded—like the Forbidden City
or the Kremlin, monuments to the grandeur of imperial power.
Adjacent to the Great Palace, Constantine built a hippodrome on
a scale that would stand comparison to the Circus Maximus, the

famous chariot-racing track in Rome. At 1,400 feet long and 400
wide, it could seat fifty thousand spectators. Above all, Constantinople was designed to impress. For one admiring provincial,
it was "the all-golden city." The midday sun, catching the walls
and terraces of some of the finest buildings in the empire, flashed
like fire from roofs sheathed in polished bronze. Viewed across
the glinting waters of the Bosphorus, the city—as if heated in a
crucible—seemed to rise out of a sea of liquid metal. The golden
dome of the imperial mausoleum glowed bright on the summit
of its highest hill. Even at night Constantinople shimmered; it
was one of the few cities in the Roman empire to have street
lighting.

The foundation of Constantinople at the beginning of the
fourth century altered the political geography of the Mediterranean world. Near the Great Palace stood the Milion, a marble
pillar marking the starting point of the major roads that ran out
of the capital and connected it with the provinces beyond. The
parallel with Rome was deliberate. In 20 BC Augustus had placed
the so-called Golden Milestone in the middle of the Roman
Forum to symbolize the city's position at the center of an imperial world. Then all roads had led to Rome. By the beginning of
the fifth century, Constantinople was the undisputed focus of the
eastern empire. Straddling seven hills and secure behind its walls,
this dazzling imperial capital more than fulfilled Constantine's
proud boast to have established a "New Rome." Even Augustus,
who once claimed to have transformed (old) Rome from a city
of brick into a city of marble, might have been impressed.

The revolt of the Tervingi—now reinforced by Greuthungi and
Huns—directly threatened this new imperial world. Constan-
tinople was only two hundred miles from the Danube frontier.
Valens had no option but to ensure the safety of the city. Forced

to cancel his plans for a campaign in Armenia, he agreed a truce with the Persian king. In April 378 he began the six-hundred-mile march from his headquarters at Antioch. Without mechanized transport, large armies with long baggage trains move slowly; on average the Roman army covered fifteen miles a day.

The six-week journey to the imperial capital was marred by a disturbing incident. As the soldiers left Antioch, they came across a man lying in the road; from the deep welts covering his body, it looked as if he had been whipped from head to foot. He was motionless and said nothing, but stared wide-eyed at all who came near. The emperor was informed, but not even Valens could command him to speak. This was a troubling moment; according to the historian Zosimus the man "could not be considered alive, because he did not move, yet he was not completely dead, because the eyes seemed bright." Then the body suddenly disappeared. Those who claimed to understand such portents had only ominous explanations to offer: "skilled interpreters concluded that this foretold the condition of the state and that the empire would continue to be beaten and whipped like a dying man."

In Constantinople, Valens' mood worsened. Appearing in the imperial box in the hippodrome, he was jeered by a crowd angry at the time it had taken to deploy adequate forces for the empire's defense—it was now nearly two years since the Tervingi had crossed the Danube. For an emperor to be insulted in public was a breach of ceremonial decorum; presiding over a morning's chariot racing, Valens expected to be welcomed by loud applause and the carefully rehearsed praises of the spectators. Instead, he was greeted with catcalls: "Give us the weapons and we'll do the fighting ourselves." Insulted, the emperor left the capital after only twelve days. Some claimed that he had threatened, after dealing with the Goths, to demolish Constantinople and plow the ruins into the ground.

Valens had good reason to be confident of success. He had received confirmation that his nephew, the western Roman emperor Gratian, was marching to join him. Withdrawing to a country estate not far from the capital, he waited for the reinforcements to arrive. By the end of July, he had held his position for three weeks, but Gratian's progress was delayed by the need to secure the Rhine frontier. He had no intention of jeopardizing the defense of the West by helping his uncle fight a war in the East. At the beginning of August, the Goths began to advance, and Valens responded by moving his forces one hundred miles northeast to the fortified city of Adrianople. This was an aggressive maneuver; Valens was concerned about the vulnerability of the army's supply lines and—despite his ill-tempered threats— the safety of Constantinople. Most of all, he was tired of waiting for Gratian. When military intelligence reported the number of enemy soldiers at around ten thousand, the emperor angrily dismissed those who questioned the estimate. On these figures, he could easily defeat the Goths on his own. Why, then, should he delay and share the glory of victory with his teenage nephew?

Valens' offensive alarmed Fritigern. He may have been concerned about the chances of winning a pitched battle against an imperial army at full strength; or he may have been playing for time, waiting for the Greuthungi cavalry, then operating independently, to return. Envoys sent to Valens offered peace in exchange for permanent settlement within the empire. A confidential letter stressed Fritigern's eagerness to become the emperor's ally, but warned that many Goths would not accept a truce without a show of force. On no account, he insisted, should Roman troops stand down until an agreement had been reached. Valens dismissed the embassy as worthless and Fritigern's offer of friendship as false, but he followed his advice. The following morning—9 August 378—thirty thousand Roman soldiers left Adrianople. Around noon the enemy camp was sighted, and the army took up position: infantry units in the center and cavalry on each wing. Fritigern delayed, still hoping for the arrival of the Greuthungi. Another embassy promising peace was rejected, but later that afternoon Valens finally agreed to talks and the exchange of hostages. The emperor's willingness to negotiate reflected a concern for the deteriorating condition of his men. They were fatigued from standing for several hours in the sun and irritated by the smoke from brush fires deliberately started by the Goths. By midafternoon it must also have become clear that the number of enemy troops was far greater than expected. Roman scouts had seen only part of the army. Once the Gothic war bands had assembled, Valens faced a force roughly the same size as his own. It must now have seemed sensible to have waited for Gratian.

But there was to be no second chance. During the exchange of hostages, one of the frontline Roman units broke ranks, probably an accident on the hot, smoke-obscured battlefield. Once the fighting started, neither side could be held back. The Roman advance was disrupted by the sudden arrival of the Greuthungi horsemen, who attacked and dispersed the cavalry covering the army's left flank. The unprotected infantry was quickly surrounded. As the Goths pressed forward, the Roman line was compressed. Amid the heat and dust, many died, crushed by their comrades. Hampered by piles of corpses, the exhausted troops were unable to regroup. They were butchered as they slipped on the blood-soaked ground. Only nightfall put a stop to the slaughter.

The Battle of Adrianople was the worst defeat suffered by the Romans for seven hundred years: out of thirty thousand troops, twenty thousand were killed. In the chilling phrase of the imperial court orator Themistius, in one summer afternoon "an entire army vanished like a shadow." The impact of this moment of destruction on Roman policymaking cannot be underestimated. Most importantly, the defeat exposed the importance of the Danube frontier to the empire's security. Valens had been critically slow to react to the disruption caused by the emerging menace of the Huns west of the Black Sea. His support of Fritigern hindered

Athanaric's attempts to restore order. The crossing of the Tervingi was poorly managed, and their internment and policing were left to barely competent officers. It took over a year to shut down the planned campaign against Persia and redeploy the army; in the meantime, the Tervingi had been joined by a large number of Greuthungi and a small group of Huns. The decision to fight at Adrianople without waiting for reinforcements from the West was one of the poorest judgment calls made by any emperor in the history of the Roman empire. The scale of the defeat was a direct result of Valens' petulant rush to seize victory on his own.

During the battle, Valens was hit by an arrow. Wounded, he retreated with his bodyguard and sheltered on the upper floor of a nearby farm building. A band of Goths, not knowing that the emperor was inside, set the building on fire. Despite his desperate attempts, Valens was unable to escape. He died a chokingly painful death, suffocated in the blaze. It seemed a final humiliation that his charred corpse was never recovered. The splendid tomb that Valens had prepared for himself in the imperial capital remained empty. He would never rest in peace in the mausoleum that glittered on the highest hill in Constantinople.

CHAPTER TWO
THE AXIS OF EVIL

The Huns did not write a single word of their own history. They can be viewed only through the distorting lens of Roman accounts. Writing in the late 380s, a decade after Valens' death, the Roman historian Ammianus Marcellinus offered his readers a vivid description of the Huns' customs and society. Twenty years earlier they had emerged from the steppes of central Asia and pushed west of the Black Sea, initiating a complex chain of events that eventually led to the Roman defeat at Adrianople. Of course, no one could blame the Huns directly for this disaster, but Ammianus' contemporaries remained fascinated by a people so barbarous that they had terrorized the Goths and forced the Tervingi to seek asylum in the Roman empire.

The Huns exceed any definition of savagery. They have compact, sturdy limbs and thick necks. They are so hideously ugly and distorted that they could be mistaken for two-legged beasts or for those images crudely hewn from tree stumps that can be seen on the parapets of bridges. Although the Huns have the shape—albeit repellent—of human beings, they are so wild in their way of life that they have no need of fire or pleasant-tasting foods, but eat the roots of uncultivated plants and the half-raw flesh of all sorts of animals. This they place between their thighs and the backs of their horses and so warm it a little.

Huns are never sheltered by buildings, but like their burial places they avoid them as they play no part in the business of everyday life. Not even a hut thatched with reeds can be found among them. Rather, the Huns roam freely in the mountains and woods, learning from their earliest childhood to endure freezing cold, hunger, and thirst. They wear garments made of linen or stitched together from the pelts of mice found in the wild; they have the same clothes for indoors and out. They cover their heads with round caps and protect their hairy legs with goatskins. Once they have put on a tunic (that is drab colored), it is not changed or even taken off until it has been reduced to tatters by a long process of decay and falls apart bit by bit.

Huns are not well adapted to battle on foot, but are almost glued to their horses, which are certainly hardy, but also ugly. From their horses by night and day they buy, sell, eat, and drink. Slumped over their horses' narrow necks, they relax into a deep sleep. No one in their own country ever plows. Like refugees—all without permanent settlements, homes, law, or a fixed way of life—they are always on the move with their wagons, in which they live. In wagons their wives weave for them the horrid clothes that they wear. There, too, wives sleep with husbands, give birth, and look after their children right up until they become adults. No one among them, when asked, can tell you where he comes from, since he was conceived in one place, born far from there, and brought up even farther away.

The Huns are not subject to the direction of a king, but are satisfied with the improvised leadership of their chief men, and batter their way through anything in their path. In agreeing truces, they are faithless and fickle, swaying from side to side in every breeze as new possibilities present themselves, subordinating everything to their impulsive desires. Like unthinking animals, they are completely ignorant of the difference between right and wrong. They burn with an unquenchable lust for gold, and are so capricious and quick to anger that often without any provocation they quarrel with their allies more than once on the same day, and then just as easily make up without anyone winning them around. Fired with an overwhelming desire for seizing the property of others, these swift-moving and ungovernable people make their destructive way amid the pillage and slaughter of those who live around them.

Ammianus Marcellinus' description is the only surviving account of the Huns before Attila. It underlies most modern explanations of their customs and society. But there is a problem: despite its apparently compelling detail, this version cannot be taken at face value. In fact, Ammianus is unlikely ever to have seen a Hun. He was not an anthropologist; his information was not based on eyewitness research in the field. Rather, in putting together this picture of the Huns, Ammianus was playing a clever literary game. He intended that his readers should recognize a set of ideas and images, some stretching back to the very beginning of classical history writing.

Many of Ammianus' references were obvious. They reflected a widely held belief in Rome's divinely sanctioned mission to establish order through the imposition of empire. For patriots, it was the obligation to ensure the spread of civilization that justified often brutal wars of conquest. This was Rome's imperial burden.

> Roman, remember through your empire to rule
> Earth's peoples—for your arts are to be these:
> To pacify, to impose the rule of law,
> To spare the vanquished, and war down the proud.

These are some of the most-quoted lines from the great Roman poet Virgil. They capture an attitude that four centuries later Ammianus' readers would still have applauded. Those who had not been fortunate enough to be subjected to the benefits of Roman rule were, by definition, barbarians. According to this worldview, the empire was surrounded by lesser breeds without the law. Beyond its frontiers lived ignorant savages lacking morality, good government, and self-discipline. Barbarians were brutal, dishonest, irrational, ferocious, violent, fickle, and arrogant: all adjectives used by Julius Caesar in his own account of his campaigns in France in the 50s BC to describe Ariovistus, one of his chief native opponents. Barbarians lived a primitive existence without cities, proper religion, education, culture, or decent food. They were recognizable by their ugly faces, their unwashed bodies, and their outlandish clothes. No civilized person ever wore trousers.

Above all, the integrity of the empire was guaranteed by its military superiority. In 113 a white marble monument one hundred feet high was dedicated in Rome to celebrate the emperor Trajan's two campaigns across the Danube in the preceding decade. Trajan's Column (still standing in the center of the city) is decorated with a narrow band of sculpture in low relief—like an outsize cartoon strip—which spirals twenty-four times around the shaft. In all, 2,500 figures make up 154 recognizably separate scenes. Rather than give a straightforward account of Trajan's campaigns, these images offer a more idealized narrative of the conflict between Romans and barbarians. In this picture-book world, the Roman army appears in good marching order: energetic and disciplined legionaries construct camps, forts, roads, and bridges; they besiege and capture a hostile fortress; they are unfailingly victorious in battle. Defeated barbarians grovel, begging for mercy; some are imprisoned, others tortured. Villages are torched, their defenseless inhabitants butchered along with their animals. The imposition of civilization is a bloody business.

In one scene, trophy-hunting Roman soldiers display the severed heads of their enemies to the emperor and his staff.

Violent images of imperial domination were commonplace. Coins commemorating Roman military success showed barbarians being dragged by their long hair or trampled to death by a victorious emperor on horseback. Roman emperors presented themselves as standing against a tide of barbarism that, if unchecked, threatened to engulf the civilized world. On the sculptures of a triumphal arch dedicated in Rome in 315 to celebrate Constantine's campaigns, the empire's enemies are shown not as warriors but as prisoners. The arch still stands (just next to the Colosseum); its modern viewers, like their ancient counterparts, are tempted into a self-satisfied sense of their own superiority by the sight of pacified barbarians in chains or as stunted figures kneeling at the feet of huge winged Victories (see figure 3). The subjugation of those who opposed Roman rule was always to be applauded. Scratched across the squares of a gaming board from Trier, not far from the Rhine frontier, is the simple slogan VIRTVS IMPERI, HOSTES VINCTI, LVDANT ROMANI, "Strength of the empire; enemies bound; let the Romans play!"

Certainly it would be wrong—at least for those wishing to think like Romans—to waste any sympathy on the defeated. To approve of victory over chaos, of a superior system of government over a confused rabble, or of the grandeur of empire over primitive barbarity was simply to affirm the proper order of things. What concerned many of those loyal to the empire in the 360s and 370s was how to ensure the maintenance of Roman rule against the threat posed by the Goths and other barbarians north of the Rhine–Danube frontier. One of the most remarkable survivals from those decades is a short pamphlet titled, by its modern editors, *On Military Matters*. The unnamed author offered the emperors advice on administrative, fiscal, and taxation reform as well as presenting plans for ingenious improvements to the

figure 3
Pacified barbarian: relief sculpture from
the Arch of Constantine in Rome.

empire's military hardware. Among the designs were an easily transportable floating bridge, a scythed chariot with retractable blades, and, most extraordinary of all, a warship powered by oxen. The oxen—so it was explained—walked in a circle on the main deck turning capstans, which through a simple set of gears operated six paddle wheels on the outside of the vessel. (However impractical the design, this unknown inventor is the first person in recorded history to have presented a worked-out proposal for propelling ships other than by oars or sail.) The need for such war machines was pressing, the anonymous author argued, because of the increased risk of barbarian invasion. The empire no doubt had the upper hand in morality and culture, but its survival also depended on the maintenance of its technological superiority. Now was the time for decisive imperial action. "Above all else, it must be recognized that savage nations are pressing hard on the empire and howling around it on all sides . . . every frontier is assailed by treacherous barbarians."

The crushing defeat of the Roman army at Adrianople confirmed this heightened sense of an embattled empire. The Goths had always been thought of as barbarians. In 369, at the end of an inconclusive three-year war, Valens and Athanaric formally ratified a peace settlement at a meeting on a boat moored in the middle of the Danube. This carefully negotiated agreement between Romans and Goths was transformed by the orator Themistius into a collision between civilized order and barbarian chaos. He invited his audience to picture both banks of the river: "one glittering with the ordered ranks of Roman soldiers who looked on calmly and with pride at what was being done, the other crowded with a confused rabble. . . . I have not heard the barbarian war cry, but I have heard their laments, their wailing, and their entreaties—utterances better suited to prisoners of war than peacemakers." In an equally uncompromising image, Ammianus compared the Tervingi's crossing of the Danube to a volcanic eruption. This was an explosive moment when the barbarian world threatened to flow unchecked across the frontier. Hostile armies covered the land "like ashes from Mount Etna." Defeat two years later shook many Romans' confidence in the ability of the empire to defend itself, but not their conviction in the rightness of their cause. Neither their conversion to Christianity nor their victory at Adrianople made the Goths any less barbarous.

For Ammianus, the Huns were also indisputably part of the barbarian opposition to Rome. The images are unmistakable. In appearance, the Huns are half human. ("They are so hideously ugly and distorted that they could be mistaken for two-legged beasts.") Their clothes are filthy, tattered, and strange. ("They cover their heads with round caps and protect their hairy legs with goatskins.") They are deceitful and dishonest. ("Like unthinking animals, they are completely ignorant of the difference between right and wrong.") They have no proper system of government. ("The Huns are not subject to the direction of a king.") Incapable of honoring alliances, they are driven only by a lust for wealth and an insatiable appetite for plunder. ("Fired with an overwhelming desire for seizing the property of others, these swift-moving and ungovernable people make their destructive way amid the pillage and slaughter of those who live around them.")

On this view, there can be no doubt that the Huns are barbarians. What is striking about Ammianus' account is his firm refusal to think beyond a repetitively recycled set of conventional stereotypes. Ammianus shows no interest in offering anything other than a traditional perspective on a people who were clearly—at least in his view—beyond the civilizing reach of the Roman empire. He is disinclined to follow those (admittedly few) writers who attempted to imagine what it might be like to be a barbarian. Around 100, a long decade before the dedication of Trajan's Column, the subtle and brilliant historian Tacitus wrote a brief ethnographic study on the tribes living in unconquered Germania, on the other side of the Rhine frontier. Much of the material is predictable: the Germans prefer war to peace, pillage to agriculture; they live in wooden huts rather than villages or cities; they wear clothes sewn together from animal skins; their children grow up naked and filthy; they are slothful (typically not getting out of bed until late morning), and their behavior is often irrational and uncontrolled. "To drink both night and day shames no one. Fights are frequent, as is common among the intoxicated, and they rarely end just with abuse, but more often in slaughter and bloodshed." But Tacitus' readers are not permitted to rest easily with a comfortably smug sense of the inferiority of the Germans. In a clearly disapproving commentary on contemporary Roman society and morality, Tacitus warmly praises these barbarians for the high value they place on the sanctity of marriage, for the low incidence of adultery, and for their sexual restraint. "For no one among them finds vice amusing, nor dismisses the corruption of themselves or others as 'fashionable.'"

By contrast, Ammianus' black-and-white description of the Huns does not force its readers to ask any difficult questions. Rather than follow Tacitus' ambiguous and challenging version of the barbarian world, Ammianus preferred to draw on an older and well-established literary tradition. Those knowledgeable enough to appreciate the references would have noted the deliberate parallels with the Greek historian Herodotus writing in the fifth century BC, eight hundred years before Ammianus. Herodotus' *Histories* included detailed accounts of the customs of the Egyptians and the Persians. In his opinion, they could both be thought of as civilized (at least in some respects), although certainly not as civilized as Greeks. Scythians living north of the Black Sea offered a sharper contrast. The vast wilderness of the steppes, stretching out to the horizon, was a harsh and forbidding place, far away from the familiar comforts of the Mediterranean world. In many ways, the Scythians were a disquieting inversion of the Greeks: they lived in wagons rather than in cities; they herded cattle and sheep rather than cultivating the land; they fought as archers on horseback rather than on foot with sword and shield. There were also unmistakable signs of savagery; head-hunting Scythian warriors made drinking cups out of the skulls of their enemies; grief-stricken mourners marked the death of a king by strangling his servants and burying them alongside the royal corpse under a great mound of earth.

For Herodotus, these were some of the characteristic traits of nomads: the modern English word simply takes over the classical Greek term, *nomades*. Beyond the Scythians in the featureless expanse of the steppes were men who in their appearance were nearer to beasts and in their habits were scarcely human. Here lived the Androphagi (literally, the "Man-eaters"), who feast on human flesh. Here might be found the Agathyrsi, who pass their women indiscriminately from man to man, and the Neuri, who turn into werewolves for a few days each year. On the steppes lived another strange race, "who are all said to be bald from birth (both men and women) and snub-nosed and with long beards" and who eat only a kind of fruitcake. Here, too, were the Issedones, who serve up the flesh of their dead at funeral banquets; and beyond them one-eyed men and great griffins guarding huge piles of gold. *Nomades* ringed the civilized world. To the east, beyond India, lived the Padaei who ate raw flesh and killed any of their number who fell ill. Herodotus' views on *nomades*—a mixture of the fanciful, the weird, and the imaginary—neatly capture a wider set of attitudes and habits that both Greeks and Romans regularly attributed to peoples living on the edges of the known world. On the steppes, civilization was turned upside down: the farther away from the Mediterranean, the stranger the inhabitants, the more inexplicable their customs, the more chaotic their societies, and the more unprocessed their food. And between these opposites there could be no easy reconciliation.

Such perceptions of the world beyond civilization had long been part of classical culture. In the eighth century BC, three hundred years before Herodotus, they were important themes in the *Odyssey*, Homer's epic poem that narrated the ten-year-long struggle of Odysseus and his companions to return home after the Trojan War. Blown off course by a storm, their ships finally found safe harbor in a country far from Greece. But this was no island paradise; Odysseus and some of the crew were captured and imprisoned by the Cyclops Polyphemus. Every morning and evening, this one-eyed giant seized two of the men, smashed their heads on the ground, and ate them—raw, of course. Escape was possible only after Polyphemus, falling into a drunken sleep, was blinded by Odysseus, who drove a sharpened stake into the Cyclops' eye.

Homer's story is not only about the cunning of Odysseus; it is also about a confrontation between civilization and barbarity. Polyphemus and the Cyclopes are *nomades*. Homer and Herodotus use precisely the same word. The Cyclopes inhabited a land without cities, agriculture, or government. They tended their sheep, lived in caves, and ate their food uncooked. Odysseus and his comrades could not hope to communicate with their captor; they could neither recount their own unfortunate history nor negotiate their release. Violence was the only language Polyphemus understood. In this biting morality tale of the brutal clash between anarchy and order, the Cyclopes are unsurprisingly one-eyed. Like other nomads inhabiting the edges of the known world, they are blind to the benefits of civilization.

It is in this rich context, which set the civilized against the nomadic, that Ammianus' account of the Huns must be read. It is not a straightforward description of their habits or society, but one deeply indebted to long-standing classical prejudices and well-worn literary stereotypes. Certainly the educated would have caught the echoes of Homer and Herodotus. They could also be expected to be sensitive to a version of the Huns that went beyond the traditional images of the hostile barbarian. What made the Huns so threatening was their utter rejection of the benefits of a settled society. For Ammianus, they were a primitive menace to be feared by all those who peaceably plowed their fields, valued the rule of law, lived permanently in settled communities, and cooked their food. Even among barbarians, Huns were the ultimate outsiders.

CHAPTER THREE
A BACKWARD STEPPE

Ammianus' account of the Huns had its own clear agenda, its own literary spin. That said, it should not immediately be discarded as worthless, especially in the absence of any other contemporary report. Some of the information may have had a reliable foundation, even if distorted to fit conventional ideas of *nomades* or exaggerated in the terrified telling by Goths eager to explain away their failure to withstand this new enemy. It might, for example, be possible to salvage something from Ammianus' description of the Huns as "so hideously ugly and distorted that they could be mistaken for two-legged beasts or for those images crudely hewn from tree stumps that can be seen on the parapets of bridges." This disgust may reflect a genuine Roman reaction to the Huns' strange appearance. In common with other steppe peoples, the Huns artificially flattened the front of their skulls. It is not known how widespread the practice of cranial deformation was, but some newborn babies had their heads tightly bound with strips of cloth. These bandages held in place a flat stone or piece of wood that pressed hard against the infant's forehead. The results were striking: the root of the nose was squashed and widened, while the forehead itself was exaggerated and greatly elongated.

Some of Ammianus' bizarre remarks also make better sense in the light of what is known of other steppe nomads. His claim that the Huns do not ever change their clothes "until they have been reduced to tatters by a long process of decay and fall apart bit by bit" has a parallel in the thirteenth-century injunction (traditionally ascribed to Genghis Khan) requiring Mongols to wear their clothes without washing them until they were worn out. Something, too, may be made of Ammianus' assertion that the Huns placed half-raw animal flesh "between their thighs and the backs of their horses and so warmed it a little." Modern scholars have speculated that raw meat may have been used as a poultice to relieve saddle sores on the backs of horses. But Ammianus may be right in insisting that it was for the riders. Hans Schiltberger, a fourteenth-century mercenary and adventurer from Bavaria, claimed to have observed that among the Tartars, nomadic neighbors of the Mongols who captured Kiev in 1240, horsemen preparing to travel long distances placed raw meat under their saddles. "I have also seen that when the Tartars are on a long journey they take a piece of raw meat, cut it into slices, place it under the saddle, ride on it, and eat it when they are hungry. They salt it first and claim that it will not spoil because it is dried by the warmth of the horse and becomes tender under the saddle from riding, after the moisture has gone out of it." Tenderized raw meat seems to have been something of a steppe signature dish. A distant descendant still survives in restaurants (although its preparation requires neither horse nor saddle) as steak tartare.

On other points of detail, Ammianus is certainly wrong. His view of the Huns as living in wagons, where "wives sleep with husbands, give birth, and look after their children right up until they become adults," ignores the everyday use of tents. His claim that the Huns have "no need of fire or pleasant-tasting foods" passes in silence over their copper cauldrons. One example, found in 1869 at Törtel-Czakóhalom, in western Hungary, stands just under three feet high and weighs ninety pounds (see figure 4). These large vessels are most likely to have been used for cooking. Rock drawings near Minusinsk, on the southern edge of Siberia,

figure 4
Cauldron from Törtel-
Czakóhalom.

show how one nomadic community in the first century AD set up cauldrons on campfires outside each family's tent (see figure 5). Like the people of Minusinsk, the Huns also preferred their meat stewed.

What is most important in Ammianus' account is his observation that Hun society was fundamentally pastoralist, without agriculture and without permanent settlements. In its essentials, life on the semiarid steppes that stretch across Asia from Mongolia to the Black Sea has changed little in sixteen hundred years. It is still a fragile existence, vulnerable to shifts in rainfall, sharp variations in the productivity of the grassland, and sudden outbreaks of disease. Prosperity and, in hard times, survival depend on sheep and horses rather than on cattle. The Huns were shepherds on horseback, not cowboys. Every year, they drove their flocks across the open plains from winter quarters to summer pasture. For the Huns, in common with other nomadic societies, the ownership of land was of little consequence; what mattered was the right to move across it.

figure 5
Rock drawings from Minusinsk.

Groups of Huns traveled slowly. Heavy wooden wagons carried their possessions and tents, predictably of sheepskin or felt made from sheep's wool. A monotonous diet of mutton, horse meat, milk, and sheep's cheese was supplemented by foraging, hunting, and fishing. Successful exploitation of the steppe required collective organization and the wide dispersal of population to prevent overgrazing. A large area of pasture was needed to support a small number of people. The basic social unit was the extended family. If they could afford it, some Huns took more than one wife and, in turn, up to twenty families may have formed a larger group. Comparisons with modern nomads in central Asia suggest that clans of between five hundred and one thousand members make good economic sense. It would certainly not be right to think of a great mass of Huns moving together across the steppes. In ecological terms, that would have been unsustainable.

Above all, nomads rely on horses. To Roman eyes, the Huns' horses, like their riders, were squat and ugly. According to Ammianus' fourth-century contemporary the Roman vet Flavius Vegetius, the Huns' horses had hooked heads, protruding eyes, narrow nostrils, shaggy manes hanging down below the

knees, overlarge ribs, wide-spreading hooves, bushy tails, and
thin angular bodies. These were not stall-fed chargers requiring shelter, special winter feed, and warm stabling; rather, they
were hardy, range-fed animals that could be put out to pasture
all year round. Vegetius particularly admired these steppe-bred
horses for their patience, perseverance, and ability to endure
cold and hunger. "The thinness of these horses is pleasing, and
even in their ugliness there is a kind of beauty." For the Huns,
horsemanship was a key survival skill. It allowed them not only
to manage their livestock but also to harass their more settled
neighbors. On horseback, a small mobile force could choose
the time and place for battle, ambush the enemy, and quickly
vanish into the steppes. As their attacks on the Goths west of
the Black Sea frighteningly demonstrated, the Huns were best
at smash-and-grab raids. They appeared as if from nowhere
and melted away, leaving only destruction behind them. It was
impossible to establish an effective early-warning system. In
modern warfare, satellite and aerial reconnaissance have greatly
reduced the impact of speed and surprise. In the ancient world,
only a cloud of dust on the horizon signaled the approach of a
raiding party.

The Huns combined rapid mobility with deadly firepower.
Hun warriors were able to shoot arrows repeatedly and accurately from horseback. They used a composite short bow about
five feet long, its wooden core backed by sinews and bellied
with horn; bone strips stiffened both the grip and the extremities
(the "ears"). That combination of materials, the back resistant to
stretch, the belly to compression, made for a powerful weapon.
Modern studies of composite bows from pharaonic Egypt show
them to be effective at ranges of up to two hundred yards. The
same principles of construction, in this case using light-colored
yew sapwood and darker heartwood, were fundamental to the
success of the early fifteenth-century English longbow used to
devastating effect against the French army at Agincourt. Hun

bows were precious items, and it is not surprising that they were considered too valuable to be buried as grave goods. With very few exceptions, only broken bows and discarded bone stiffeners have been found.

The use of horse and short bow, and the reliance on unexpected raids and equally swift retreat, helps to explain why the Huns were so feared. It was this combination—rather than any marked technological superiority in their weapons—that was key to the Huns' success. These were not standard Roman or Gothic tactics. Ammianus' description of the Huns in battle may draw on reports of those who had seen them in action against the Goths in the 370s. The Huns relied on the disorienting effect of flights of arrows. This destructive volley was quickly followed by hand-to-hand fighting and the throwing of "strips of plaited cloth." The skillful use of the lasso—a military novelty Ammianus carefully describes for his readers—was another example of the Huns' ability to counter heavily armed infantrymen with a series of rapidly executed and unconventional maneuvers. "At first, they fight from a distance with arrows . . . then they advance rapidly over the intervening ground and engage at close quarters with swords, regardless of their own lives. While enemy troops are protecting themselves against injuries from sword thrusts, the Huns throw strips of plaited cloth over them and ensnare their opponents' limbs, depriving them of the ability to ride or walk."

To be successful, these tactics demanded both well-disciplined warriors and an effective chain of command. While Ammianus is insistent that the Huns were not "subject to the direction of any king," he does grudgingly allow "they were content with the improvised leadership of their chief men." Ammianus is vague when it comes to who these "chief men" were, but it seems he envisaged some kind of council in time of war, uniting a few clans rather than a whole people. As always, Ammianus must be read with care. While he offers some credible information on the Huns' organization in the field, his main point is to contrast this temporary imposition of control with their normally anarchic way of life. Again, the comparison is overdrawn. The Huns, even when not at war, were more orderly in their arrangements than Ammianus was willing to concede. At its most basic, survival on the steppes depended on the close control of grazing rights and established routes to summer pastures. The westward migration toward the Black Sea must also have been the result of some kind of collective decision.

Most importantly—as Ammianus himself notes—the Huns possessed bows, wagons, and swords. In other words, they had regular access to the products of settled communities with expertise in carpentry and metalworking. The skills required for the manufacture of bows are even more specialized. According to the fourteenth-century Egyptian expert Taibugha, one of the greatest Islamic authorities on archery:

> The manufacture of a bow calls for patience, since it cannot properly be completed in less than a full year. Autumn must be devoted to the carving and preparation of the wooden core and to the sawing and fitting of the horn. Winter is the season for binding and reflexing, and in the beginning of the spring the sinew is applied. Next, in summer, the bow, as yet unfinished, is strung and rounded to the curvature required. It is then veneered and painted.

A competent craftsman could make more than one bow a year. As Taibugha's description indicates, the process itself is intensive, but not time-consuming. The different conditions in each of the four seasons are used to obtain the optimum conditions for working the various components and for glue setting. What matters most are the facilities to prepare the raw materials and to store the unfinished bows in the various stages of construction. This combination of highly specialized labor, a heavy up-front investment in materials, and a long lead time in manufacture was practicable only in a settled community. The composite short bow cannot easily be made by a steppe nomad on the move.

It is not known for certain how the Huns secured a steady supply of swords, cauldrons, bows, and wagons. They may have incorporated smiths, carpenters, wheelwrights, and bowyers into their clans. These men might have offered their services willingly or, captured on raids, been forced to work as skilled slaves. Even so, this would have been merely a stopgap, allowing for repairs and emergencies. It is likely that the main source of handicrafts and manufactured goods was trade between the Huns and those living on the more fertile edges of the steppe. For nomads, regular contact with farms and villages is essential. In good years, when there is surplus of livestock to dispose of, it is difficult to sell to other nomads—who have precisely the same surplus at exactly the same time. In poor years, purchasing food stored in granaries can be the only way to avoid starvation. On the steppes, nomads, farmers, and craftsmen were bound tightly together in a web of mutual dependence. Only through carefully managed long-term relationships could sheep and horses be converted into grain, wagons, cauldrons, and bows. It was never in the Huns' interests to wipe out agricultural communities through repeated raiding.

All things considered, it is difficult to believe that the Huns conformed as closely as Ammianus or his readers might have imagined to the conventional image of the nomad. They were no bestial horde, ugly and misshapen, forever shunning shelter, fixed to their horses even while asleep, a semihuman people without fire, laws, or morality. The Huns were better organized, more economically advanced, and less isolated than Ammianus' selective and overdrawn account suggests. It is more accurate to think of them as a loose confederation of highly mobile, well-armed clans without any permanent settlements of their own, but reliant on regular contact with farmers and expert craftsmen. Of course, even if more sophisticated than sometimes portrayed,

Hun society lacked the political and cultural complexities of an urban civilization. Huns were disturbingly different from those living in the towns that ringed the Mediterranean (in the philosopher Plato's phrase) "like frogs around a pond." On this point, Ammianus was undeniably correct: a vast distance still separated the harsh wilderness of the steppe from the more comfortable world of the Roman empire.

Yet on one matter concerning the Huns, Ammianus demonstrated admirable restraint: he refused to speculate on their origin. For Ammianus, the Huns belonged somewhere far away from civilization "dwelling in the frozen wastes that stretch beyond the Maeotic Sea" (somewhere to the east of the Crimea and the Sea of Azov). Like other nomads, the Huns were somewhere "out there" on the steppes, beyond the limits of the settled world. Modern scholarship has tried to be more precise, but as yet the Huns' homeland cannot conclusively be identified. One of the difficulties is the nature of the evidence. Material remains such as grave goods can reveal only so much about identity, lifestyle, and personal habits. And obviously nomads do not leave as many things behind as those living in settled societies. To complicate matters, the very mobility of nomads means that customs, artifacts, and decorative styles circulate across huge distances; and, in any case, many objects that survive are the products of permanent communities acquired through trade. Among European cultures, practices such as cranial deformation or items such as bone fittings for composite bows are usually reliable indications of the intrusive presence of outsiders. Not so east of the Black Sea. These seemingly distinctive features are shared by a wide range of peoples from the Crimea to Korea. From an archaeological point of view, one group of steppe nomads looks much like another. There is nothing exclusively "Hun" about flattened skulls or bone stiffeners.

One theory about the origin of the Huns is certainly open to question: that they are the descendants of the Hsiung-Nu (or, in its new-style spelling, the Xiongnu). The Xiongnu were Mongolian nomads who established an extensive empire in the late third century BC. Tension between the Xiongnu and the Han emperors, who controlled China for four centuries from 206, culminated in a series of conflicts in the first century BC. In AD 48, the Xiongnu empire was split: the southern Xiongnu, in Inner Mongolia, were incorporated into the Chinese state. The northern Xiongnu, in Outer Mongolia, were shattered by further Han victories in the 80s and by the Xianbei, a nomadic people pushing down from the north. At some point, perhaps following the breakup of their empire by the Han or under pressure from the Xianbei, remnants of the Xiongnu were thought to have moved west, preserving something of their original identity until—as "Huns"—they spilled over into Europe.

This view was most vigorously advanced in German scholarship before the First World War. Arguments were based on scarce linguistic material and on attempts to make sense out of the frequently contradictory Chinese accounts of the Xiongnu. What was missing from these discussions was any consideration of the archaeological evidence. At the time, neither Hun nor Xiongnu material had been systematically excavated or published. There was also a darker side to the debate. For some writers, connecting the Xiongnu and the Huns was part of a wider project of understanding the history of Europe as a fight to preserve civilization against an ever-present oriental threat. The Huns were a warning from history. With their Chinese credentials established, their attacks on the Roman empire could be presented as part of an inevitable cycle of conflict between East and West.

Understanding of the Xiongnu changed significantly in the 1930s with the publication of bronze artifacts from the Ordos Desert, in Inner Mongolia, west of the Great Wall. These demonstrated the striking difference between the art of the Xiongnu and that of the Huns. Not one object found in eastern Europe dating from the fourth and fifth centuries AD is decorated with the beautiful stylized animals and mythical creatures—horses, goats, fighting tigers, griffins, dragons—that are characteristic of Xiongnu design. At present, there is no reason to reject the robust conclusion reached sixty years ago by Otto Maenchen-Helfen, the most authoritative writer of the twentieth century on Hun culture:

> The Ordos bronzes were made by or for the Hsiung-nu. We could check all items in the inventory of the Ordos bronzes, and we would not be able to point out a single object which could be paralleled by one found in the territory once occupied by the Huns. . . . There are the well-known motifs of the animal style . . . not a single one from that rich repertoire of motifs has ever been found on a Hunnish object.

The most recent archaeological evidence from Mongolia further widens the gap between the Huns and the Xiongnu. Russian archaeologists working in the Transbaikal region on the Russian–Mongolian border have excavated a number of sites dating from the height of the Xiongnu empire during the second and first centuries BC. At Ivolga, near the modern city of Ulan-Ude, there is clear evidence of the beginnings of an urban civilization: ramparts enclosed a large, well-planned settlement with dwellings arranged neatly in rows. Its inhabitants were engaged in agriculture, cattle breeding, and metalworking. These prosperous Xiongnu farmers living in their fortified town do not look like Huns. The finds from the burial ground at Ivolga were meticulously published by the Russian Academy of Sciences in St. Petersburg in 1996. Although expanding the range and variety of artifacts known to Otto Maenchen-Helfen, they confirm his conclusions: there are still no convincing parallels between Xiongnu decorative styles and any objects in Europe associated with the Huns.

If a connection with Mongolia and the Xiongnu seems highly unlikely, where did the Huns come from? In default of other hard evidence, the best—although still unsatisfactory—solution would be to locate them farther west of Mongolia, somewhere between the eastern edge of the Altai Mountains and the Caspian Sea, roughly in modern Kazakhstan. Kazakhstan is a huge country, the ninth largest in the world, at just over a million square miles four times the size of Texas or France. It borders China to the east and Russia to the north, and has a western coastline on the Caspian Sea. At its center is the most extensive dry steppe region on earth, covering 300,000 square miles. The climate is similar to that of the Canadian prairies, with July temperatures in the seventies and January temperatures no higher than ten and regularly dropping to zero. With its low rainfall, the Kazakh steppe is mostly treeless grassland punctuated with large areas of sand. Across this flat expanse, the wind blows strong and cold, sometimes hard enough to knock people over.

Perhaps the homeland of the Huns lies somewhere in this monotonous vastness? For the present, it is regrettably impossible to suggest anything more precise. This may seem a disappointing conclusion, and not much improvement on Ammianus' vague claim that the Huns were originally to be found somewhere "beyond the Maeotic Sea." But to relocate the Huns to the Kazakh steppe represents a solid and significant advance on the unconvincing speculation of the last 150 years. It places them firmly within the broad context of pastoral nomadism, while recognizing that the lack of any convincing connection with the Xiongnu makes it unlikely that their homeland was ever as far east as Mongolia. Most importantly, moving the Huns away from "the mysterious Orient" liberates them from a set of modern prejudices. Without a convincing link with China and the Xiongnu, they can no longer be claimed as the first frightening wave of a "yellow peril" threatening to engulf Western civilization.

CHAPTER FOUR

ROMANS AND BARBARIANS

N o one knew why the Huns left their homeland on the steppes. Perhaps it was the result of a series of poor summers, or severe winters, or some natural disaster, or diseased flocks, or pressure from other nomad competitors, or some critical combination of factors. Whatever the causes, the effects (explored in chapter 1) were clear. After disrupting, in Ammianus' words, "obscure peoples whose names and customs are unknown," the Huns threatened the Alans, who occupied the territory between the Don River and the Caspian Sea. Some Alans joined with the Huns, and together they attacked the Goths. In turn, the Gothic resistance led by Athanaric collapsed, and a splinter group of Tervingi under Fritigern and Alavivus sought asylum within the Roman empire. The failure of the frontier command to treat these refugees humanely was a key factor in their growing hostility. The conflict that followed also involved a contingent of Huns invited by Fritigern to join his army as mercenaries. Their intervention broke Roman attempts to push the Goths back toward the Danube. In Ammianus' harsh assessment, "the barbarians like savage beasts that have broken free from their cages" spread "the foul chaos of robbery and murder, slaughter and fire," as they moved south through the Balkans. This was the bloody prelude to the Roman defeat at Adrianople and the death of an emperor.

No Roman historian mentions the Huns on the battlefield. They may have ridden with the Greuthungi against the Roman cavalry, or hung back until victory and the opportunities for looting were certain. The next day, the Goths attacked the city of Adrianople; attempts to scale the walls with ladders were repelled by defenders who dropped lumps of masonry on the enemy below. Joining forces with the Huns, the Goths moved on to Constantinople. Their progress was checked by a unit of Saracens, recruited from the Arab tribes that controlled the eastern fringes of the empire from Syria to the Sinai. One of these desert warriors, naked apart from a loincloth, his long hair streaming out behind him, rode into the thick of the advancing troops. With a chilling yell, he slit the throat of one of the Goths and, leaning down from his horse, drank the blood that spurted warm from the wound. Such brutality sapped the morale of the attackers, and, confronted with the strength of Constantinople's walls, they hurriedly withdrew.

The Goths and their Hun allies lacked the skills and resources for siege warfare, yet without capturing cities they could not press home the advantage won at Adrianople or gain access to food stored in granaries. The problems of provisioning the army (and the families that followed behind) could partly be solved by raiding villages and farms, but there is a limit to the number of times the same region can be pillaged. Faced with these shortages, the Greuthungi split off and moved west into Pannonia (modern Slovenia). Given the failure of the Goths to maintain their unity and momentum, some Romans still believed a military solution was possible. That would be the task of Valens' successor as eastern Roman emperor. In January 379, Gratian—who had halted his march eastwards, fearing to engage the Goths after Adrianople—nominated Flavius Theodosius, a general in his early thirties with campaign experience in Britain and the Balkans. Theodosius' remit was to avenge Valens and crush the Goths and their Hun allies.

In fact, Theodosius managed little more than containment. Despite his efforts at conscription and recruitment, the imperial army could not quickly be brought up to strength. Gratian, who defeated the Greuthungi in Pannonia in 380, remained unwilling to commit a large force to a war in the Danube provinces. Both emperors were aware of the risks of being locked into a lengthy conflict. Neither wished to weaken his capacity to respond to any new threat. In dealing with the Goths, the options were a continued stalemate across a devastated landscape or a truce. Theodosius chose to negotiate and in October 382 agreed that the Tervingi, Greuthungi, and their Hun allies could occupy land immediately south of the Danube. In return, they were to contribute troops to the Roman army.

In praising Theodosius' success, Themistius had to work hard to sidestep the traditional rhetoric of peace through conquest. The agreement with the Goths was still to be seen as a Roman victory: not a victory that had been brought about by sparing the vanquished and warring down the proud, but rather the result of the emperor's overwhelming philanthropy. "For such are the victories of reason and humanity, not to destroy but rather to improve the lot of those who are responsible for the suffering. . . . Was it, then, better to fill the Danube provinces with the dead or with farmers? To make it full of tombs or of men? To travel through a wilderness or cultivated fields? To count up the number of slain or of those who work the land?" Themistius' speech was a masterpiece of imperial spin. It was cozy, seductive, and knowingly false. The uncomfortable truth could quietly be suppressed: that after the defeat at Adrianople, Valens' death, and Theodosius' inability to impose a permanent military solution, the Goths and their Hun allies had been allocated land within the empire. To many in the audience—even as they applauded— it must have seemed a biting irony that it was precisely such a settlement that Fritigern had requested six years earlier when the Tervingi had first massed on the banks of the Danube.

Only a small number of Huns entered the empire as Fritigern's allies before the Battle of Adrianople and later accepted Theodosius' offer of land. The majority continued their attacks on Goths north of the Danube. After Fritigern's followers had abandoned the fight, Athanaric withdrew across the Carpathian Mountains into the Banat region (on the Romanian–Serbian border). There he held out for four years before he, too, fled across the Danube. For the next two decades, there is no detailed history of the Huns' advance. Roman writers recorded its disruptive effects only when they threatened the empire's security. In 386, another large group of Greuthungi attempted to break through the northern frontier. Ten years earlier, eighty thousand had crossed the Danube and joined the Tervingi outside Marcianople. This time, they were deceived by Roman spies. Believing them to be genuine deserters with a grudge against their commander, the Greuthungi leader Odotheus was too trusting in revealing his plans. An advance party set out on a moonless night to cross the Danube and surprise the sleeping Romans—or so they thought. They were met midstream by a well-armed fleet, and their crude rafts and dugouts sunk. Those not drowned were quickly killed.

The slaughter of the Greuthungi and the absence of any major incursion in the next decade reflect the steady recovery of the Roman army after Adrianople and its release from six years of grinding warfare with the Goths. The lack of any large-scale raid is also an indication that the Huns were occupied in securing territory north of the Danube, rather than attacking the empire. In late 386, the threat of conflict on the eastern frontier was reduced by a power-sharing arrangement that gave the Persians control of part of Armenia. Exploiting peace with Persia and the Goths, Theodosius led the eastern imperial army into Italy to deal with internal revolts: first in 387–88 against Magnus Maximus—

figure 6
Framed gold medallion of Honorius, minted in Ravenna, probably early 420s.

who in August 383 had assassinated Gratian—and then again in 393–94 against Eugenius, defeated at the river Frigidus. The Goths and Huns settled in 382 fought for the emperor in both these campaigns. After his victory over Eugenius, Theodosius never returned to Constantinople. In January 395, he died in the western imperial capital, Milan. The empire was divided between his two sons: the West was ruled by the ten-year-old Honorius (see figure 6) and the East by the eighteen-year-old Arcadius. Honorius' court was dominated by the general Stilicho, who announced that on his deathbed Theodosius had appointed him as regent. In the East, the ineffectual teenage emperor Arcadius was unable to prevent the rise and fall of power brokers, each claiming to act in his best interests. They were united only in their opposition to Stilicho's ambition to extend his influence from Milan to Constantinople.

Within a few months of Theodosius' death, the Goths rebelled. Their leader Alaric had served as an officer in the Roman army and was aware of the resentment among his men at their deployment. At the Battle of the River Frigidus, the Goths suffered higher casualties than any other units. Many suspected that Theodosius aimed to sap their military strength by using them as frontline troops. Alaric was also able to exploit a growing sense of insecurity. In the harsh winter of 394–95, Hun war bands crossed the frozen Danube and destroyed the villages built by the Goths and their Hun allies. (Clearly there was no bond between these two groups of Huns.) It must have seemed a bitter turn of events that the men who should have been defending their families were six hundred miles away in Italy fighting a civil war on behalf of a Roman emperor. Looking at their still-smoking farmsteads, many of the settlers must have wondered whether the imperial government cared about their security. Perhaps it regarded them as no more than a useful buffer: at best, forced to bear the brunt of cross-border incursions; at worst, expendable barbarians who might slow down a full-scale invasion across the Danube.

Fear of further Hun raids pushed the Goths to abandon the land they had occupied since 382. Alaric's forces pillaged the Danube provinces before moving south through mainland Greece to the Peloponnese. Troops under Stilicho failed twice to win a decisive victory, succeeding only in driving the Goths back to the Balkans. The Roman army was unable to operate at full strength or maximum effectiveness with legions that only eighteen months earlier had fought each other in the civil war that ended at the river Frigidus. Rivalry between the eastern and the western empires was again a crucial factor. In the mid-390s, the regime in Constantinople was unwilling to cooperate with Stilicho, fearing that victory against the Goths would make him even more powerful. There were also new threats to the security of Armenia. With increasing pressure on the eastern frontier, Arcadius and his advisers were reluctant to commit to a potentially costly military solution to the problems caused by the Goths. They wished to avoid fighting on two fronts at once.

The challenge in the East came not from the Persians but from those Huns who had remained north of the Black Sea. In summer 395, raiding parties crossed the Caucasus Mountains, between the Black and the Caspian Seas, and moved rapidly through Armenia and into Syria. Farther south, in Bethlehem, the Christian monk Jerome wrote as though he, too, were on the front line. But even in his terror, he held fast to his classical education: in the end,

the catastrophe of the Hun raids was most powerfully captured
in a quotation from Virgil.

> Behold, last year the wolves of the North were let loose
> upon us from the far-off crags of the Caucasus, and quickly
> swept through entire provinces. Countless monasteries were
> captured, innumerable streams that once flowed with water
> now ran red with human blood. . . . Herds of captives were
> dragged away. Arabia, Lebanon, Palestine, and Egypt were
> seized by fear. "Not even if I had a hundred tongues and a
> hundred mouths and a voice of iron could I recite the names
> of all these disasters."

The memory of the Huns' attacks was long lasting. Two centuries
later, a Christian visionary in Syria warned that the Apocalypse
would be heralded by Huns invading from the distant north.
Their weapons would be dipped in a magic potion made from
fetuses cut from pregnant women roasted alive. They would
drink human blood and eat babies. "They will move faster than
the winds, more rapidly than storm clouds, and their war cries
will be like the roaring of a lion. Terror at their coming will cover
the whole earth like the floodwaters in the days of Noah."

The aim of these Hun raids was plunder, not conquest. As long
as the bulk of Roman forces was no farther east than the Balkans,
these attacks could be carried out with impunity. Combined with
the failure of Stilicho to defeat the Goths in Greece, the continuing Hun offensive forced a peace deal with Alaric. The agreement brokered by Eutropius, Arcadius' closest adviser, recognized
that the Goths had set out not to destroy the empire but to find
a more secure place within it. In 397, Alaric received the rank
of general in the Roman army and his followers gold and grain.
Negotiations were opened for a more permanent solution, perhaps
a new homeland much farther away from the frontier than their
original settlement under Theodosius. In Milan, Stilicho's sup-

porters were outraged. The poet Claudian, his chief propagandist, imagined the return of Alaric as a Roman general administering justice in cities he had only recently besieged as a Gothic rebel: "this time he comes as a friend . . . and hands down decisions in cases brought by those whose wives he has raped and children murdered."

Eutropius' agreement allowed Roman troops—reinforced by Goths—to move east and eject the Huns from Armenia. Victory over "the wolves of the North" was celebrated in late 398 with a parade through Constantinople. An enthusiastic crowd lined the streets to cheer Eutropius as he passed by. But success was fleeting. Within a year, Arcadius had reversed Eutropius' policies and sent him into exile. After all, as his rivals were quick to point out, once the threat to the eastern frontier had been removed, there was no longer any need to appease Alaric. The shift in attitude was signaled by the termination of the Goths' subsidies and supplies. In early 401, Arcadius also strengthened his diplomatic ties with Uldin, the first Hun leader in Europe to be named by Roman historians. Uldin controlled territory close to the Danube and is unlikely to have had any close links with those Huns north of the Black Sea who had attacked Syria and Armenia. Arcadius and his advisers may have planned an alliance, with the aim of using Uldin's Huns against Alaric's Goths. Certainly it was clear that the government in Constantinople was no longer prepared to negotiate. The eastern frontier was quiet and the arrangement with Uldin had secured the Danube. If necessary, the imperial army—perhaps even reinforced by Huns—could concentrate on the Goths. These tough tactics worked: by the end of the year, Alaric had left the eastern empire and moved west.

The Goths' attempt to enter northern Italy was blocked by Stilicho, and after two hard-fought battles Alaric withdrew to Dalmatia and Pannonia. Given the impossibility of a conclusive military solution, Stilicho faced a problem similar to Theodosius' after Adrianople. The Goths were too strong to be subdued by force and too dangerous to be left unchecked. It was an indication of the seriousness of the threat that the western imperial court abandoned Milan and moved to Ravenna, on the Adriatic coast. The new capital was well defended and could be approached only by a narrow causeway across treacherous and stinking salt marshes. (In more peaceful times, the waterlogged ground had made Ravenna famous for its asparagus.)

Like Theodosius and Eutropius before him, Stilicho aimed to neutralize the Goths through negotiation. On offer in 405 was a generalship for Alaric and payments for his followers. Alaric's acceptance allowed Stilicho to concentrate on countering an invasion of northern Italy by a substantial number of Goths. These Goths were not connected to those led by Alaric. They had remained north of the Rhine–Danube frontier since the Hun invasions in the 370s, but by moving deep into the empire they now sought safety from the disruption caused by the Huns' intrusive presence west of the Black Sea. It must then have seemed to their leader Radagaisus a vicious twist of fate that in seeking to avoid one group of Huns, he should have to face another. The Roman army was strengthened by Hun mercenaries commanded by Uldin, who, after Alaric's Goths moved west, had offered his services to Stilicho. There was nothing unusual in either Uldin's offer or Stilicho's acceptance. The Roman army had always been supplemented by troops from outside the empire. Only recently Theodosius had used Goths to defeat a usurper at the river Frigidus; Eutropius had used Alaric's Goths against one group of Huns in Armenia; and, after Eutropius' exile, Arcadius had been prepared to use another group of Huns against Alaric's Goths in the Balkans. Stilicho's latest combination of Huns and Romans proved effective. In late 406, Radagaisus' Goths were wiped out. So many of his followers were taken prisoner and sold into slavery that the Italian market was flooded and the price of slaves dropped steeply. The revenue raised helped pay for Uldin's Huns. If well rewarded, they would continue to fight for the empire; if not, they would turn against it. Certainly, at least for the moment, Stilicho felt safest when surrounded by his Hun bodyguard. In the deadly game of court politics, he preferred to rely on those whose loyalty he had purchased in advance.

But Stilicho's military success was short-lived. He failed to prevent a much larger movement of people across the Rhine in December 406, the likely result of the continued disruption caused by the Huns' westward advance, which displaced not only Goths but also others, including large numbers of Vandals and Alans. (Regrettably, nothing is known of this group of Alans, nor their reasons for breaking their long-standing alliance with the Huns.) The Rhine crossing was a serious incursion that, according to one fifth-century account, "ripped France to pieces." In the following year, France and Britain broke away from the empire and proclaimed a new emperor, Constantine III. The official regime in Ravenna was unable to halt the usurper's advance, and by the end of 407 Constantine had strengthened the Rhine defenses, garrisoned the Alpine passes into Italy, and established his own court at Arles. There was little Stilicho could do to restore Honorius' authority. Even with Uldin's Huns, he had insufficient forces either to reestablish imperial rule or to secure the frontier. He was also well aware that his continued willingness to discuss terms with the Goths aroused suspicion. Yet (as Stilicho might have argued) compromise was the only realistic option. His detractors disagreed: Stilicho's lack of success was to be explained not by Roman weakness but by a covert alliance with the ultimate aim of using Alaric's Goths to further his own ambitions. These were wild and unsubstantiated accusations. There is no good evidence that Stilicho had ever concluded a secret pact with Alaric. Rather than accuse him of double-dealing, it is easier to believe that he was no more able to defeat the Goths than Theodosius was, and in the end—like Theodosius—he had no choice but to negotiate.

Honorius chose to back Stilicho's critics. The western emperor had always been suspicious of the general, who had once sought to force his regency on the whole empire. Those around Stilicho made their own choices: in late August 408 his Hun bodyguards were secretly killed, and a few days later he was arrested and executed. Prudently it was thought worthwhile to maintain cordial relations with at least some Huns. In 409, negotiators agreed on the emperor's behalf that the sons of prominent families at court in Ravenna should be sent beyond the Danube as hostages; in return, later that same year, Honorius called up ten thousand Hun mercenaries. It is not clear whether these troops ever arrived in northern Italy; in the end, it is likely that the emperor was unable to pay or supply them properly.

After the death of Stilicho, Alaric again invaded northern Italy and marched on to Rome. He was not bent on destruction, but aimed, in the face of an intransigent imperial government, to compel negotiation. For eighteen months the Goths blockaded the Eternal City, and for eighteen months Honorius refused to make any major concessions. Finally, on 24 August 410, frustrated by the military and political deadlock, Alaric's Goths sacked Rome. For three days they looted the city's mansions and seized priceless treasures from its sacred sanctuaries. St. Peter's, on the Vatican Hill, was crammed with terrified citizens seeking refuge. In all the destructive chaos, the cathedral was left untouched. Yet for many, next to the shock at the fall of the city, such public gestures of compassion by a barbarian leader—even if now a Christian—were to be dismissed. "When the brightest light on the whole earth was snuffed out," lamented an overwrought Jerome, "when the Roman empire was decapitated, when—to speak more accurately—the whole world perished in one city, then I was dumb with silence and my sorrow was stirred."

The sack of Rome was a disaster that could and should have been avoided. It was not a surprise attack, nor was it the dramatic result of a bloodthirsty horde streaming down the Italian peninsula intent on grabbing gold and violating virgins. Rather, it represented a double failure: the failure of Alaric to force a viable agreement for the permanent settlement of the Goths, and the failure of the Roman government to deal reasonably with a people who had, after all, been permitted to enter the empire. The Goths were not permanently settled for another eight years, and the stalemate that had led to their attack on Rome continued as they moved slowly north into France. There negotiations were opened with Stilicho's successor, the general Flavius Constantius, who finally granted them land in the Garonne valley between Toulouse and Bordeaux, forty years and twelve hundred miles away from their crossing of the Danube.

The lack of cooperation between the East and the West hampered any earlier solution to the disruption caused by the Goths, as did the shortage of military manpower that after Adrianople arguably made their settlement within the empire a necessary risk. The inability of either imperial government to impose a resolution between Alaric's revolt in 395 and the Goths' settlement in southwestern France in 418 starkly exposed the difficulty of attempting to suppress an internal revolt while defending the empire from external enemies. The need to secure the northern and the eastern frontiers was a continual drain on resources. It forced the Roman army in both the East and the West to employ mercenaries, and placed a critical limit on the number of troops that could prudently be deployed on any one front or against any one threat. Only Theodosius managed to strike a workable balance, and he had negotiated peace with both the Persians and the Goths.

The continued instability along the Rhine–Danube frontier was the direct result of the westward push of the Huns. This was a gradual process. There is no sign of a solid block of Huns marching west from the Black Sea and systematically propelling the Goths and other peoples into the Roman empire. There is no evidence to support what some German scholars, rather splendidly, have called the *Hunnensturm*. The Huns moved into Europe in stages, consolidating their hold on territory disrupted through raiding and the displacement of some of its original inhabitants. Their piecemeal progress can be traced by the pressure on the Roman empire's northern frontier: in the 370s and 380s, groups of Goths were pushed toward the Danube; in 395, there were raids across the Danube and in Armenia (a sure indication that at least some Huns were still north of the Black Sea); in 401, Uldin controlled territory close to the Danube and was also able to move his men west to fight for Stilicho. The presence of Huns on the middle Danube is also indicated by Honorius' levy of mercenaries in 409. The overall pattern is clear: across forty years from 370 to 410, the focus of Hun activity slowly moved seven hundred miles, from the Don to the Dniester to the middle Danube or, in modern terms, from Ukraine to Romania and finally westward to Hungary.

CHAPTER FIVE
HOW THE WEST WAS WON

By the beginning of the fifth century, the Huns were firmly established on the Great Hungarian Plain in the heart of Europe (see figure 7). The Hungarian Alföld, or *puszta*, is the most westerly extension of the central Asian steppe, separated from it by the Carpathian Mountains. These fertile lands stretch in an arc from eastern Slovakia through Hungary and northern Serbia and into western Romania. The Great Hungarian Plain is a fragment of the steppe marooned in central Europe. It is a landscape of wide horizons shimmering in the summer heat and of endless flat fields—a treeless, grassy expanse broken only by swamps and bright-green algae-rimmed lakes. The open plain offers a stark contrast to the terrain south of the Danube with its narrow valleys and heavily forested mountain slopes. As a home for the Huns, the Great Hungarian Plain was self-selecting. West of the Black Sea it is the only area of grassland large enough to support horses on any scale. Located in the middle of Europe, it is an ideal base from which to launch attacks both north and south of the Danube. Yet compared with the vast wildernesses of central Asia, the Hungarian Plain hardly merits the description "great": it covers an area of about 40,000 square miles, as opposed to the 300,000 of the Kazakh steppe. These physical limitations are important. Survival in this more constrained European environment forced a social and political revolution among the Huns.

figure 7
The Plain *(1900), painting by Károly Kótasz (1872–1941).*

Failure to adapt would mean defeat or compel a slow and dangerous retreat back to the steppes.

In their initial westward push, the Huns relied on their superior
fighting skills and rapid mobility to raid local communities; the
unfortified Gothic villages were sitting targets. Yet while the
Great Hungarian Plain offered grazing for their horses, it was
simply not extensive enough to sustain the nomadic life the Huns
had followed on the steppes. In their new European homeland,
the Huns could no longer operate, year in year out, as pastoral
nomads driving their flocks from winter to summer pasture and
supplementing their income by a mixture of trading and opportunistic attacks. Rather, the Great Hungarian Plain offered the
Huns a different set of possibilities. In this richer, more densely
populated, and more productive land, they were able to use their
military advantage over the local population to establish themselves as an effective and permanent occupying force.

The crucial change in Hun tactics came at the beginning of the fifth century. Instead of leaving shattered villages, slaughtered farmers, and burned-out buildings behind them, it was more profitable to demand regular tribute from prosperous agricultural communities against the threat of reprisals. The Hun empire as it expanded across Europe was successful in systematizing the extraction of wealth and manpower from conquered territory. Its main concern was to ensure the maintenance of an army. Provided that recruits and supplies were delivered in full and on time, and suitable land was made available for grazing and breeding horses, the empire's interference in the economic and social arrangements of those it conquered was minimal. It was to the Huns' advantage to exploit rather than wreck Gothic society. The Hun empire in Europe was not an interventionist Roman-style empire relying on the close administrative control of subjugated provinces and peoples. Rather, it was a protection racket on a grand scale.

It is this sense of a society in transformation that is entirely absent from Ammianus Marcellinus' account of the Huns with its emphasis on many of those elements of their traditional nomadic lifestyle that did not survive their migration into Europe. Ammianus missed—or at least chose to ignore—the potential of the Huns to establish an empire. He persisted in forcing his description of their customs and lifestyle to conform to conventional literary stereotypes of barbaric outsiders. No contemporary Roman writer was interested in tracing the rise of the Huns' power beyond the northern frontier or in offering any account of how their society was changed by their contact with the Goths. Aside from a few chance remarks, this process of steady consolidation must be reconstructed from archaeological evidence and from thinking about the constraints imposed on the newcomers by the resources available on the Great Hungarian Plain.

figure 8
Csorna diadem.

According to Priscus of Panium, the Hun empire at its height stretched as far as "the islands in the Ocean"—that is, as far as the Baltic Sea. This may be correct, although it is impossible to tell whether the scatter of objects from northern Europe associated with the Huns and other steppe peoples is the result of conquest, alliance, or trade. The bulk of the archaeological material comes from north of the Black Sea (southern Ukraine and the Crimea) and from the heartland of the Hun empire stretching from western Romania across Hungary and Slovakia to eastern Austria. Finds of cauldrons are concentrated in this middle Danube region. Here, too, there are a small number of burials, datable to the fifth century, of men and women whose skulls show clear signs of artificial flattening. Characteristic items (not all found in graves with individuals displaying cranial deformation) include bone stiffeners for reflex bows, gold diadems, and decorative horse trappings.

The diadems are magnificent. The most beautiful was found in the late 1880s in an unrecorded burial site somewhere near the town of Csorna, seventy miles east of Budapest. When the grave was opened, the diadem was still in place, proudly encircling the skull of its owner. The Csorna diadem consists of a single sheet of gold twelve inches long and two wide, folded around a strip of bronze. Traces of copper oxide on the skull indicate that it was worn without any padding or leather lining. At the center of the gold band are two smoky-purple carnelians flanked by a row of blood-red garnets and three of similarly shaped red glass (see figure 8). Equally impressive are the splendid decorations for a horse's reins found twenty miles away in 1979 in the sandy soil of the vineyards around the tenth-century Benedictine monastery at Pannonhalma. Twelve strips of gold foil two inches long and three in the shape of a four-leaf clover were found intact. They were attached to leather trappings with small bronze tacks (see figure 9). Certainly no one could doubt the wealth or status of the rider whose shining golden reins glittered so brightly in the sunlight, flashing with every movement of his horse.

Such objects are eye-catching evidence of an intrusive, foreign presence. Yet it is important to emphasize that in the middle Danube finds of Hun (or perhaps better "steppe") material are

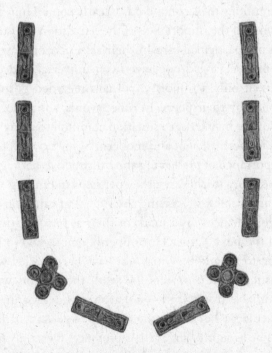

figure 9
Gold harness decoration from Pannonhalma.

rare. What is most remarkable about the presence of the Huns in Europe is the striking lack of archaeological evidence. Only some seventy burials have been identified that, on the basis of their characteristic features, might be thought to belong to Huns. This small number could simply be a reflection of their relatively brief domination of the middle Danube—roughly from 410 to 465, ten years after the death of Attila. The chances of survival play a part, too: leading Huns, as Priscus' description of Attila's funeral confirms, were interred beneath great earthen mounds, that—despite the brutal precautions taken at the time of burial—acted as prominent markers for tomb robbers.

Of course, the apparent absence of steppe finds in Europe is puzzling—or demands an explanation—only if Hun burial practices and objects are expected to be different from the settled communities they conquered. Clearly some Huns retained a strong sense of the importance of their traditional customs and habits, taking particular care in their selection of grave goods. But such practices need not have been universal; indeed, they may represent only a minority, perhaps regarded as stuffy and old-fashioned by their peers. In other words, the history of the Huns in Europe may reflect a situation common to many migrant communities both ancient and modern. Some no doubt insisted on the importance of preserving their distinctive heritage. They clung tenaciously to old ways: they persisted in binding the foreheads of their babies, in stewing their meat in cauldrons, and in wearing gold diadems as a mark of their superior status in this world and the next. Other Huns openly embraced Gothic culture and customs, and they may not have been buried with any characteristically Hun objects. In death these Huns would be indistinguishable from Goths—a sharp reminder that in dealing with archaeological evidence the absence of certain artifacts can sometimes be as significant as their presence. Certainly it would help to explain why there is only a small number of identifiably "Hun" burials in Europe.

The suggestion that from the early fifth century many Huns began to appear like Goths (at least in their burial practices) is also attractively consistent with the apparent lack of any major disruption to Gothic culture in the same period. Goths still lived in unfortified villages situated along fertile river valleys; they continued to cultivate millet, rye, and barley and raise livestock; they used much the same sorts of glassware and dull, wheel-made gray pottery. There were some changes in the appearance of the wealthiest, most fashion-conscious Goths, who began to wear large semicircular brooches, gold necklaces, and belts with big flat buckles. These developments had no certain origin on the steppes. They are more likely to have been the result of the intermixing of ideas and styles that followed the displacement and resettlement of peoples within Europe. In other words, changes in Gothic culture may reflect some of the consequences of the disruption caused by the migration of the Huns, but these changes did not draw directly on the heritage of the steppe itself.

The continued vitality of Gothic culture under Hun domination in the fifth century contrasts with conventional modern expectations of empire: that conquerors will impose their culture on the conquered. This is often a painful process, well known—as the imperial adjectives themselves attest—from the histories of Roman Britain, Spanish America, or British India. The imposition of Roman, Spanish, and British rule shattered local customs and beliefs. Defeated elites were among the first to reject traditional ways of life, advertising their willingness to collude with their conquerors by openly embracing their language, culture, and habits. This adoption of new ways was actively encouraged by imperial powers keen to maintain and support a local ruling class. In Roman Britain, country villas, with their mosaics, wall paintings, and central heating, did not house Italians sent out to govern a recently subdued province; rather, these new and ostentatiously Roman-looking buildings were the grand residences of a cooperative British-born elite.

Europe under Hun rule was strikingly different. It was not "an empire" in the way the Romans would have thought of (and praised) their own conquest of the Mediterranean world. North of the Danube, Gothic culture remained largely unchanged, nor is there any clear indication that leading Goths adopted Hun customs. This lack of cultural interaction might be explained by thinking of the Huns and Goths as isolated groups, but this is unsatisfactory: it is difficult to see how the Huns could ensure a regular flow of tribute without establishing a close relationship with the local elite, many of whom, in turn, benefited from the association with their new Hun overlords. It is better to assume that the culture of the rulers had no significant impact on the culture of the ruled. In other words, Gothic culture continued largely uninterrupted precisely because it was adopted by many Huns.

The Hun empire—as it deserves to be called—is, then, a significant exception to the usual pattern of imperial domination. Again that reflects the very different circumstances surrounding the conquest of settled communities by nomads. The successful establishment of an empire was in great part due to the Huns' abandonment of many of the customs and practices that had served them well on the steppes, but were either redundant or unsustainable in their new homeland. Once in permanent occupation of the Great Hungarian Plain, the Huns transformed themselves into an imperial power whose success relied on the systematic exploitation of existing Gothic society. The Hun empire was, above all, a parasitic state; its success lay in its ability to mimic the culture of those it ruled, to cream off their wealth, and to consume the food they produced. A minority of Huns, with their distinctive and recognizable grave goods, persisted in their adherence to the old ways; the majority became more like the settled Goths they had conquered. That shift made the conquerors archaeologically invisible. As Yeh-lü Ch'u-ts'ai, administrative reformer and adviser to Genghis Khan, would

shrewdly observe seven centuries later, "a country can be conquered but not governed from the saddle." By building an empire
in Europe, the Huns ceased to be nomads.

Back on the steppes, at least according to Ammianus Marcellinus,
the Huns were not "subject to the direction of a king"; clans of
perhaps five hundred to one thousand might group together in
time of war under "the improvised leadership of their chief men."
As pointed out in chapter 3, even in peacetime, Hun society was
much better organized than Ammianus was prepared to allow.
But aside from his sketchy and sometimes misleading remarks,
there is little information on the Huns' political organization.
Parallels with other nomads are again worth considering. If the
Huns were organized in ways similar to those of the Mongols
before Genghis Khan, then it is unlikely that all clans had equal
influence; some were more powerful, others subordinate, perhaps
as a result of military defeat, the lack of resources, or the need for
protection. Collective decisions were probably driven by a few
dominant clans, but within that broad framework the decision-
making process and its enforcement were loose enough to allow
particular clans or clan groups to pursue their own policies. This
is consistent with what is known of the westward movement of
the Huns into Europe: a general migration, not the tightly regi-
mented advance of a whole people.

It is possible, too, that clan membership was not fixed. Among
the Mongols, clans most commonly consisted of a number of
closely related families, but kinship was not the only way in
which a clan might be defined. Mongol custom also recognized
the possibility of *anda*, or sworn brotherhood, which allowed
clan members to move by being accepted in another clan as
the equivalent of a blood relative. Key to the establishment of
Genghis Khan's powerbase was the *nöker* system, a less binding

form of association in which a member of one clan could declare himself the "comrade" of a powerful person from another clan. The *nöker* system allowed a charismatic warrior to build up a following; equally that following could quickly dissolve if he failed to live up to his promise. The possibility that ambitious individuals from any clan could choose to offer or withdraw their support permitted the rapid rise—and sudden fall—of prominent leaders. It also undercut the establishment of the more permanent institution of kingship. Allowing loyalties to shift freely works against two of the fundamental assumptions of monarchy: that, whatever the circumstances, rulers should always be able to rely on their followers, and that authority and allegiance should pass from royal father to princely son.

The fragile position of Hun leaders is neatly demonstrated by the rise and fall of Uldin. Uldin had profited greatly from the Roman empire's inability to find a solution to the problems created by Alaric's Goths. In 401 he dealt directly with Arcadius, who may have planned to use Hun troops against the Goths in the Balkans, and in 406 he took his followers west to serve as mercenaries in Stilicho's army, defending the empire against another group of Goths led by Radagaisus. Three years later Uldin and his men were back in the East, but this time as a hostile force. In 408 he led a Hun war band across the Danube, raiding deep into Roman territory. Initial offers of peace were rejected, and Uldin demanded a large payoff before he would agree to withdraw. His threats were expansive: pointing to the sky, he declared that his Hun army could conquer all the lands on which the sun shone. Confronted with such arrogance, Roman negotiators tried a different tactic, opening discussions with Uldin's senior officers. According to the Christian historian Sozomen, writing thirty years later in Constantinople, Uldin's men were moved by the intervention of God to recognize the superiority of "the Roman form of government, the philanthropy of the emperor, and his swiftness and generosity in rewarding the best men." It may, of course, have been through a heated debate on political philosophy that Uldin's followers were won over, or, perhaps more likely, it was a result of the solid prospect of the emperor's generosity. Either way, the Roman plan worked; the Huns were bought off and peace concluded. Abandoned by most of his comrades, Uldin barely made it safely back across the Danube. Many of those who decided to stay with him on his desperate dash to the frontier were captured and sold into slavery.

Only as long as they were successful could Hun leaders expect to rely on their followers. This arrangement allowed those Huns important merely within their clans to support whoever might seem to offer the best prospect of immediate advancement and reward, whether by attacking the Goths or by fighting as mer- cenaries in the pay of a Roman emperor. Such a volatile sys- tem was vulnerable to manipulation. Against Uldin in 408, the Romans achieved a double victory: they both purchased peace and undermined a prominent Hun. That latter tactic was repeated four years later when the historian Olympiodorus was sent on an embassy to the Huns on behalf of the eastern court. No coherent account of this mission survives. Olympiodorus' lengthy history covering events from 407 to 425 is preserved in only forty-three fragments, some only a brief paragraph. Worse still, the few lines that deal with his own embassy to the Huns come from a sum- mary of his original text made four hundred years later by an unsympathetic scholar in Constantinople who found Olympio- dorus' work "laid back and loosely organized with a tendency toward the banal and vulgar—so much so that it is not worthy of being classified as history."

Olympiodorus left the imperial capital in late 412 or early 413 and sailed in stormy weather around Greece and up the Adriatic Sea, a good indication that the Huns he was to meet were located on the middle Danube. He was accompanied on the voyage by his parakeet. He was very proud of this bird, at least according to the impatient scholar who also recorded Olympiodorus' praise of his

pet's abilities, no doubt as proof of his triviality: "Olympiodorus
also mentions a parakeet he had with him for twenty years. He
says there was scarcely any human action it could not imitate. It
could dance, sing, call out names, and do other things." Regrettably, the reaction of the Huns to the arrival of this bird-fancying
Roman ambassador and his performing parakeet is not known.
Perhaps some realized, too late, that this was the colorful front
to serious diplomatic business.

The much reduced version of Olympiodorus' history that survives makes it is impossible to reconstruct events securely, but
it seems that he was involved in the assassination of one prominent Hun, called Donatus, and in buying off the objections of
another, called Charaton. Like Olympiodorus' parakeet, Charaton's anger may have been a decoy to divert suspicion from his
own involvement. Perhaps Charaton had invited the Romans and
conspired with them to rub out a rival, promising for a price to
promote friendly relations with the empire; or perhaps Donatus was eliminated by a competing faction because of his close
involvement with the Roman ambassador. More than this it is
difficult to say, but it seems likely that Olympiodorus' embassy
is another example of Roman exploitation of the unstable nature
of Hun leadership. Clearly, whatever the advantages of allowing
a talented individual from any clan to acquire a following, there
were also drawbacks in fueling fierce competition that could suddenly flare up in fatal feuds. Ever-changing loyalties encouraged
division and internal conflict. Temporary support for one leader
might work well in times of war—at least for a short and victorious expedition—but the uncertainty of any continuing obligation
made it less suitable for the conduct of a longer campaign or for
the management of a settled society.

During the fifty years in which the Huns had migrated from
the Black Sea to Hungary, they had operated as a series of loosely
connected clan groups. This had been sufficient to disrupt and
displace those living north of the Danube and for some Hun war

bands to take advantage of the Roman army's need for mercenaries. In effect, the Huns both created a persistent security problem for the empire and offered themselves as part of the solution. Yet, as the Huns extended and consolidated their control over new territories and peoples, it was clear that there was a limit to the effectiveness and profitability of continual raids. An unregulated cycle of opportunistic violence was inadequate to meet the demands of a permanent state. If tribute were systematically to be extracted from conquered territory, then it was necessary to establish a more stable form of government. In addition, any expansion of Hun dominance, especially against the Roman empire, required a greater concentration of military effort focused on a single objective, the closer coordination of individual clans, and well-planned campaigns. It was not until all clan groups could be united under one leader, to whom his followers owed lasting and unquestioned allegiance, that the destructive potential of the Huns could be fully realized. Remarkably, this was substantially achieved in the next thirty years. Key changes mark out the difference in the organization of Hun society between Uldin and Attila. More widely, they are part of the extraordinary transformation during the first half of the fifth century of a nomadic people who had moved westward from the vast wilderness of the steppes to settle permanently in the confines of the Great Hungarian Plain.

PART TWO

HUNS AND ROMANS

CHAPTER SIX
A TALE OF TWO CITIES

In Constantinople in May 408 Arcadius died. The emperor, shrouded in purple, lay in state in the Great Palace. Senior courtiers (in strict order of precedence) filed slowly past, their impassive faces briefly illuminated in the flickering light of the candles that surrounded the golden coffin. The city went into mourning; shops and public buildings were closed. In a solemn procession, Arcadius' body was carried from the Great Palace up the hill to the imperial mausoleum. A huge crowd stood listening to the heavy, rhythmic tread of the dead emperor's guard of honor and to the rising lamentations of the choirs of nuns and priests that followed the cortège. The air was sweet with the purifying smell of incense. At the rear of the funeral procession—in the place of highest honor—was Arcadius' son, the new ruler of the eastern Roman empire, Theodosius II (see figure 10).

Theodosius was then only seven years old. His unchallenged elevation was assisted by Arcadius' foresight; six years earlier he had made his infant son his imperial equal. Following Arcadius' death, there was no "succession crisis": Theodosius was already an emperor. For the first years of his sole reign, the real business of government was carried out by Anthemius, praetorian prefect of the East. The prefecture—which had its distant origin in the praetorian guard that had once been responsible for the safety of emperors in Rome—had overall responsibility for judicial and

figure 10
Emperor Theodosius II, marble bust
(10 inches high), probably carved in
Constantinople, 430–40. This is
the only known bust of the emperor.

financial matters, taxation, army recruitment, public works, and administrative affairs in a vast territory that covered most of the eastern empire. After a successful career, working his way steadily through the senior administrative posts at court, the Egyptian-born Anthemius had been appointed prefect three years before Arcadius' death. He was one of the emperor's most trusted advisers and well known as a capable consensus politician. In the judgment of one contemporary, the prefect "was the most resourceful man of his time and held in high regard. He never undertook anything without first taking advice, and on matters of state he sought the opinions of most of his close friends."

Anthemius not only managed the smooth transfer of imperial power from father to son; he also ensured the confirmation of a nonaggression pact with Persia. In 400 Anthemius had been one of the ambassadors sent to the Persian capital, Ctesiphon, to congratulate Yazdgard I on his accession the year before. In 408 Yazdgard affirmed his intention to maintain cordial relations with the Roman empire and threatened war on any who dared rebel against its new boy emperor. It was also made known that the Persian king had agreed to act as an executor of Arcadius' will and to look after his young son's interests until he came of age. This might have been true, or it might have been a useful exaggeration of Yazdgard's diplomatic expressions of brotherly affection for Theodosius. Certainly for the prefect and his supporters, the apparent intervention in Roman dynastic politics of such a strong ruler was to be welcomed. It helped prevent a repeat of the distrust and disunity that had followed Stilicho's claim to have been named as regent by the dying Theodosius I. Fifteen years later, it was to everyone's advantage that Theodosius II's powerful protector should be not at court at Constantinople but safely distant, over one thousand miles away in Ctesiphon.

The knowledge that the eastern frontier was stable and the Persian king personally friendly allowed more resources to be directed to the defense of the northern frontier and the security of Constantinople. In 412 Theodosius authorized the refitting of the Danube fleet. A carefully worked-out system of repairs, rolling replacements, and additions ensured that 225 river patrol craft would be commissioned over seven years. The emperor also approved Anthemius' proposal to build a second line of walls to protect the imperial capital. In 324, as part of his original foundation, Constantine had planned a wall enclosing an area of roughly two and a half square miles. Ninety years later, Constantinople had outgrown these defenses. The project to construct another set of fortifications was an ambitious one. The aim was to safeguard the whole of the peninsula on which Constantinople was sited and to allow for the further expansion of the city within that protected zone. Anthemius' scheme nearly doubled the area defended by Constantine by building a new belt of walls just over half a mile beyond the old and running shore to shore from the Golden Horn to the Propontis.

The Theodosian Walls—named in honor of the young emperor who commissioned them—were among the most formidable military structures ever built in the Roman empire (see figure

figure 11
Theodosian Walls, Constantinople.

11). The raw statistics are impressive enough. A series of parallel
defenses 180 feet deep ran for three and a half miles. The inner
wall was 36 feet high (roughly four stories) and 16 feet thick at its
base. A strong rubble core was faced with blocks of white limestone set with bands of red brick. The inner wall was punctuated
by ninety-six towers, 60 feet high and set at irregular intervals. In
front was a raised terrace 50 feet wide. In turn, this dead ground
was screened by an outer wall 26 feet high and reinforced by
ninety towers, offset from those in the inner wall. Finally, in
front of the outer wall, another broad terrace and a dry moat 20
feet deep and 60 wide. The ongoing maintenance and repair of
the newly constructed Theodosian Walls was financed through
their partial privatization. The towers were leased back to those
who owned the land on which they were built. In return for these
valuable properties—all with stunning city views—tenants were
required to pay for their upkeep. In the words of the imperial
regulations issued in April 413, "Thus the splendor of the work

and the fortifications of the capital shall be preserved, as well as their use for the benefit of private citizens."

The Theodosian Walls have been steadily restored over the last decade. Long stretches of the inner wall and many of its towers now stand at near their original height. Little remains of the great moat; it has mostly been filled in. The raised terrace is no longer visible; its stone has long since been carried away. This once vital defensive space is now a green mosaic of suburban allotments: here vines flourish and fruit ripens against the white, sun-warmed limestone. Too few visitors to Istanbul take the time (about half a day) to walk the length of the Theodosian Walls. For those living in Constantinople at the beginning of the fifth century, this solid fortified line represented the power and security of the Roman empire. The walls' protective presence added to the magnificence of the imperial capital. Thanks to its massive defenses, no other city in the Mediterranean world was so well shielded from attack. Even if the frontier provinces south of the Danube fell to an invading army of Huns or Goths, Constantinople would be able to stand firm.

In Ravenna in August 423, the western emperor Honorius died, fifteen years after his elder brother, Arcadius. It is probable that Honorius, like his father, Theodosius I, suffered from edema, traditionally known as dropsy, a condition in which the body is unable to regulate the intake and excretion of fluid. Death commonly follows kidney failure or a pulmonary edema, a heart attack brought on by the pressure of fluid retained in the lungs. Theodosius II, who had carefully prepared for his uncle's death, moved quickly to assert his authority over the West. But his attempt to return to a united Roman empire did not run according to plan. In Ravenna, leading courtiers and military officers backed a senior bureaucrat, named John. In Constantinople,

figure 12
Framed gold medallion of Galla Placidia,
minted in Ravenna, 425–30.

Theodosius had to reckon with the claims of his aunt Galla Placidia and her young son Valentinian.

Galla Placidia was a princess of impeccable imperial pedigree: she was the daughter of Theodosius I and his second wife, Galla, and so half sister to Honorius and Arcadius (see figure 12). She was accounted a great beauty by many who met her, although flattering convention always insists that princesses are beautiful. More astute observers were struck by her sharp wit, shrewd political judgment, and ruthless ambition. In 395, at the age of seven, Galla Placidia was in Milan when her father died and had remained in the West with its new emperor, Honorius. She had been taken hostage by the Goths during Alaric's siege of Rome in 410. On New Year's Day 417, under pressure from her half brother, she reluctantly married the general Flavius Constantius, who, after the execution of Stilicho in August 408, was Honorius' most trusted commander and responsible for the permanent settlement of the Goths in France.

The marriage between Flavius Constantius and Galla Placidia had clear dynastic implications, particularly since the childless Honorius, in a public display of Christian piety, had declared himself strictly celibate. In late 417 Galla gave birth to a daughter, Justa Grata Honoria, and eighteen months later to a son, Valentinian. In 421 Honorius made Constantius co-emperor and conferred the impressive title of *nobilissimus* ("most noble") on

Valentinian, marking out the two-year-old boy as his successor. Theodosius, who regarded himself as Honorius' rightful heir, refused to recognize either Valentinian's title or Constantius' new imperial rank. The stalemate did not last long. Death and exile altered everything. After only seven months of joint rule with Honorius, Constantius died. Two years later, in early 423, his widow and her two young children fled Ravenna to seek safety in Constantinople. Justly or not, Galla Placidia had been accused by Honorius of plotting his downfall. Having carefully designated a successor, Honorius now regretted it. While he was content to be followed by Valentinian, he had no intention of being replaced by him.

Galla Placidia received a cool reception at the eastern court. Although offering her protection, Theodosius declined to support Valentinian. Following Honorius' death, he still intended to assert his own claim over the West and make Constantinople— as it had been briefly under his grandfather Theodosius I—the capital of a unified empire. That was a vain and outdated ambition. In the thirty–five years since Theodosius I had marched into Italy to defeat the usurpers Magnus Maximus and Eugenius, too much had changed: Rome had been sacked by Alaric, the Rhine frontier had been seriously breached, the Goths had found a new homeland in France, and the Huns had occupied the Great Hungarian Plain. The West could not be ruled from the other side of the Mediterranean; it was now too unstable and its defenses too fragile. Moreover, after Honorius' death, the strong support for the bureaucrat John was a telling indication that influential courtiers in Ravenna would resist any attempt to force them to shift their allegiance nine hundred miles east to Constantinople.

Confronted with John's rebellion, Theodosius speedily changed his views. He retrospectively recognized the dead Constantius as emperor and Valentinian's status as Honorius' legitimate heir. The connection between the East and the West was to be confirmed by the future marriage of Valentinian to Theodosius' daughter, Licinia Eudoxia, then only two years old. In 425 a rapidly assembled force, commanded by Flavius Aspar, was sent to northern Italy. The city of Aquileia, on the Adriatic coast, sixty miles east of modern Venice, was captured, and Ravenna fell soon after. Those who saw the advance of the imperial army as confirming the will of God claimed that an angel disguised as a shepherd had shown Aspar a secret pathway across the marshes surrounding the city. Others, more skeptical, thought that the shepherd—well rewarded for his services—had been precisely what he seemed.

This theological dispute was of little consequence to John. Dragged back to Aquileia, the failed usurper was led around the hippodrome on a donkey. The crowd jeered as he was forced to take part in a crude pantomime reenactment of his downfall. After this humiliating entertainment, John's right hand was cut off and he was beheaded. From their seats, shaded by purple hangings trimmed with gold, Galla Placidia and her two children, it may safely be assumed, watched the vicious spectacle with a pitiless indifference. It was a grim reminder that the risks of court politics were fatally high. The losers, mutilated like criminals, deserved to die in the arena; the winners had earned the privilege to watch their execution from the splendor of the imperial box.

Despite these victory celebrations, the war was not yet over. A few months earlier, John had sent a middle-ranking palace official, Flavius Aetius, with a large sum in gold to seek the help of the Huns. Aetius was a good choice; he came from a wealthy and influential family with a distinguished record of administrative and military service. His father, Gaudentius, had governed a province in North Africa, before commanding imperial troops in France, where he was killed during a mutiny. Those who favored Aetius described him in admiring terms.

He was of average height, manly in appearance with a well-toned body, neither too slight nor too stocky. . . . He was never deflected from his goal by those who encouraged him to act improperly. He was at his most patient when wronged. He was always eager to take on work. He was undaunted when facing danger, and his ability to endure hunger, thirst, and lack of sleep was remarkable. From an early age, he seemed aware that he had been marked out by destiny for great power.

In 409, while still a teenager, Aetius had been sent along with other aristocratic hostages as part of Honorius' surety for a levy of ten thousand Hun mercenaries. Beyond the Danube, Aetius seems to have been well treated, spending his time in the company of the sons of the Hun elite. He returned an excellent horseman and a deadly accurate bowman. He had also formed a number of genuine friendships with Huns whom—contrary to Roman prejudices—he found he could both respect and trust. In 425 it was precisely this privileged relationship that John hoped to turn to his own advantage. The mission was successful. The persuasive combination of Aetius' connections and John's cash raised a sizable army. Some claimed in panicked exaggeration that sixty thousand Huns were marching on Ravenna. But help came too late: the mercenaries entered northern Italy three days after John had been decapitated. Following a costly encounter with Aspar's troops, Aetius abandoned John's cause and instead furthered his own. Galla Placidia had no option but to negotiate; reluctantly, she agreed to pay off the Huns and appoint Aetius commander of imperial forces in France.

When news of John's execution reached Theodosius in Constantinople, he was presiding over chariot races in the hippodrome. Immediately he canceled the rest of the program and ordered a service of thanksgiving. A victory procession was hur-

figure 13
Gold coin of Valentinian III, minted in
Rome. The emperor is shown triumphing
over his enemies in the form of a human-
headed serpent.

riedly formed, and the chanting of the city's sports fans soon gave way to the singing of hymns in praise of the ever-triumphant Christ. In Ravenna, Galla Placidia, while also giving thanks to the divinity, no doubt wished that John's defeat had been followed by the elimination or exile of his supporters. She resented having to promote her enemies to powerful posts. It is unlikely that this was the all-conquering return she had prayed for. In successfully extorting a senior military command, Aetius had exposed the damaging possibility that Hun mercenaries might be used not to defend the empire but to advance the factional interests of ambitious Roman generals. For the moment, all at court proclaimed themselves loyal to the new boy emperor, Valentinian III, and his formidable mother (see figure 13). Yet all must have been uncomfortably aware that had Aetius and his Huns arrived in Italy only a few days earlier, it might be John and his military backers who now ruled in Ravenna.

CHAPTER SEVEN

WAR ON THREE FRONTS

The greatest threat faced by the Roman empire was war with more than one enemy. Military operations on two fronts inevitably stretched manpower and resources, and made an inconclusive outcome more likely. It heightened the risk of a long conflict—as time dragged on, an expected quick victory might erode into an expensive and demoralizing stalemate finally forcing withdrawal or compromise. These possibilities could also be exploited by those hostile to the empire. With Roman forces committed on one front the chances of an invasion on another— perhaps hundreds of miles away—was significantly increased. For Roman commanders, maintaining a balance between defense and offense was always difficult: should troops be deployed on active service in a war zone or stationed in reserve along a frontier against the possibility of an attack? In the 420s and 430s, this problem repeatedly confronted Theodosius II as he faced tough campaigns in Mesopotamia and in North Africa while attempting to ensure the security of the Balkan provinces in the face of the continued threat of Hun incursions across the Danube. No matter how powerful an empire, there is always a limit to the number of wars it can fight at the same time.

In 420, five years before the restoration of Galla Placidia and Valentinian in Ravenna, the fanatical leader of a martyr brigade set fire to a temple in the Persian province of Khuzistan, in the south of modern Iraq. This radical extremist expected to be killed on the spot by guards. The aim of his suicide mission was to strike a dramatic blow against Zoroastrianism, the main religion of the Persian empire. Abdaas, a Christian bishop, succeeded in destroying the temple, but not in securing his immediate death. Arrested, he was taken before Yazdgard I, who for the last twenty years had been tolerant toward Christianity. Abdaas and his followers changed the Persian king's mind. They rejected his suggestion that, as a gesture of reconciliation with other faith communities in Khuzistan, they should rebuild the burned-out temple. Abdaas' refusal convinced Yazdgard that some Christians in his empire had no intention of integrating into Persian society; rather, they had taken advantage of his liberal policies to pursue their subversive activities. Reluctantly he authorized severe countermeasures: Christians were to be rounded up and executed, and their churches demolished. In the face of systematic Persian reprisals, some Christians chose to die for their faith; others fled across the frontier to seek refuge in the Roman empire.

Yazdgard's persecution was denounced in Constantinople. When in the following year it was intensified by his son and successor, Bahrām V, Theodosius ordered a tough military response. This is an important moment in the history of the Roman empire: it marked the first time that an emperor had declared war explicitly to protect Christians. Theodosius' supporters claimed that God was on the Roman side: 100,000 desert Arabs on their way to fight for Persia were reported to have been seized with a divinely inspired terror and thrown themselves into the Euphrates River. Yet, despite the support of such well-timed miracles and some initial success in the field, Roman forces in northern Mesopotamia failed to achieve any decisive superiority. In 422, negotiations were opened and peace restored. Both sides agreed not to add to the fortifications along the frontier and proclaimed mutual toleration of Christians in Persia and the far fewer Zoroastrians in the Roman empire.

One significant factor in the abandonment of Theodosius' crusade after less than a year was a sudden attack across the Danube. In early 422, the Huns took advantage of Roman troop commitments in Persia and marched south into Thrace (roughly modern Bulgaria). How this offensive was organized is not known, nor is there any record of the name of its leader. The incursion is reported only in one brief entry in a sixth-century chronicle: "The Huns laid waste Thrace." The scale of the incursion, clearly more than a cross-border raid, forced the immediate recall of units from Mesopotamia. There were strict strategic limits to Theodosius' religious fervor. Only peace with Persia could ensure that sufficient manpower was available for the defense of the Balkans. A law issued on 3 March 422 formed part of the provisions hurriedly put in place to cope with such large troop movements. The emperor instructed landowners leasing towers in the Theodosian Walls to assist with the provision of emergency accommodation: "Our most loyal troops returning from active service or setting out to war shall take for their own use the ground floor of each tower in the new walls of this most sacred city."

The redeployment of troops was sufficient to force an agreement with the Huns, who withdrew on the promise of an annual payment of 350 pounds of gold. In Constantinople the settlements with both the Huns and the Persians were claimed as successes. A statue of the emperor was put up at the Hebdomon, the military parade ground on the shores of the Propontis, just outside the Theodosian Walls. The statue has not survived; on its base (the fragments are now in the Istanbul Archaeological Museum), an inscription praised Theodosius as "everywhere and forever victorious." That, of course, was not true; but given the failure to defeat either the Persians or the Huns, it was shrewder to negotiate peace and then to celebrate this as a Roman triumph.

The next crisis that faced Theodosius was unlikely to be resolved so swiftly or simply. It had its origins in the disruption caused by the westward advance of the Huns a generation earlier. In December 406, the Vandals had crossed the Rhine; they had then moved through France and by 409 reached Spain. Twenty years later, having failed to find land on which they could settle safely, they crossed the Strait of Gibraltar. The Vandal push into North Africa was a more serious threat to the integrity of the empire than their presence in Spain. These provinces were among the most prosperous in the Mediterranean. The large agricultural estates that ran along the wide coastal strip produced wine, oil, grain, and tax revenue in abundance. This was the granary of the Roman world. Carthage, North Africa's main port, was a wealthy city, its great harbor ringed by warehouses and well-equipped dockyards. With a population of 200,000, it was rivaled in size and importance only by Rome, Constantinople, Antioch, and Alexandria, on the Nile Delta. The Vandal invasion in spring 429 threatened to shatter this imperial world unified around a single sea. The Romans referred to the Mediterranean simply as *mare nostrum*—"our sea"—and for nearly five hundred years the empire had completely encircled its shores. The loss of the North African coast would expose Italy to attack. From Carthage the Vandals could launch an invasion fleet against Rome or Ravenna and even reach Constantinople. The fortifications along the eastern and northern frontiers might provide protection from the Persians and the Huns, but against an attack from Africa they were—quite literally—facing the wrong way.

In the division of the Roman empire in the fourth century, North Africa (apart from Egypt and Libya) had been allocated to the West. Yet in the face of the Vandal invasion, Theodosius decided to step in, unwilling to leave the direction of such a critical conflict to the eleven-year-old Valentinian III and his mother. In 431 Flavius Aspar, who had captured Aquileia and Ravenna in 425, was sent with an army to reinforce troops under Boniface,

the western imperial commander. This close military cooperation was in stark contrast to previous frictions. The threat posed
by the Vandals was too great to risk disunity. It was hoped that
the combined resources of the eastern and the western empires
might result in a rapid and decisive victory. But the Vandals under
their leader Geiseric were not so easily suppressed. Boniface and
Aspar were able to halt their advance, but no more. Defeated in
battle on open ground in early 432, Roman troops withdrew to
Carthage. Two years later it was clear that, if the Vandals were
to be dislodged, Theodosius would need to commit additional
resources to the African front. For governments determined to go
to war in distant lands, justifications for an ongoing commitment
can always be found. To pull out after three years of hard fighting
was politically unattractive, and this time there was little chance
of presenting withdrawal as a military triumph. By abandoning
North Africa, Theodosius, who had once proclaimed himself
"everywhere and forever victorious," could be seen to be turning
his back on the West.

Nor was there any evidence of a significant threat on the northern frontier. Diplomatic relations had been established with the
Hun leader Rua. Along with his brother Octar, who died in
430, Rua is the next Hun leader to be named by Roman writers
after Uldin, Donatus, and Charaton. (Either Rua or Octar may
have been the unnamed Hun leader responsible for the invasion
of Thrace in 422.) In early 434, through Eslas, the Huns' ambassador at court in Constantinople, Rua declared his intention
to attack a number of tribes north of the Danube. He insisted
that any young men who had already fled across the frontier
and joined the Roman army should be handed over without
delay. Negotiations on a final resolution to these demands were
in progress, and ambassadors had only recently been dispatched
for a further round of talks. Theodosius and his advisers took a
carefully calculated risk: on balance they judged the chances of a
Hun invasion to be low. Under these circumstances, it was in the

empire's best interests to continue the war against Geiseric. The task force would not be recalled for the defense of the Danube provinces. It would remain in Africa and finish the job.

A few months later, in the summer of 434, the Huns attacked. Perhaps negotiations over asylum seekers finally broke down; perhaps Rua had misled the ambassadors all along, his diplomatic wrangling masking his real intentions; perhaps the change of plan was sheer opportunism once it was clear that Roman troops in Africa would not be redeployed. As the Huns devastated Thrace, moving steadily toward Constantinople, the city's terror-stricken citizens expected a long and bloody siege. Their safety would depend on the strength of the Theodosian Walls. It would be the first time that the capital's new defenses had been tested in action. At court those criticized for failing to foresee Rua's invasion would have regarded such censure as unjustified. After all, as they perhaps hurried to assure Theodosius, they had reached a reasonable conclusion after a careful consideration of all the available evidence. It is a harsh political truth that some judgments, however correct they may appear at the time, can in hindsight turn out to be completely wrong.

It is equally true that, in the resolution of a crisis, good luck can sometimes be just as important as good judgment. Without warning, the Huns withdrew. The reasons for this abrupt change in tactics are unclear. The best explanation is the sudden death of Rua. It may be that his successors did not feel confident in establishing their authority while on campaign, and particularly before the walls of the imperial capital. Theodosius believed that the Huns' retreat was an act of God in direct answer to his prayers. In Constantinople, it was rumored that Rua had been incinerated by a providential lightning bolt. His followers were said to have been killed by plague and scorched by fireballs. Proclus, bishop of Constantinople, in a sermon giving thanks for the city's deliverance, was convinced that these events had been foretold in the visions of the Old Testament prophet Ezekiel, whose prediction of the defeat of Gog could now be understood to refer to the Huns: "Thus says the Lord God: 'Son of man, set your face toward Gog, of the land of Magog. . . . With pestilence and bloodshed I will enter into judgment with him; and I will rain upon him and his hordes, and the many peoples that are with him, torrential rains and hailstones, fire and brimstone.'"

The imperial capital had been saved either by chance or by the well-directed intervention of the divinity. Theodosius, now parading piety rather than policy, took full credit for the achievement. Two narrow escapes (the rapid reversal of the crusade against Persia and the unexpected death of Rua) had prevented major military disasters. Perhaps the Persian campaign could have been avoided, although as a committed Christian Theodosius had no doubt of his obligation to protect his persecuted fellow believers. The war in Africa was more pressing. To relinquish control to the Vandals without a fight would be to stand aside while the empire was dismembered; the emperor and his advisers had no option but to risk an African campaign; yet to misjudge the situation was to imperil Constantinople itself. To his credit, Theodosius remained willing to accept a compromise that allowed troops to be withdrawn. In 435, the year after Rua's death, a treaty formally ratified by Valentinian—North Africa was part of the western empire—granted the Vandals the land they had already occupied in the province of Numidia. The more fertile territory (roughly modern Tunisia), along with the vital port city of Carthage, remained safe in Roman hands.

Theodosius had no option but to accept these concessions. The need to defend the Danube and the imperial capital against the Huns critically restricted the eastern Roman empire's ability to pursue its wider strategic goals. Improved fortifications, more river patrol craft, and the building of the Theodosian Walls reduced, but did not eliminate, the pressure on the northern frontier. These measures helped slow the enemy's advance, rather than preventing a full-scale invasion. All the more reason, then, to celebrate Rua's fiery demise. For those who remembered the defeat of Uldin or Olympiodorus' embassy and the murder of Donatus, the sudden withdrawal after Rua's death also held out the possibility that the Hun problem might be solved by opposing clans exhausting themselves in a lengthy civil war. Those, like the bishop of Constantinople, who argued that contemporary events had been predicted by Ezekiel no doubt drew some cheer from his words: "Thus says the Lord God: 'Behold, I am against you, O Gog. . . . I will strike your bow from your left hand, and will make your arrows drop out of your right hand.'"

But this was cold comfort. Ezekiel may have foreseen the destruction of Gog, but his vision was of the coming of the Antichrist and the end of the world. Nor could the emperor, for all his religious convictions, be expected to formulate the empire's foreign policy on the basis of a Christian bishop's reading of the Old Testament. Perhaps Gog would eventually be defeated, but analysis of the latest reports indicated that the Huns had regrouped and Rua had been replaced by two of his nephews. Much now depended on their ability to assert their joint authority. And that was difficult to predict—even with the prophetic assistance of Ezekiel. More information was needed by Theodosius and his military advisers before the situation beyond the Danube could be fully understood and its security implications properly assessed. For the moment, the new Hun leaders were no more than two strange and unfamiliar sounding names: Bleda and his younger brother, Attila.

CHAPTER EIGHT

BROTHERS IN ARMS

Attila the Hun was no son of the steppes. He was probably born at the beginning of the fifth century somewhere on the Great Hungarian Plain. Attila's father was called Mundiuch, his mother's name is not known. Mundiuch was brother to Octar and Rua, joint leaders of the Huns in the late 420s and 430s. As a member of the most powerful family north of the Danube, Attila had a highly privileged upbringing. Certainly he was not the homeless, half-starved barbarian child of Ammianus Marcellinus' imagination: "Huns are never sheltered by buildings. . . . Not even a hut thatched with reeds can be found among them. Rather, the Huns roam freely in the mountains and woods, learning from their earliest childhood to endure freezing cold, hunger, and thirst." Nor, perhaps to Ammianus' disappointment, is Attila ever likely to have worn goatskin leggings or to have been sewn into clothes made from the pelts of wild mice until they fell to pieces bit by bit.

The young Attila spent most of his time in the company of his elder brother, Bleda. Together they were taught archery, how to fight with sword and lasso, and how to ride and care for a horse. Both were likely to have been taught to speak, and perhaps to read, Gothic and Latin: Latin for conducting business with the Roman empire, Gothic for controlling conquered territory in central and eastern Europe. Attila and Bleda also learned something of military and diplomatic tactics. They may have been present, somewhere quietly in the background, when Rua and Octar received Roman ambassadors. As young men, they took a leading part in Hun raids across the Danube and north of the Great Hungarian Plain. No doubt some high-ranking Huns assumed that one day, like their uncles, Bleda and Attila would rule the Huns together.

This cannot have been certain. After Octar's death, Rua resisted any pressure to share power. His own sudden death deep in Roman territory must have been a dangerous moment for his nephews. Perhaps they had the support of those who wished to see joint rule restored; perhaps others were less confident than Rua of the strategic wisdom of advancing on Constantinople and were prepared to follow new commanders brave enough to lead an orderly retreat. Perhaps it was Rua's unexpected death on campaign that really mattered. It allowed Attila and Bleda to secure the loyalty of the army before it returned home. No doubt, back on the Great Hungarian Plain, there were rival candidates. In seizing power, Attila and Bleda are likely to have had blood on their hands. Rua may well have had sons of his own. If so, nothing is known of them. After their father's death, they may not have survived for long.

Both Octar and Rua had strengthened Hun control over territory north of the Danube. Of this process—again owing to the lack of interest of Roman writers—only a few fragments of information survive. According to Priscus of Panium, prior to the invasion of 434, Rua was concerned to keep refugees from "the Amilzuri, Itimari, Tounsoures, Boisci, and other tribes living near the Danube" from crossing the frontier and joining the Roman army. Nothing is known about these tribes; the best conjecture is that these were some of the steppe peoples settled around the Black Sea who were swept into Europe by the Huns' westward migration in the fourth century. Now their loyalty could not be guaranteed, and it might have been to their advantage to side with the Romans. That was to be prevented by force. Before suddenly changing his plans and marching against the empire, Rua claimed to be considering an agreement with Theodosius that would allow Hun troops to campaign on the northern bank of the Danube without Roman interference.

A few years earlier, in 430, Octar had attempted to push Hun rule farther west by attacking the Burgundians who occupied territory on the Rhine around modern Worms, in southwestern Germany. The account of this expedition is buried in the story of the Burgundians' conversion to Christianity as told a decade later by the historian Socrates (christened by his parents in honor of the great Greek philosopher who had died 850 years earlier):

> There is a nation of barbarians known as Burgundians who live beyond the Rhine. . . . The Huns, by repeatedly attacking these people, devastated their territory and often killed large numbers of them. In this crisis the Burgundians decided not to seek any human help, but to entrust themselves to some divinity. As they were clear in their minds that the god of the Romans offered the greatest assistance to those who feared him . . . they went to one of the cities in France and asked the bishop there to baptize them as Christians. . . . Then they marched against the Huns, and were not disappointed in their hopes. For when Uptaros, king of the Huns, burst during the night as a result of his overindulgence, the Burgundians attacked the Huns, who were now leaderless. . . . The Burgundians were only three thousand men, but they destroyed around ten thousand of the enemy. From then on, the Burgundians were fervent Christians.

For those who believe in miracles, much may be salvaged from this pious text. The explosive death of Uptaros, painfully ruptured after a night of gluttonous excess, is a delightful moment of divine comedy in a serious tale of the triumph of Christianity. For those less certain of humorous heavenly interventions in the course of history, it is still possible to see in the outline of Socrates' account a memory of the defeat of Octar (here called Uptaros) in his attempt to push the Hun empire as far west as the Rhine.

Rua's need to bring tribes along the Danube into line and Octar's failed expedition against the Burgundians are reminders that Attila and Bleda inherited an empire established by military force. Moreover, its stability could not always be guaranteed. While some peoples fled in the face of the Hun advance, others were capable of putting up a fight. The Hun migration into Europe was no walkover. That said, their superior horsemanship and continual raids, mostly against unprotected farming communities, meant that local resistance was eventually broken. The victory of the Burgundians was an exception, and that was possible only with well-disciplined troops able to take advantage of an unexpected situation.

Octar's and Rua's efforts to strengthen the Huns' hold over central Europe were continued by Attila and Bleda. Again, aside from campaigns along the Rhine (discussed in the following chapter), during the first six years of their joint rule (434–40), it is difficult to trace in any detail their part in the expansion of the Hun empire. It was perhaps by the late 430s that it extended, in Priscus' vague description, as far as "the islands in the Ocean," that is, as far north as the Baltic Sea. Alongside the acquisition of new territories, Attila and Bleda also promoted the consolidation of Hun rule. As suggested in chapter 5, the regular payment of tribute depended on the cooperation of the locally powerful. Some acted out of fear; others, out of self-interest. Faced with the options of fleeing into the Roman empire or taking to the hills as freedom fighters, they preferred to come to an arrangement with the Huns. Attila and Bleda allowed these collaborators to retain control over their own affairs and welcomed them as friends and companions. For many, the decision to side with the enemy was a pragmatic choice. Not everyone confronted with conquest always joins the resistance.

The extent to which it was possible for local rulers to accumulate considerable wealth is spectacularly revealed by the Pietroasa treasure. This hoard was found buried under limestone boulders near the Romanian village of Pietroasa, in the foothills of the Carpathian Mountains. Among the objects now on display in National Museum of Romanian History in Bucharest are four large brooches, one bowl, two cups, three necklaces, a great circular tray, and a tall pitcher. All are solid gold, together weighing over forty pounds. The Pietroasa treasure has a checkered history. The two peasants who discovered it in 1837 divided the twenty-two finds between them by cutting some of them up. The dealer to whom they sold these now badly mutilated objects was interested mainly in their value as bullion. He was responsible for prying out most of the precious stones and for breaking up some of the objects with an ax. By the time the treasure was seized by the Romanian authorities, it had been severely damaged; only twelve items were recovered. Following repairs, they were put on display in 1842 in the National Museum of Antiquities.

Then, one winter night in 1875, during a heavy snowstorm, the treasure was stolen by a young novice priest. The theft was cleverly planned. A small hole was cut in the ceiling of the gallery and an umbrella inserted. The umbrella was then opened and used to catch the plaster as the hole was enlarged. Next, the thief lowered himself on a rope, easily opened the display case, and, concealing the contents in an improvised sack made from his underclothes, left the museum quietly by a side door. Attempts to sell pieces to a local jeweler allowed the police to trace the culprit. The golden objects, now bent and flattened, were found

figure 14
Eagle brooch from the Pietroasa treasures.

jammed inside an upright piano. Repaired for a second time, the treasure remained in Bucharest until 1916, when, to protect it from advancing German troops, it was taken to Russia. It was only returned to Romania by the Soviet government in 1956.

The largest brooch in the Pietroasa treasure is a remarkable piece of workmanship. Its size, ten and a half inches long and six inches wide, suggests that it was worn on the shoulder to pin together the folds of a man's heavy cloak. What survives, battered and twice repaired, is the brooch's framework, made from thick gold plate in the shape of an eagle: the broad body of the bird (with the clasp underneath), its elegantly curved neck, its sharp-eyed stare, and cruelly hooked beak. The eagle's tail is suggested by four chains of thin, twisted gold wire that hang down from the bottom of the brooch. Each gold chain terminates in a translucent teardrop of rock crystal. The other stones that once encrusted all the visible surfaces are now sadly missing: the great oval gem in the middle of the eagle's back, a necklace of small stones encircling the throat, and for the eyes, most splendid of all, perhaps deep red garnets glinting with the cold, unblinking gaze of a bird of prey. The man whose cloak was fastened by this magnificent brooch may have hoped that those who saw him parading such finery would also think of him admiringly as possessing noble, aquiline features and perhaps, too, an eagle-like character: unruffled, ever watchful, and deadly accurate in seeking out and destroying his enemies (see figure 14).

The brooch's wearer was probably also the owner of the other precious objects, including the two drinking cups, the tall pitcher, and the great circular tray (see figure 15). On the basis of stylistic parallels and method of manufacture, it is likely that the gold tableware, like the eagle-headed brooch, was made somewhere north of the Danube in the first half of the fifth century. The exception is the most beautiful object in the treasure, a shallow bowl just over eleven inches in diameter and three inches deep. At its center is a statuette of a seated woman about five inches high; around the inside of the bowl runs a vigorous scene of gods and goddesses. Individual deities can be identified: a half-naked Apollo sits holding his lyre, and the goddess Isis (originally Egyptian, but worshipped throughout the Mediterranean) stands next

figure 15
Drinking cup from the Pietroasa treasure.

figure 16
Shallow bowl from the Pietroasa treasure.

to her husband, Serapis. The meaning of the scene is unclear, but the quality of the piece is undoubted. Both its design and its decoration indicate that it was made by one of the finest goldsmiths in the eastern Roman empire, perhaps working in Antioch or Alexandria (see figure 16).

The owner of the Roman bowl and the rest of the Pietroasa treasure is unknown. The best guess is that these were the proud possessions of a leading Goth. On one of the necklaces there is a short inscription in Gothic. The translation is much disputed—the damage to the fragmentary piece makes a definitive reading impossible—but the words "sacred" and "Goth" are clear. Situated on the fertile lower slopes of the Carpathian Mountains, now a prosperous wine-growing region, Pietroasa had always been an important Gothic settlement. It was dominated by a substantial stone fort and farmhouse whose extensive storage facilities suggest that it was the center of a large estate. It is certainly attractive to think that the Pietroasa treasure might have belonged to a powerful Gothic leader who had found a secure place within the Hun empire. As a mark of his superior status, he wore a great eagle-headed brooch and dined in splendor at a table glittering with gold plates and cups. Perhaps this Goth had joined Attila on campaign. That might offer an explanation for the presence of such a valuable bowl. Taken as plunder on some raid across the Roman frontier, it was the share of spoils allotted to a trustworthy subordinate.

That Attila and Bleda allowed such wealth to be distributed to the leaders of subject peoples is one of the keys to the success of their empire. It would be wrong to think of the Huns as grabbing all the gold for themselves. Nor did they seek to dominate the locally powerful by threats and violence alone. Collaboration has its benefits. The wealthy Goth who owned the Pietroasa treasure clearly prospered under Hun rule. Looking back over the violent history of the preceding seventy years, he must have been pleased that his father or grandfather had refused to join Fritigern. As things had turned out, it had proved much more profitable to fight alongside Attila and Bleda than to seek asylum among the Romans on the other side of the Danube.

Alongside the regular payment of taxes, the maintenance of an army, and the cooperation of local rulers, the promotion of a state-sponsored religion is one of the engines of empire. Theodosius II was committed to the close coalition between Christianity and Roman rule firmly established by Constantine a century before. It was the emperor's God-given responsibility to support the Church and all who followed its teachings. Heretics were to be persecuted and unbelievers made to suffer for worshipping false gods. In 427, five years after the hurried cancellation of the crusade in Mesopotamia, Nestorius, the newly appointed bishop of Constantinople, pointedly reminded Theodosius of his duty as a Christian monarch: "Give me the earth undefiled by heretics, and I will give you heaven. Help me to destroy the heretics, and I will help you to destroy the Persians."

To the pious frustration of both Nestorius and Theodosius, the empire's enemies remained stubbornly faithful to their own religions—it was only in their desperation to be allowed to cross the Danube that the Goths had become Christians. Despite the persistent efforts of missionaries, the Huns had refused to convert. At the beginning of the fifth century, Theotimus, bishop of Tomi on the Black Sea coast, attempted to inspire conversion by giving the Huns who lived nearby food and other gifts. Unfortunately this kindly, if not particularly spiritual, tactic backfired. Given his generosity, the Huns assumed that Theotimus must be a rich man and worth kidnapping for a ransom. A trap was laid and a meeting arranged with the bishop, who perhaps thought that he had at last attracted some converts. As Theotimus approached, one Hun suddenly raised a rope in his right hand and made to lasso him and drag him away. But the lasso was never thrown. The Hun remained motionless with his arm outstretched until Theotimus prayed for him to be released. Despite, or perhaps because of, this dramatic demonstration of divine power, the Huns who had tried to seize the bishop remained hostile to Christianity. One afternoon when riding upcountry, Theotimus saw some Huns in the distance. The situation was dangerous. As his servants panicked, the bishop prayed and the Huns passed by without noticing anything. This was a miraculous escape. Even so, it is a fair indication of the failure of Theotimus' missionary work that he had to make himself invisible to avoid meeting the very people he was trying to convert.

The Huns' steadfast refusal to abandon their traditional beliefs was a direct challenge to a Christian Roman empire. Attila went further. Against Theodosius' conviction that, as Constantine's imperial successor, he was especially beloved of Christ, Attila defiantly advanced his own claim to be favored by a powerful deity. One day, or so the story recorded by Priscus of Panium goes, a poor herdsman noticed that one of his prize heifers had gone lame. Anxiously he followed the trail of blood left by the animal. It led back to a sword that was almost completely buried in the ground (see figure 17). The herdsman, fearing to keep or

figure 17
The Warlord's Sword *(1890), painting by Béla Iványi*
Grünwald (1867–1940).

sell such a magnificent object, took the sword to Attila, who at once recognized it as sacred to the war god. This sword had disappeared long ago and was thought by many to have been lost forever. Attila was clear about the significance of its extraordinary rediscovery. "The king rejoiced . . . and, as he aspired to greatness, he supposed that he had been appointed ruler of the whole world, and that through the sword of the war god he was assured supremacy in all armed conflicts."

For the Huns, as for other steppe peoples, swords had great symbolic significance. Of this Priscus was well aware: Herodotus had noted that the Scythians worshipped their war god "in the form of a sword set up on a platform made from bundles of brushwood." Hun ceremonial weapons were beautifully made by highly skilled craftsmen. The sword found in 1979 near the

figure 18
Sword from Pannonhalma.

monastery at Pannonhalma, in Hungary, had a scabbard covered
in delicately embossed gold foil; its grip was encircled by three
decorated gold bands (see figure 18). Attila's striking innovation
was to take these traditional beliefs in the importance of the
sword and link them to his own claim to rule over the Huns. This
was an astute political move. The miracle of the herdsman and
the lost sword allowed Attila to assert that he was the one leader
whose authority had been confirmed by the direct intervention
of the gods. His rise to power was no accident of fate; rather, it
was part of a divinely ordained plan. Nor is there any reason to
think that Attila was any more (or less) genuine than Constantine
or Theodosius in believing that heaven was on his side and had
proclaimed the legitimacy of his rule.

How much Bleda cared about all this is uncertain. He may not
have felt any need to establish a religious justification for his
rule or to contest Theodosius' belief that the Christian Roman
empire was uniquely blessed. For the most part, Bleda expected
to strengthen the Hun empire by force. No doubt he prided
himself on being a man of action. He put his faith in real swords,
not sacred ones. Close companions sensed a growing tension

between the brothers. In this dangerous game of sibling rivalry, those who sided with Attila alleged that on important matters of state Bleda took advice from a Roman captive called Zercon, cruelly delighting in his strange appearance and sniggering at his halting speech. According to Priscus, "Attila could not stand the sight of Zercon, but Bleda was pleased by him, not only when he was telling jokes but even when he was not, because of the weird movements of his body as he walked. . . . He was rather short, hunchbacked with distorted feet and a nose that, because it was completely flat, was indicated only by the nostrils."

On one occasion Zercon escaped with some other prisoners of war. Soon recaptured, he was put in chains and brought before Bleda. So terrified that he could hardly stammer out a single word, Zercon excused his flight, blaming his master for not finding him a wife. Laughing, Bleda immediately gave him the daughter of a high-ranking Hun. She had been a close companion of one of Bleda's wives, but had fallen out of favor following some indiscretion. Attila (it may be assumed) turned away in disgust. Perhaps he felt that this was no way to treat a wellborn woman. If guilty of misconduct, she ought then to be punished properly, not suddenly married off for Bleda's amusement. For the moment, Attila controlled his anger. Always a shrewd strategist, he would continue to rely on his blood ties with Bleda until his own position was secure. Only then would he fulfill the promise of the war god's sacred sword and seek to rule the Hun empire alone.

CHAPTER NINE
FIGHTING FOR ROME

Flavius Aetius was the most feared man in the western Roman empire. He owed much of his success to his long-standing association with the Huns. After Honorius' death, they had backed his bid to put the bureaucrat John on the throne. When that failed, they had compelled the new regime in Ravenna—the boy emperor Valentinian III and his mother, Galla Placidia—to avoid civil war by paying them off and appointing Aetius to a senior military command. Successive victories enforcing imperial rule in France confirmed his increasingly powerful position. In addition, there was always the threat that, if challenged, he might once again persuade the Huns to march on Ravenna in support of his cause.

In the decade before the sudden death of Rua in 434, court politics in the West were dominated by Galla Placidia's attempts to curb Aetius' growing influence. Galla preferred to rely on Aetius' main rival, Boniface, commander of imperial forces in North Africa. Boniface had always supported Galla and her son, sending them money when they were forced to flee Ravenna for Constantinople. After Honorius' death, Boniface had refused to join Aetius in supporting John. Given this unstinting loyalty, it was with some sadness and much skepticism that in 427 Galla Placidia faced Aetius' claim that Boniface was planning a revolt. Rather than trust Aetius, she decided to test the truth of his allegations by recalling Boniface from North Africa and giving him an opportunity to clear his name. This was precisely what Aetius had predicted Galla would do. He had already written to Boniface, warning him of a conspiracy to deprive him of his command. To return to Ravenna, Aetius advised, would be to walk into a carefully laid trap. Rather than act immediately, Boniface decided to wait and see whether he would be ordered back to court. When Galla's instruction arrived, Boniface, now believing that there really was a plot against him, refused to comply.

At court, Aetius pointed to Boniface's failure to follow a clear imperial directive as certain proof of his intention to revolt. Boniface now had few options. Once he had disobeyed Galla, he doubted he could convince her of his innocence. Reluctantly, he declared North Africa independent of the empire. Ironically, Aetius' false accusation had turned out to be true. For two years, troops loyal to Boniface held off reinforcements sent from Italy to suppress the "rebellion," as Aetius always insisted it should be called. The stalemate was broken in spring 429 by the Vandal invasion. Aetius also blamed this on Boniface. It was, he alleged, all part of the same treasonous pattern of disloyalty: Boniface had concluded a secret pact with Geiseric, and they had agreed to divide North Africa between them. It was Boniface who had connived to help the Vandals cross the Strait of Gibraltar and then deliberately failed to defend Roman territory.

There was no substance to Aetius' slurs. If Boniface had been slow to prevent the Vandal advance, it was due to the need to keep units in reserve to protect himself. No doubt, too, Geiseric had taken advantage of the Romans' failure to present a united front. Given the seriousness of the Vandal invasion, no one could reasonably object to Galla Placidia's seeking to reach an agreement with Boniface, whom she now believed the excusable victim of Aetius' intrigue. All, even Aetius' strongest allies, would recognize the overriding importance of ensuring that North Africa remained Roman. Envoys sent to Carthage easily settled the matter, and Boniface was restored to his command. In 431 the army in North Africa was strengthened by the arrival of the task force from the East under Theodosius' trusted general Flavius Aspar.

Aetius, despite the revelation of his dirty dealing, which he strenuously denied, remained in post. He was powerful enough to resist any opposition. With a large part of the western imperial army committed against the Vandals, Galla Placidia was not prepared to risk destabilizing Italy or chance the possible intervention of the Huns. As she was all too well aware, no other general could claim such privileged access to military assets outside the empire. In 430 Aetius, as he had done five years earlier, extracted a high price for keeping the peace: he demanded and received supreme command over all Roman troops in the West. For Galla Placidia, this was one humiliation too many. She was, after all, the daughter, half sister, and mother of emperors. It was intolerable that she should suffer the threats of a man who was prepared to use the empire's enemies for his own ends. She had not struggled to put Valentinian on the throne to have him overshadowed by an upstart general who had once supported a usurper.

Two years later, Galla decided on confrontation. In 432 the situation in North Africa was stable—after an initial setback, Roman forces had blocked any further Vandal advance—and, critically, news of Octar's death and the massacre of the Hun army by the Burgundians had reached Ravenna. Galla calculated that, following such a defeat, Aetius would not be able to rely on the support of his friends beyond the Danube. Boniface was recalled from North Africa. This time, there was no doubt that he would obey the summons. In Rome, the ancient capital of empire, he was made joint supreme commander in the West. He was also invested with the hallowed title of "patrician." A thousand years earlier, this hereditary rank had marked out the oldest and most important families in the Roman republic. Now it was a coveted honor conferred only on the most senior courtiers and generals. As joint supreme commander, Boniface was Aetius'

equal; as a patrician, technically his superior. It was a nicely calibrated insult, deliberately intended to provoke a response.

Aetius, on campaign in France, hurried back to Italy to challenge his newly promoted rival. Suspecting this, Galla had urged
Boniface never to travel without a large bodyguard. The clash
took place in late 432 outside the town of Ariminum (modern
Rimini), thirty miles down the coast from Ravenna. This was
an intensely personal conflict; in the middle of the battle, the two
Roman generals faced each other. It was later rumored that, in
anticipation of confronting his rival, Aetius had ordered his lance
to be lengthened so that he could attack while remaining out of
reach of Boniface's sword. Aetius, it was said, had no intention
of offering a fair fight, especially if that meant compromising
his chances of killing his opponent. In the struggle, Boniface
was fatally wounded and Aetius forced to flee. Galla Placidia
had given Boniface good advice. His troops had defeated Aetius'
men, yet even she had not foreseen that in single combat Aetius
might cheat to win.

Now a rebel, stripped of his commission and fearing for his
life, Aetius had only one option left. Traveling in secret, he made
it by boat to the Croatian coast. Riding mostly at night, he did
not rest until he had passed the Danube frontier and reached the
Great Hungarian Plain. It was nine years since Aetius had visited the Huns. Then he had brought John's gold to back up his
promises of victory; this time he could offer only the prospect
of plunder. Some of his former supporters, perhaps Attila among
them, were persuaded of the merits of sending forces west to
attack Italy while a large part of the Roman army was engaged in
North Africa. Rua remained unconvinced; his concern was with
those tribes north of the Danube still resisting Hun domination.
No doubt he listened closely to Aetius' account of the Vandal
invasion and the extent of Theodosius' military commitment.
Indeed, it may be that this information was one important factor
in Rua's sudden decision the following year to attack the eastern

empire. After all, compared with Ravenna, Constantinople was the bigger prize.

Rua offered to help, but it is unlikely that he was prepared to risk more than a small force. Aetius' response was to chance everything on an outrageous gamble. He brilliantly exploited the Huns' terrifying reputation. They had marched against the western Roman empire once before, and who was to say they would not do so again? Returning to northern Italy in autumn 433, Aetius dismissed any suggestion that the Huns had been weakened by Octar's defeat. Thousands of Huns, he confidently claimed, would soon follow behind him. When reports of Aetius' triumphal progress reached Ravenna, Galla Placidia feared that she might lose everything. After all, in 425 a real Hun army had missed rescuing John by only seventy-two hours. With large numbers of imperial troops still on active service in North Africa, she could not risk calling Aetius' bluff. Galla Placidia knew when to cut her losses: Aetius was reinstated as supreme commander with the title of patrician, taking possession of Boniface's estates and marrying his widow. In return, Aetius agreed to halt the Hun advance. His was certainly the easier half of the bargain.

Success in politics is often as much a matter of dare as of truth. Real political skill lies in the persuasive presentation of unproven possibilities as though they were facts. Subsequent investigations matter little: they are the dusty business of historians and judicial commissions. Those in power have long since moved on to new concerns. In the following year, when Rua suddenly died while advancing on Constantinople, Galla Placidia may have wondered whether the Huns had ever consented to march their army westward to support Aetius. Had they given him victory with only a few horsemen? This was the bitterest of speculations. Perhaps then it occurred to Galla Placidia that, had she held her nerve in the face of Aetius' most audacious falsehood, she might have eliminated him and gained undisputed control of the West for her son.

If not particularly loyal to Valentinian, Aetius believed in a united and coherent western Roman empire. This was still an imperial ideal worth fighting for, although increasingly difficult to defend. Despite his many victories in the last ten years, Roman rule in France was far from secure. The Goths, now settled in the southwest with their capital at Toulouse, were dissatisfied with their landlocked territory and threatened to push through to the Mediterranean. The Burgundians, who had successfully fought off Octar's Huns in 430, remained a dangerous presence on the Rhine, where they had recently seized more land on the Roman side of the river. Lastly, the Bagaudae, a blanket term for a loose alliance of small landholders and their supporters concentrated north of the Loire, refused to recognize the authority of the imperial government. In their rebellious view, it was too distant and too weak to protect them or collect their taxes.

Aetius was aware that Roman forces in France were insufficient to deal with all these difficulties. In 435 he again turned to the Huns, hoping that their new rulers Attila and Bleda might be persuaded to commit troops to a campaign in the West. Perhaps he reckoned that the Hun retreat after the death of Rua might have made the prospect of another expedition against the eastern empire less immediately attractive. No doubt, too, Aetius felt safer commanding Huns rather than those Roman soldiers who had fought loyally under Boniface in North Africa. The Huns' presence would also silence rumors at court that his much advertised special relationship was no more than threatening talk. In inviting Attila and Bleda to send troops, Aetius aimed to confound his critics. He would demonstrate that he could still rely on the Huns, and he would use them to support, not undermine, Roman interests in France.

Attila and Bleda, or perhaps mainly Attila, considered Aetius'

figure 19
View of Pest and Buda *(1870s), Hungarian School.*

proposition. The brothers were unwilling to divert significant military resources away from the immediate aim of consolidating their own authority. Recognizing these concerns, Aetius offered a guarantee that Roman troops would not contest the extension of Hun control into part of two frontier provinces, Pannonia and Valeria. In effect, the western empire conceded a broad belt of land about a hundred miles wide, facing the Danube as it turns sharply upriver from modern Budapest (at the so-called Great Danube Bend) and runs south for two hundred miles before again turning, more gradually, and flowing east through Serbia (see figure 19). Aetius, with or without Valentinian's approval, was prepared to sacrifice ultimately indefensible territory along the frontier. This was neither an easy nor, as Aetius' critics were quick to point out, a particularly patriotic solution to the problem of the Goths and Bagaudae. Aetius' response was simple: the western empire could either retain its core possessions in France or protect its less prosperous Danube provinces, but not both.

What clinched the deal was Aetius' offer of a joint offensive against the Burgundians. For Attila the campaign made good sense. On balance, rather than deal with the instability that might result from an aggressive Burgundian kingdom, he could see the benefits of a clear and defensible western border with the Roman empire. After all, for the last four centuries the Romans had shown no interest in holding territory across the Rhine. Attila had also learned much from studying the difficulties that had dogged Theodosius' campaigns in Mesopotamia and North Africa. The history of the Roman empire in the century after Constantine had starkly exposed the dangers of fighting on two fronts at once. To Attila the benefits of eliminating the Burgundians and strengthening his alliance with Aetius were clear. With the Rhine frontier secured, and the western empire relinquishing its responsibility to defend part of Pannonia and Valeria, he could again think of crossing the Danube farther east and pushing toward Constantinople.

The alliance of Romans and Huns was an overwhelming success. In 436 the Burgundians were checked, and a truce agreed. The next year they were wiped out. Roman writers, all too aware that the Burgundians had only recently converted to Christianity following their defeat of Octar, were horrified at the inhumanity of the Hun death squads. The monk Prosper of Aquitaine, who published the final edition of his *Chronicle* in Rome in the 450s, noted grimly that "the Huns destroyed the Burgundians root and branch." In a pitiless act of ethnic cleansing more than twenty thousand men, women, and children were said to have been butchered. Only the briefest account of this extermination survives. The details must be left to the imagination: terrified families pulled out of hiding, the cruel certainty of death, the corpses of the slain left in heaps to rot. Roman commanders failed to prevent the slaughter. Perhaps they regarded it as a necessary cost of ensuring the preservation of the Roman empire, the bloody price to be paid for a joint expedition with the Huns.

At the same time as the liquidation of the Christian Burgundians, Hun and Roman troops under Litorius, one of Aetius' senior officers, moved west to terrorize the Bagaudae into submission. Pacification followed swiftly as the Bagaudae's leaders were rounded up, perhaps following the selective targeting of a few villages. A laconic notice by one Roman historian offers only the brutal bottom line: "when some of the leaders of the revolt had been thrown into chains and others killed, the insurrection caused by the Bagaudae was suppressed." Litorius then turned south to deal with the Goths. As the army marched through the rich countryside of the Auvergne, in central France, Hun raiding parties split off from the main column to attack farms and villages. Litorius did nothing to restrain them. Perhaps, like Aetius, he regarded the looting of the estates of even the most loyal of the empire's supporters as part of the unavoidable cost of maintaining Roman rule in France.

Certainly, if challenged, Aetius and Litorius could rightly claim that without the help of the Huns, neither the Burgundians nor the Bagaudae would have been defeated, nor could the Goths in France have been brought back into line. In 436, while Hun and Roman forces were fighting the Burgundians, the Goths took the opportunity to attack Narbo (modern Narbonne), eighty miles southeast of Toulouse. Founded nearly six centuries earlier, Narbonne was a prosperous Mediterranean port at the mouth of the river Aude. It stood at the intersection of two great highways, the *via Domitia*, which connected Italy to Spain, and the *via Aquitania*, which ran northwest to the Atlantic coast, following the Aude through Toulouse and Bordeaux. Something of Narbonne's substantial trading wealth is still visible beneath the rue Roger de Lisle in a vast underground warehouse, the only surviving part of one of the large covered markets that once crowded the town center.

For the Goths, aiming to dominate the main access routes

between southwest France and the Mediterranean, control of Narbonne was a prime objective. This they hoped to achieve by blockading the town and starving it into submission. It was only the arrival of Litorius' troops in late 437 that broke the siege. The hungry citizens cheered the Hun horsemen, who, according to Prosper of Aquitaine, each carried a sack of grain. In the following year, both Aetius and Litorius continued to press the Goths. In 439 Litorius, now instructed by Aetius to continue the campaign alone, reached Toulouse. Not all Romans applauded his success. In Marseille, the commercial rival of Narbonne 150 miles along the coast, the monk Salvian doubted God's continuing support for a Roman empire willing to use pagan Huns to subdue Christian Goths. In Salvian's view, something was fundamentally wrong when "the Romans presumed to put their hope in Huns and the Goths dared to trust in God."

Those committed Christians who shared Salvian's concerns must have been further dismayed by Litorius' behavior. He refused to negotiate with bishops sent by the Goths as peace envoys. Before the walls of Toulouse, he permitted the Huns to sacrifice to their gods and agreed to consult their soothsayers. The Huns predicted the outcome of significant events by scapulimancy, a ritual in which the shoulder blades of a sacrificed animal are carefully cleaned and then exposed to fire. It is the pattern of cracks and fissures in the bone caused by the heat that the soothsayer interprets. This method of divination was not used by either the Romans or the Goths within the Hun empire; it was a survival of an ancient religious practice from the steppes of central Asia.

The performance of these alien rites must have been an extraordinary sight for both the Christian Romans in Litorius' army and the Christian Goths looking down from the battlements. This was the last time in the long history of the Roman empire that one of its generals would consult the old gods on the outcome of a battle. In approving these sacrifices, Litorius may not have intended any polemical purpose; at worst, he may have had to square his own faith with the need to ensure the Huns' continued loyalty. Allowing the Huns freedom of religious expression may have weighed less heavily on Litorius' Christian conscience than having to turn a blind eye to their raiding parties. More intolerant antipagan campaigners like Prosper of Aquitaine or Salvian of Marseille allowed no such latitude. Litorius, it was claimed, had ignored the advice of his junior officers and, trusting in Hun soothsayers and the evil demons they had consulted, was determined to attack Toulouse and crush the Goths. For a while, the battle hung in the balance. To some it seemed that the Huns might break through and the Goths suffer the cruel fate of the Burgundians. But then some good luck (or perhaps a miracle): Litorius was captured, and the battle turned as the Goths steadily advanced. By nightfall the Huns had been routed, and a few days later Litorius was executed. In case his readers had been slow to draw the correct moral conclusion from this clash between patient God-fearing Goths and arrogant Hun-loving Romans, Salvian, quoting from the Gospel of Luke, pointedly observed that the truth of the New Testament had been vindicated: "Everyone who exalts himself will be humbled, and he who humbles himself will be exalted."

The year before the Huns had been humiliated beneath the walls of Toulouse, Theodosius and his advisers had discussed the possibility of a treaty. The timing was right and the arguments persuasive. Since Rua's death four years earlier, there had been little activity on the Danube frontier. Attila and Bleda may also have recognized the greater degree of unity between the East and the West. A joint expedition had halted the Vandals, and the treaty that followed ensured that Carthage and the richest provinces in North Africa remained part of the empire. In 437, the same year in which both the Burgundians and the Bagaudae were suppressed, Valentinian journeyed to Constantinople to claim the long-promised hand of Theodosius' daughter, Licinia Eudoxia. The imperial couple honeymooned at Thessalonica, in northern Greece, before returning to Ravenna.

Attila, and perhaps Bleda as well, could see the benefits of an agreement. A secure border along the Danube would allow them to continue with the consolidation of the Hun empire. It was probably the unwelcome news of the defeat of Litorius that finally convinced them. Peace would give the Huns a breathing space to recover their military strength. It would enable the brothers to restore their damaged authority by attacking carefully selected targets in northern and eastern Europe, campaigns more likely to end in victory than an expedition across the Danube. A treaty with Theodosius would also mark a significant policy shift away from involvement in the internal politics of the Roman empire. Rua—Attila might now have admitted—had been right to offer only limited help to Aetius. It would have been wiser for the Hun troops to have returned home after destroying the Burgundians. Hun forces operated best under their own leaders and when pursuing their own objectives. They should never have been at Toulouse fighting someone else's war.

Hun and Roman envoys met in winter 439 at Margum (modern Orašje), an important market town at the confluence of the Morava and the Danube, forty miles west of modern Belgrade. Theodosius sent Flavius Plinta, one of his senior commanders, and Epigenes, an experienced court official responsible for drafting imperial legislation. The Huns were represented by Attila and Bleda. The summit opened with a dispute over protocol: the Huns refused to dismount from their horses, while the Romans declined to stand and look up at them. In the end, Plinta reluctantly conceded that all talks should be held on horseback. Already saddlesore, Epigenes, more accustomed to the comforts of Constantinople, must have felt himself at a painful disadvantage. After some negotiation, the parties ratified a four-point peace plan.

The Romans were to return all Hun refugees and not offer any assistance to those who crossed the Danube. They were not to enter into an alliance with any people who were enemies of the Huns. Trading rights between the two states were confirmed on an equal basis. The Romans were to make an annual payment of seven hundred pounds of gold directly to Attila and Bleda.

This was a good deal for both sides. In addition to the agreement reached with Aetius in 435 on the extension of Hun rule into territory once part of the western empire, Attila and Bleda had now reduced the threat of hostile military action along a substantial part of the Danube frontier. They strengthened their own position by ensuring that they received the payments of gold personally and by demanding the repatriation of asylum seekers whose loyalties might be suspect. No risks were taken, particularly with those who had been in Roman custody for some time. Their very presence across the frontier was evidence of their hostility to Attila and Bleda and their regime. There was always a danger that they might agree to lead a rebellion financed by the empire. As soon as they were handed back, two young boys, both blood relations of Attila and Bleda, were impaled. Their execution was a warning to any potential rivals, or to those who might seek to use junior members of the ruling family as a focus for opposition.

For their part, the Romans, in agreeing to the treaty at Margum, had paid a reasonable price for a peace that allowed troops currently committed to the defense of the Balkans to be released (if needed) for deployment elsewhere. It offered a more immediate solution to border control than another expensive investment in recruitment or upgraded fortifications. A secure northern frontier gave the empire the strategic flexibility it needed, especially with the Vandals now occupying part of North Africa. Following the talks with Attila and Bleda at Margum, Theodosius might have been satisfied that—after nearly a century of intermittent conflict—he could at last proclaim with confidence that he had achieved peace on the Danube.

CHAPTER TEN

SHOCK AND AWE

A few weeks after peace broke out on the Danube, war was resumed in North Africa. On 19 October 439 the Vandals, led by Geiseric, seized Carthage in direct violation of the treaty agreed in 435. This was another challenge to the integrity of the empire. As one contemporary noted, it had been 585 years since Carthage was conquered by Rome. That victory was achieved after nearly a century of fighting. Three long conflicts, known as the Punic Wars, had stretched the Romans to their limits. In the Second Punic War they almost lost to the great Carthaginian general Hannibal, who in 218 BC marched his army of fifty thousand men, nine thousand cavalry, and thirty-seven elephants out of Spain, across southern France, and over the Alps into Italy. Two years later at Cannae, Hannibal almost wiped out the Roman army, killing fifty thousand men in a single day's fighting. This was the severest defeat ever inflicted on the Romans. The casualty rate was not matched again until the Battle of Adrianople when, in one sun-baked afternoon in August 378, the Goths killed twenty thousand troops and the emperor Valens.

The Romans recovered from Cannae. Forcing Hannibal to withdraw from Italy, they went on to crush Carthage seventy years later at the end of the Third Punic War and establish one of the greatest empires in history. It was questionable whether they

would ever recover from Adrianople. Since then the Eternal City
had been sacked and the West reduced to a rump. In Ravenna,
the twenty-year-old Valentinian III could not claim to control
more than Italy and France, and the latter only thanks to Aetius
and his Hun allies, and even they had not been able to dislodge
the Goths. The loss of Carthage in the same year as Litorius was
defeated at Toulouse was a strategic and financial body blow. For
six centuries North African grain had helped feed the citizens
of Rome. North African tax revenues had made its rulers rich.
Now the city of Hannibal and some of the wealthiest provinces
in the Mediterranean no longer belonged to the Romans. The
empire would have to survive without them or confront Geiseric
to get them back.

With the fall of Carthage, the Vandals gained access to one of
the best harbors on the African coast. This was a great prize to
be exploited. In both the East and the West, additional measures
were taken to protect major ports against an attack by sea. In late
439 work was begun to improve Constantinople's defenses. The
sea wall built by Constantine along the Propontis was extended
to connect with the Theodosian Walls. In Italy, Valentinian, who
spent the winter in Rome, ordered the city's fortifications to be
repaired. Citizens were to be organized into a home guard to
ensure that all towers, walls, and gates were properly manned. As
predicted, soon after capturing Carthage, the Vandal armada set
sail for Sicily. In an imperial edict issued on 24 June 440, Valentinian declared, "Geiseric, the enemy of our empire, is reported
to have issued forth from the port of Carthage with a large fleet
whose swift transit and capacity for opportunistic marauding is
to be feared along all coastlines . . . as it is by no means certain,
particularly given the advantages of navigation during the summer, how far enemy ships may be able to sail."

In Constantinople, Theodosius was ready to go to war. The
case for military action was clear. The invasion of Sicily might
be the beginning of a wider Vandal offensive that could further

weaken Roman control of the Mediterranean. If Geiseric chose to advance eastward along the African coast, his army could split Egypt off from the empire. The great commercial harbor of Alexandria might be blockaded, disrupting the shipments of grain on which Constantinople depended. The dangers of sending a task force were obvious, but it could plausibly be argued that the policies pursued over the last twenty years had brought a new stability to the Danube provinces. The Huns had not crossed the frontier since Rua's incursion in 434. That attack had followed lengthy, but inconclusive, talks conducted through envoys. By contrast, the recently ratified treaty had been negotiated with Attila and Bleda in person, and confirmed by the immediate handover of high-ranking refugees and the promised annual payment of seven hundred pounds of gold.

The general Flavius Aspar is likely to have disagreed. He had fought Geiseric in North Africa in the early 430s and a decade earlier defeated the usurper John in Ravenna. He was aware of the Huns' frightening ability to muster large numbers of men quickly and to move them rapidly across great distances. On this view, as long as the Vandals did not march into Libya and then Egypt, a campaign in North Africa was not worth the risk. There was no guarantee that Attila and Bleda could be trusted to respect their treaty obligations, any more than Geiseric had respected his. The Huns had crossed the Danube in 422, when the empire's troops were fighting in Mesopotamia, and again in 434, when they were in North Africa. History, Aspar may tartly have observed, can have an unpleasant habit of repeating itself. The emperor was unconvinced. In his opinion, those who argued against war had too hastily dismissed the treaty with Attila and Bleda. Nor had they grasped fully the pressing need to counter Geiseric. The safety of Constantinople and the security of its food supply demanded that Carthage be returned to Roman rule. Theodosius was not prepared to wait and see whether Egypt was threatened. The expedition against the Vandals would go ahead, and Aspar—who had failed in North Africa before—would not be in command.

The army did not set sail from Constantinople until spring 441, the year's delay an indication of the lengthy and careful preparation insisted on by Theodosius. This was not a high-spirited adventure by a reckless ruler in search of military glory. Success depended on two critical factors: the state of the northern frontier and the speed at which the Vandals were defeated. Theodosius believed that his treaty with Attila and Bleda would hold. That was a crucial calculation: units released from Danube defense made up the bulk of the task force. It was hoped that, by the deployment of these experienced legionaries, any Vandal resistance could be quickly overcome. As the emperor reviewed the fleet, safely moored in the harbor built by his grandfather Theodosius I, he was increasingly confident of victory. In the bright spring sunshine, all looked full of promise. Led by three capable generals—Flavius Ariobindus, Ansila, and Germanus—it would not be long before the army landed in Sicily and then advanced on Carthage. If the reconquest of North Africa went as planned, the troops would be back home in Constantinople by Christmas.

As soon as Attila and Bleda received reliable intelligence that the fleet had left for Sicily, they opened their Danube offensive. Given the recent heavy losses at Toulouse, the brothers had been reluctant to cross the border while the Roman army was at full strength. Under those circumstances, a treaty had suited their interests. The transfer of units to the North African expeditionary force altered the balance of advantage. The Huns' first objective was Constantia, across the river from Margum, where, barely two years earlier, Roman ambassadors had settled the terms of the peace. Then both sides had agreed to facilitate cross-border commerce. Constantia, one of the few remaining Roman forts on the northern bank of the Danube, was officially designated a secure trading post. On a crowded market day, the Huns struck without warning, easily taking the town in a carefully coordinated attack on its Roman garrison.

Theodosius refused to believe that Attila intended all-out war. Rather, it was now a matter of skillful negotiation, of understanding the Huns' grievances and moving quickly to reach an acceptable settlement. With a nice sense of irony, the emperor appointed Flavius Aspar as his envoy. Aspar's instructions were to arrange a truce and to investigate the reasons for the Huns' apparent breach of the peace accord. Arriving at the frontier, Aspar found to his discomfort that Attila regarded the treaty as void. In his view, it had already been broken by the Roman authorities at Margum. The accusations were striking. The town's bishop was alleged to have crossed the Danube at night to steal valuables from Hun tombs. Even more seriously, this Christian treasure hunter was said to have desecrated burials belonging to members of Attila and Bleda's own family. (If the *strava*, as in Attila's case, had included the slaughter of servants involved in the funeral rites, this had apparently not been sufficient to conceal the location of these rich graves.) Attila demanded that the tomb-raiding bishop of Margum be handed over, along with other refugees who, it was claimed, had been offered protection, contrary to the terms of the treaty.

The facts behind these allegations are impossible to establish, and it may not have been much easier for Aspar at the time. Given the Huns' open hostility to Christianity, it might be thought just too suspiciously neat that they should accuse a bishop of violating their dead. No doubt Aspar was shown evidence of looting (soil disturbed, coffins damaged, and bones displaced), but there was no proof linking the bishop, or any other resident of Margum, with these crimes. Nor could Aspar be sure that these were really the tombs of Attila and Bleda's relatives, or that they had ever contained any precious grave goods worth taking. Whether the authorities at Margum were at fault in failing to hand over Hun fugitives was also unclear. The terms of the treaty ratified in 439 had been vague, falling short of imposing any formal obligation on the Romans to round up and regularly repatriate asylum seekers. But now was not the time to argue the point. Aspar is most likely to have attempted a compromise: questioning the nature and relevance of the Huns' claims, but also welcoming negotiation on issues of mutual concern. If Theodosius was right in believing that Attila did not want war, this approach would at least offer the opportunity for a fresh round of meetings and the possibility of agreement.

Attila did not stay to talk. For him, Aspar's failure to hand over the bishop of Margum and the refugees was the confirmation he needed that the treaty was no longer in force. In the next nine months (from summer 441 to spring 442), the Huns attacked, captured, and destroyed almost all the major cities on the middle Danube and southeast along the Morava River valley. Roman writers, preferring not to dwell in any detail on the collapse of imperial authority along the frontier, offer only the names of the places besieged and sacked: Sirmium (modern Sremska Mitrovica), Singidunum (Belgrade), Margum (Orašje), Viminacium (Kostolac), Naissus (Niš), Serdica (Sofia). Of the hundreds of unfortified settlements that must also have been plundered and set on fire, there is no record, not even a name. Many who risked death in protecting their families and livelihood have no memorial to their courage. The cowardly, the craven, and the terror-stricken are also unknown. The arrival of a Hun raiding party at farmstead after farmstead is a story of repetitive brutality and suffering. At first a smudge on the horizon; gradually through the dust the horses and their riders take shape, then the sickening realization that this is not help but destruction; the harsh shouts of anonymous men blankly uniform in their helmets and armor, the cruel flash of swords, and the hot flow of blood. There is nothing new about the horrors of war; they do not shock until a brief list of cities destroyed becomes—at least in our imagination—a roll call of thousands of individuals raped, enslaved, or killed.

At Margum, the citizens debated how best to face the Huns. Once Attila had rejected negotiation, Aspar left the city. To any who might have complained that he was deserting his post, he could point out that he did not wish to give the Huns a valuable hostage and that, in any event, a general is no use without an army. It was his duty, as an imperial envoy, to carry the news back to Constantinople. With Aspar gone, some wondered whether it might be worth trying to reach an agreement with Attila. As a gesture of goodwill, they could hand over the bishop. The less pious perhaps suggested that God would be certain to approve: if the bishop was guilty, then justice would be done; if he was innocent, he would undoubtedly embrace martyrdom at the hands of the Huns in return for saving his fellow Christians.

The bishop did not wait to find out whether his congregation would turn into a lynch mob. Slipping quietly out of the city and across the river, he offered to betray the town to the Huns in return for guarantees of protection. Attila accepted and no doubt smiled as he swore a binding oath on his sword, calling on the war god to preside over his pact with a Christian. That night, mindful of his own pledge invoking the saints, the bishop of Margum kept his word. He convinced those manning the town's defenses that he was returning with urgent information from an undercover reconnaissance mission. (As he perhaps pointed out, his very presence before the walls demonstrated that he had not gone over to the Huns.) His story was believed: after all, he was still a bishop. He then seems to have urged a surprise attack against Attila and his men. He may have claimed that the Huns were preparing to cross the Danube and could be caught at their most vulnerable while landing. The inevitable followed: the ambush by Attila's troops who lay concealed by the riverbank, the slaughter of the remaining defenders, and Margum's destruction.

Not every city fell through treachery. Part of the success of

Attila's Danube campaign lay in his army's skill at siege warfare. Seventy years earlier, the inability to take Roman strongholds, and to seize the treasure and grain stored there, had hampered the Goths' offensive after Adrianople. Attila ensured that the Huns mastered siege technology and were able to attack and capture fortified cities by means of textbook Roman military tactics. It is likely that these were learned from prisoners of war. Some, like the bishop of Margum, willing to strike a bargain to ensure their survival. It was this new expertise that made Attila's Huns a much more formidable enemy than any that had previously penetrated the Danube cordon. The Romans could no longer depend on well-defended cities to act as islands of security in a hostile countryside, protecting supplies, people, and wealth.

In attacking Naissus, the Huns first crossed the river that protected part of the walls and then brought up tall cranes mounted on wheels. Shielded by light willow screens covered with rawhide, men positioned high up on the arm of each crane were able to fire arrows directly over the battlements. Once a stretch of walls had been cleared of defenders, the cranes were replaced by battering rams. Priscus of Panium, who described the siege in detail, was particularly impressed by the rams' size and effectiveness. "The ram is a very large machine. A beam with a sharp metal point is suspended on chains hung loosely from a V-shaped timber frame. . . . With short ropes attached to the rear of the ram, men vigorously swing the beam away from the target and then release it, so that as a result of the force the section of wall opposite the ram is completely demolished."

Naissus was wiped off the map. Its population was killed, dispersed, or captured and sold as slaves. The city would not be rebuilt for another century. Seven years after Attila's attack, Priscus found it deserted, save for a handful of monks whose unceasing prayers rose thinly above the desolation. His traveling companions took some time to find a clean place to pitch camp. The ground toward the river, where the battering rams had smashed through, was strewn with the bleached bones of the slain. A look back at the shattered walls made it difficult to believe that only 150 years earlier Naissus had been the birthplace of the emperor Constantine, who had cherished and beautified his hometown. All that had been brutally obliterated by Attila and his Huns. Now the ruins sheltered only religious fanatics who looked forward with joyous expectation to the end of the world. For these Christian holy men, the burned-out shell of a once great imperial city must have seemed a fitting place to wait patiently for the Apocalypse.

In the golden throne room of the Great Palace in Constantinople, Theodosius sat in sullen silence. Each day messengers brought news of the Huns' steady progress. Unable to assemble an army large enough to oppose them in the field, the emperor had little option but to hope that Attila's insistence on taking each city in turn would slow his advance. Under the circumstances, there was only one possible course of action: peace would have to be concluded swiftly with Geiseric and the task force recalled. Roman troops had been in Sicily for the best part of a year and had not yet attempted to capture Carthage. Aware of the deteriorating situation on the Danube frontier, their commanders had been understandably reluctant to commit to what they knew might be a long and difficult war against the Vandals.

Geiseric certainly did not overplay his advantage. He was all too aware that, if the northern frontier was stabilized, there could be another attempt at reconquest. It was in the Vandals' long-term interests to compromise and allow themselves time to consolidate their hold over the territory they had seized. The partitioning of North Africa, first sanctioned under the treaty of 435, was rene-gotiated. The most fertile part (an area slightly larger than mod-ern Tunisia), with Carthage as its capital, was formally recognized

as Vandal territory. The rest of the African coast (roughly Algeria
and Morocco), including some of Numidia originally ceded in
435, was retained as part of the western Roman empire. Geiseric
also agreed to pay an annual sum to Valentinian's government,
reducing the immediate consequences of the loss of African tax
revenue.

The fleet returned to Constantinople in spring 442, too late
to prevent the fall of Naissus. Attila—by then as far forward
as Serdica—decided not to chance any direct conflict with the
newly reinforced Roman army. The Huns marched in good order
through a devastated provincial landscape back to the Great Hungarian Plain. This had been a substantial victory. The destruction
of the main cities in the central sector of the Danube had punched
a hole in the empire's frontier defenses. The capture of Naissus,
and raids east of Serdica, had opened the way to Constantinople.
Attila used the loot brought back from the Danube provinces to
his own advantage. Booty and captives were distributed to reward
and reinforce the loyalty of leading Huns and their supporters.
The golden bowl from the Pietroasa treasure, with its delicately
modeled scenes of gods and goddesses, may have been snatched
from a grand house in Sirmium, Singidunum, or Naissus. It
may have been taken by a Goth fighting alongside the Huns, or
it may have been a generous gift from Attila, part of a carefully
calculated distribution of spoils intended to tighten his personal
control over the Hun empire.

Of Attila's steady strengthening of his own authority, Roman
writers—focused on the wreckage that followed the Huns'
attacks—have almost nothing to say. At some point in the three
years after the campaign, Attila decided to challenge Bleda. This
may have been a long and bitter struggle. Bleda may also have
secured his own position by giving lavish presents of Roman
gold to comrades and relatives. Many may have felt that, as the
elder brother, he had every right to demand an equal share of
empire. On the other hand, Bleda could have been unaware

that Attila had any intention of ruling alone. Perhaps Bleda—boorish, violent, vulgar—never noticed a thing. Or perhaps Bleda—hearty, hospitable, open-handed—laughingly dismissed the idea that his kid brother was capable of such treachery. Or perhaps Bleda—shrewd, nasty, cunning—fought viciously like a trapped animal to hold on to power.

Regrettably, these rivalries cannot be reconstructed. In the years immediately following the Huns' invasion, the Romans had only the haziest idea of events on the Great Hungarian Plain. That is reflected in the terse notices in the histories of the mid-440s that do no more than register a scatter of matters outside the empire. It is as though all that remained of a newspaper were a few torn headlines. The detailed stories are lost; the particular circumstances and precise chain of events open to endless speculation. Only one thing is sure: in the brief words of the most reliable Roman account, in 445, three years after Hun troops had returned home from their Danube offensive, "Bleda, king of the Huns, was assassinated as a result of the plots of his brother Attila."

CHAPTER ELEVEN
BARBARIANS AT THE GATES

In Constantinople, on 26 January 447, Theodosius II refused to wear his glittering imperial regalia; he set aside his heavy purple robes, bejeweled diadem, pearl earrings, and gem-encrusted shoes. He dismissed his golden carriage and his body-guards in their scarlet uniforms and shining parade armor. Instead, the emperor set out into the city dressed only in a simple white tunic. He walked barefoot, his feet bleeding and his forehead glistening with sweat, the seven long miles along the hard marble-paved streets of Constantinople from the Great Palace to the military parade ground at the Hebdomon beyond the Theodosian Walls. He was followed by high-ranking dignitaries and a great crowd of citizens. At the Hebdomon, they all chanted the Trisagion, the invocation (still in daily use in the Eastern Orthodox Church) that a decade earlier was said to have been revealed by angels: "Holy God, Holy Mighty One, Holy Immortal One, have mercy upon us."

The normally prosperous and self-confident residents of the imperial capital, who assumed as a matter of course that God was on their side, were in penitent and prayerful mood. In the dark hours of the early morning of 26 January, a severe earthquake had shaken the city. Educated people in the fifth century knew how earthquakes happened (that had been worked out eight hundred years earlier by the Greek philosopher Aristotle): they were the result of the sudden movement of vast bodies of air in huge voids deep underground. For many Christians, Aristotle might have explained what caused the earth to shake, but not what caused the air to move in the first place. These tremors, it was believed, were in accordance with the will of God, who sought to turn sinners to repentance. An earthquake was a warning from heaven—not a notion that would have appealed to Aristotle. The sight of a barefoot emperor walking painfully through the city was an indication of how seriously God's purpose was to be taken.

On the way to the Hebdomon, the scale of the destruction was clearly visible. The recently completed sea wall along the shores of the Propontis was severely damaged. Great stretches of the Theodosian Walls were now heaps of rubble; fifty-seven towers had collapsed. The city lay wide open to any invading army. That alone was sufficient reason for an emperor to cast off his royal robes and join his people in prayer. This was a spectacular act of public penance that might ensure divine protection for the city. Yet only Theodosius and his closest advisers appreciated how desperate the situation was. They looked at the defenseless capital in the terrifying knowledge that, shortly before the earthquake shattered the Theodosian Walls, the northern frontier had been breached. According to the latest military intelligence, Attila and his Huns had already begun a new Danube offensive. "Holy God, Holy Mighty One, Holy Immortal One, have mercy upon us."

Toward the end of 446—a few months prior to the earthquake—Attila sent diplomatic letters to the imperial court, again insisting that any asylum seekers who had crossed the Danube be handed over. He also demanded the back payment of the seven hundred pounds of gold a year that had been agreed in 439 at Margum. (Perhaps only one or two installments had been received before war broke out in 441.) Theodosius refused to hand over either the money or the refugees. He proposed instead to send ambassadors and begin talks on these disputed issues. The emperor knew the risks involved: five years earlier Flavius Aspar's offer to discuss the nighttime activities of the bishop of Margum had been brushed aside with an immediately hostile response.

This time Theodosius was confident of containing any Hun attack. The legions protecting the Danube provinces were now back to strength, and the frontier defenses had recently been reviewed. In September 443, senior officers had been instructed to ensure that those under their command were properly trained and fully paid. The emperor, seeking to encourage the permanent settlement of land near the border, confirmed that rank-and-file soldiers were permitted to own farms along the Danube free of all rents and taxes. An annual audit of troop strength and condition reports on both river patrol craft and army camps were now to be submitted to officials at the imperial court every January. Theodosius was robust in setting out the benefits he hoped would flow from these reforms. "For we believe that if military affairs are organized exactly as we have decreed, then in whatever territory an enemy might be tempted to invade, a victory that is advantageous to us (according to the will of God) will be proclaimed—even before any battle."

Undaunted by such grand claims, Attila rejected outright Theodosius' suggestion of negotiation. The Huns opened their offensive by taking Roman forts along the frontier, including Ratiaria, the headquarters of the Danube fleet. This was a more rapid and damaging attack than had been expected. With the Huns only sixty miles northeast of Naissus (or at least its blackened ruins), Theodosius may still have been prepared to chance war, or he may now have preferred to offer concessions in return for peace. Whatever the emperor's plans, they were wrecked by the earthquake in January 447. The priority was now the security of the imperial capital. The pious chants of its citizens and their barefoot ruler might move the divinity to support the Roman cause and protect the city. As some of the emperor's advisers quietly observed, it would take a miracle to repair the Theodosian Walls before Attila reached Constantinople.

Although never doubting the power of prayer, the praetorian prefect of the East, Flavius Constantinus, had no intention of waiting for God to come to Constantinople's rescue. He speedily organized gangs of skilled artisans and laborers to work on the walls. These were joined by members of the Blues and the Greens, the two main sporting associations in the city, whose fanatical followers were more accustomed to cheering on their teams in the chariot races held in the hippodrome. Like modern football or baseball clubs, the Blues and the Greens were both well managed. They each had a professional staff of highly trained charioteers involved in talent spotting, coaching, selection, and the running of the games. More visible were the fans, who at the races sat together in designated rows. The most dedicated had identical haircuts and wore green (or blue) tunics with huge, baggy sleeves that billowed out like flags whenever they waved their arms to urge on their favorites.

Successful charioteers were celebrities in Constantinople. Statues were erected in their honor and their lavish lifestyles admired and imitated. In the hippodrome, the entry of these superstars might be greeted with as much applause as the appearance of the emperor; after all, it was the races that the crowd had come to see. Excited supporters shouted in praise of their heroes and their athletic prowess—both on and off the racetrack—and insulted their opponents. The rhythmic chanting of the cheer squads and their obscene verbal sparring were all part of the entertainment. They added to the thrill of watching charioteers expertly maneuver their horses along the narrow straights and around the dangerously tight turns at either end of the course. Sometimes the intense competition between the Blues and the Greens spilled out into the city. Residents of Constantinople regularly blamed fires, street fights, and vandalism on hooligans leaving the hippodrome.

It was, then, all the more remarkable that the praetorian prefect was able to marshal these rowdy sports fans. Unsurprisingly, the Blues refused to cooperate with the Greens. That, too, the prefect turned to his advantage, allocating the rival clubs different sections of the broken defenses and encouraging them to compete against each other. They worked without break for sixty days; during the night masons cut and laid stones by torchlight. For all involved, this was a deadly serious race: not between pampered charioteers and their sleekly groomed horses, but between terrified Romans and advancing Huns. The Romans were victorious —but only just. The Theodosian Walls were repaired in time to discourage Attila from attacking the imperial capital.

The memorial to this extraordinary feat by an exhausted populace is still visible. Before reaching the impenetrable confusion of Istanbul's vast and dusty bus station, Millet Caddesi, one of the city's main thoroughfares, cuts its way through the Theodosian Walls. Just to the south is the Mevlevihane Gate. Yeni Mevlevihane Kapısı (as it is called in Turkish) belongs to an older and less hurried world. It is just wide enough for a donkey, or for a swiftly skillful moped rider who knows that the passage through the walls—as an extra defensive measure—sharply narrows. To the left of the gateway in the outer wall is a grayish marble slab, cemented securely into the stonework precisely where Flavius Constantinus ordered it fixed more than fifteen hundred years ago. On the slab, a laconic inscription in Latin is still clearly legible (see figures 20 and 21).

THEODOSII IVSSIS GEMINO NEC MENSE PERACTO
CONSTANTINVS OVANS HAEC MOENIA FIRMA LOCAVIT
TAM CITO TAM STABILEM PALLAS VIX CONDERET ARCEM

By Theodosius' command, Constantinus triumphantly built these strong walls in less than two months. Pallas could hardly have built such a secure citadel in so short a time.

figure 20
Mevlevihane Gate, Theodosian Walls.

This was a proud boast. In the scale and speed of the undertaking, the restored Theodosian Walls surpassed any fortifications that might have been raised by Pallas Athene, the divine protectress of cities and patron of Athens. (Athens' natural citadel, the great limestone rock of the Acropolis, was still dominated by Athene's wondrously beautiful temple, the Parthenon, built nine hundred years earlier.) Constantinus had every reason to be satisfied with his achievements. He had seen off his critics—as always, there were some who regarded the whole scheme as ill advised—and accomplished more than those who had prayed for some heaven-sent deliverance. By rebuilding Constantino-

figure 21
Mevlevihane Gate, inscription of Flavius Constantinus.

ple's defenses, the prefect had outdone even a Greek goddess. By completing the project in only sixty days, he had actually made a miracle happen.

Despite the damage caused by the earthquake in January 447, Attila was not prepared to jeopardize the success of his offensive with a sudden push to Constantinople. Two obstacles lay between the frontier and the capital. First, Attila was reluctant to leave any well-defended cities in Roman hands. At the end of the campaign, or if a rapid retreat were needed, these might compromise the safe return of his troops to the Danube. Second, and more important, Attila must have been aware that, although he had broken through the frontier defenses, as he marched toward Constantinople he would face a Roman army that had not been depleted by the need to oppose either the Persians or the Vandals. Rather than rush to the capital, it was a more prudent strategy for the Hun army to advance steadily and then meet—or choose to avoid—any serious opposition.

So after taking Ratiaria, the Huns moved to attack the major cities and forts that stood between them and Constantinople. As in 441–42, Roman historians, as if too shocked to offer more than the briefest account of the Huns' success in "plundering no fewer than seventy cities," again record only a small number of the places destroyed: Philippopolis (Plovdiv), Arcadiopolis

(Lüleburgaz, in Turkey, one hundred miles northwest of Istanbul), Callipolis (Gelibolu, in the north of the Gallipoli Peninsula), Sestus (Eceabat, to the south near Çanakkale), and Athyras (Büyükçekmece, on the northern shore of the Sea of Marmara). The last place on the list gives a striking indication of how close the Huns came to Constantinople. The fort of Athyras was less than twenty miles from the Theodosian Walls.

But this attack on the Balkans was not a lightning raid by swift-moving Huns. Philippopolis was protected by substantial walls and, like Naissus in 441–42, could have fallen only after a siege. Attila also had to deal with more effective resistance the closer his army came to Constantinople. Two cities managed to beat off their attackers: the well-fortified Adrianople (Edirne), near the site of the great battle between Romans and Goths, and Heraclea (Mamara Ereğli), sixty miles along the seashore from Constantinople. These slight successes might also be connected with the activity of the Roman army, which was now directed by three veterans: Flavius Aspar, who must have been relieved to abandon diplomacy for an armed response, Flavius Ariobindus, one of the leaders of the expedition against the Vandals in 441, and Arnegisclus, who commanded imperial troops in Thrace.

The army was divided between these three generals in order to cover all possible land routes to the capital. Their defensive strategy failed to halt the Hun advance, but did slow it down. While Roman troops were never victorious in the field, they may have been able to harry the Hun marching column and compel it to move more cautiously. The capture of Callipolis and Sestus on the Gallipoli Peninsula is evidence of further deliberate diversion. Although some Roman units were defeated, their Gallipoli campaign across difficult and broken terrain did deflect Attila from the imperial capital. The cost of such tactics was high: soldiers and cities were repeatedly sacrificed to save Constantinople. Moreover, Aspar and his fellow generals were not prepared to stake all on one decisive encounter. They elected instead to sustain severe and demoralizing losses over two long and weary months to win the time needed for the rebuilding of the capital's defenses. Only when that had been completed would Constantinople again be safe.

Attila and the Huns never saw the Theodosian Walls. Their assault on the Roman empire had been too successful for them to risk attacking the best-defended city in the Mediterranean world. The outbreak of disease in the capital and its surroundings added to Attila's unwillingness to attempt what was certain to be a long siege. He recognized the problem of provisioning a stationary army in a region already ruined by invasion and earthquake. The Huns now swung away from Constantinople and moved north to Marcianople. Like other cities obliterated in the 440s, it would not be rebuilt for another century. The need for supplies dictated that the Huns return to the Great Hungarian Plain, avoiding land that had already been pillaged. About 150 miles to the west of Marcianople, near the Utus River, Roman forces under Arnegisclus blocked the Huns' homeward march. Only with Constantinople secure was a Roman commander prepared to deploy a substantial number of troops in such an aggressive action. During a long and exhausting engagement, both armies suffered heavy casualties. Arnegisclus' horse was killed beneath him. Trapped in the middle of the fray, he fought on bravely until his death. In the end, the Huns gained the upper hand, but Arnegisclus—in a final bid for glory—almost managed to register the only Roman victory of the whole campaign.

Despite Arnegisclus' heroic last stand, the Huns' Danube offensive was a devastating success. Attila had smashed through the empire's frontier defenses and brought his army within twenty miles of Constantinople. According to the sixth-century historian Marcellinus, the Huns had "attacked and pillaged forts and cities, lacerating almost all the territory surrounding the capital." Twice Attila had skillfully exploited Roman weaknesses: in 441 the transfer of troops to deal with the Vandals in North Africa and in 447 the disruption following a serious earthquake. Perhaps Aspar and his colleagues should have had more confidence in meeting the Huns in a set-piece battle, but there was always the possibility of another Adrianople. If in February or March 447 the Roman army had been wiped out in an afternoon's fighting, Constantinople would have fallen soon thereafter and the eastern Roman empire come to an abrupt and bloody end. Even so, the narrow defeat of Arnegisclus on the banks of the Utus River showed what might have been achieved. It also demonstrated that Attila was right to be wary of the Roman army. There was always the chance that he might lose.

In 447, the Huns were not set on an unstoppable craze of slaughter and destruction. Careful strategic thinking on Attila's part prevented a dash for Constantinople. That would have provoked a dangerous confrontation with Roman forces in the Balkans and forced—no matter what the strategic risk—the emergency recall of crack troops from the eastern frontier. Nor was Attila prepared to expend the time and resources a siege of Constantinople would have demanded. The Huns could have found themselves trapped before the Theodosian Walls, short of food, threatened by disease, and too far from the safety of the Danube. Without a fleet, they could not have imposed an effective blockade. The decision not to attack Constantinople ensured that they returned to the Great Hungarian Plain with their plunder and captives. Certainly with its defenses repaired—even with the Huns' new skills in siege warfare—the empire's capital was too formidable a target. History confirms Attila's judgment. The Theodosian Walls shielded the city for another eight hundred years: they withstood the Avars in 626, the Arabs in the 670s, Krum the Bulgar in 813, the Russians in 860, and the First Crusade in 1097. They were scaled by the Venetians in their attack during the Fourth Crusade in 1204. The Theodosian Walls were finally breached in 1453 by Mehmet the Conqueror, whose Ottoman army had one explosive advantage that Attila would have envied: gunpowder.

CHAPTER TWELVE
THE PRICE OF PEACE

After the defeat of Arnegisclus, Theodosius sent the senior general Flavius Anatolius to negotiate peace with Attila. For most of the last fifteen years, Anatolius had been responsible for the security of the eastern frontier. He may also have been accompanied by Nomus, master of the offices, one of the most powerful officials at court, whose duties included the oversight of all imperial business and the regulation of access to the emperor. Attila was impressed by such high-ranking envoys. He indicated that he was prepared to discuss terms and withdraw from Roman territory. Central to his demands—as on every occasion in the preceding decade—was the prompt return of refugees and continued annual payments of gold.

Given the success of Attila's attack, the Roman negotiators were in no position to object. They agreed to the extradition of any Huns sheltering in the empire and settled on a payment of 2,100 pounds of gold a year with an additional 6,000 to cover arrears. This lump sum may also have included a tariff per head to ransom prisoners of war. It was a substantial increase on previous payments set at 350 pounds of gold annually in 422 and raised to 700 under the treaty agreed at Margum in 439. Anatolius and Nomus also conceded that the Danube would no longer mark the extent of Roman imperial rule. Attila demanded the evacuation of a broad belt of territory running from Singidunum (modern Belgrade, in Serbia) 300 miles east along the river to Novae (Svishtov, in Bulgaria) and, at its maximum, five days' journey wide. This depopulated buffer zone protected the Huns from a surprise attack and deprived the Romans of the natural defensive advantages of the Danube. In some places the border was pushed back up to 120 miles. The ruins of Naissus were now right on the frontier.

For many contemporaries, the peace settlement was an outright humiliation. Priscus of Panium—the most important historian of the Roman empire's conflicts with Attila—was clear in his condemnation of Theodosius' cowardice.

> Because of the overwhelming terror that gripped their generals, the Romans were compelled to accept cheerfully every injunction, no matter how harsh, in their eagerness for peace. . . . Even senators contributed a fixed amount of gold. . . . They paid only with difficulty . . . so that men who had once been wealthy were putting up for sale their wives' jewelry and their furniture. This was the disaster that happened to the Romans after the war, and the result was that many killed themselves either by starvation or by hanging. The imperial treasuries were also emptied.

Priscus is correct in emphasizing the size of the agreed annual payout to Attila: 2,100 pounds of gold is equivalent to 151,200 solidi (there are 72 solidi, or gold pieces, to a pound). Even one solidus was no small amount. A single working person could live for several months on such a sum. Upon enlistment, an army recruit in the fourth century received six solidi to cover his uniform, equipment, and other initial expenses. Personal documents, wills, leases, and bills of sale surviving from the sixth-century village of Nessana (in the south of modern Israel) show that on a provincial market one solidus purchased a donkey, two solidi a colt, three a slave girl, five a camel, and six a slave boy. Set against this scatter of figures, 151,200 solidi was a vast sum—but did it, as Priscus claims, threaten the financial integrity of the imperial government?

Regrettably, there is insufficient evidence to allow any detailed reconstruction of state revenue and expenditure in the Roman empire. Only the roughest of estimates is possible. In 445 a law issued by Valentinian III, after the partitioning of Africa with the Vandals, estimated the annual revenue from Numidia at 78,400 solidi, or just under 1,100 pounds of gold. On a crude calculation, reckoning Numidia as an average province—some, such as the Egyptian provinces, were much more prosperous; others, such as the war-damaged Danube provinces, significantly less so—the annual tax take from the sixty provinces that made up the eastern Roman empire was 66,000 pounds of gold. In other words, the payment to Attila was somewhere around 3 percent of revenue. That is still a large sum, but even with the addition of a heavy burden of arrears, it is unlikely to have emptied the imperial treasury or resulted in any lasting financial instability. Indeed, in 457, ten years after the peace settlement with the Huns, Theodosius' successor, Marcian, was said to have left a surplus of 100,000 pounds of gold.

Nor is it likely, if the funds to pay Attila were clawed back through increased taxation, that this would have bankrupted senators, among the richest men in the empire. In Rome, where old, aristocratic families had accumulated property over generations, middle-ranking senatorial households are reported to have enjoyed an annual income of 1,000–1,500 pounds of gold, the few super-rich considerably more, perhaps as much as 4,000. In other words, an annual payment of 2,100 pounds of gold to Attila put him on a par with the wealthiest families in the Roman empire. It was by any measure a huge sum, but—despite Priscus' exaggerated claims—it is most unlikely to have resulted in a tax hike that forced senators to dispose of their furniture and their wives' jewelry, and then go out and hang themselves.

If the lurid detail of Priscus' objections to the treaty of 447

is open to serious question, the general thrust of his criticism is
clear: Theodosius was an ineffectual ruler unable to cope with the
problems that confronted him. Rather than fighting his enemies,
he pursued a supine policy of appeasement. For Priscus, war was
the most effective way for a dynamic superpower to defend its
interests. To avoid battle and instead to purchase peace undermined the self-confident superiority of the Roman empire. As
with many morally forthright views, these arguments are super-
ficially attractive, but ultimately incorrect. Above all, they mis-
understand the complex international situation that Theodosius
faced in the first half of the fifth century. The risks were high
and the losses, especially in the Danube provinces, punishingly
heavy. Even so, over three decades the eastern Roman empire
managed to contain not only the Huns but also the Vandals,
as well as an ever-present Persian threat. Securing a thousand
miles of frontier from Armenia through Syria to the Sinai put a
continual strain on resources. Roman historians focus on major
wars; they tend to ignore the frequent firefights and low-grade
incursions along the often ill-defined edges of empire. Yet, from
a military point of view, to deal effectively with these incidents
required a significant commitment of manpower stationed in
forts and garrison towns.

Given these constraints, Theodosius' master plan was fundamentally sound. He resisted calls to transfer more troops to the
northern frontier or to risk them in a major strike against the
Huns. No doubt, too, financial considerations played a crucial part
in the formulation of policy. To mount an effective military operation across the Danube would have been hugely expensive. In 468,
eleven years after the emperor Marcian's death, his successor, Leo,
sent a task force in yet another attempt to dislodge the Vandals
from North Africa. The bill for the campaign was estimated at just
over 100,000 pounds of gold—and it ultimately failed. At 2,100
pounds per year, the price paid by Theodosius to secure peace was
high, but modest compared with the cost of war.

The result of these careful calculations was a grim strategy of containment. As a matter of cold realism, unless or until the imperial capital was directly threatened, it made both military and financial sense to allow the Huns to plunder the Danube provinces. The alternatives were either to risk Roman forces in an offensive that might end disastrously in a second Adrianople or—by refusing to send reinforcements to other areas of conflict—to offer a weak response to potentially more damaging threats. It was precisely this problem that confronted Theodosius in 421–22 in attacking Persia, in 431–34 in dealing with the first phase of the Vandal invasion, and again in 441–42 when Geiseric seized Carthage. Hence, too, the importance of the Theodosian Walls and the crisis following their collapse. It was the sheer strength of Constantinople's defenses that allowed the legions to be deployed elsewhere. In an emergency, no matter how severe the situation south of the Danube, there would always be time to recall the army or send reinforcements from the eastern front to protect the imperial capital.

What amounted to a strategic willingness to sacrifice Roman territory was never likely, as Priscus' complaints underline, to be a popular policy. For the local population whose cities and farms were wiped out, the empire's response to Hun aggression was inadequate and inept. It seemed that the army had not put up much of a fight; the three generals—Flavius Aspar, Flavius Ariobindus, and Arnegisclus—had been reluctant to chance a major pitched battle. Only when it was clear that the Huns were on their way back to the Great Hungarian Plain did Roman troops go on the offensive, and then not entirely successfully. The hard-fought encounter at the Utus River cost Arnegisclus his life.

Aspar and Ariobindus also paid for their caution; by the end of 447, neither was still in post. It is easy to see why Theodosius decided to let these generals go. Above all, he was not prepared to admit publicly the cruel consequences of his frontier defense policies. Removing Aspar and Ariobindus from their commands was an immediate and pragmatic response to the devastation of the Danube provinces. It deftly shifted responsibility away from the emperor—but it was also unjust. Like Priscus' accusations of cowardice, it refused to recognize that Aspar's and Ariobindus' prudent tactics had prevented any major confrontation and ensured the safety of Constantinople while the Theodosian Walls were hurriedly rebuilt. To attempt more would have been to risk too much. Yet in politics the well-judged avoidance of defeat is not always enough. Aspar's and Ariobindus' achievement fell far short of a decisive victory. For their failure they were unfairly forced to take the blame.

The carefully considered deployment of military assets, even if at times unpopular, and the construction of massive defenses for the imperial capital were not the only keys to the preservation of empire. As Theodosius and his advisers recognized, the well-targeted payment of gold was just as important. (For governments in need of a policy fig leaf to justify the transfer of large sums to sometimes unfriendly regimes, these funds may more diplomatically be termed "subsidies" or "development aid.") Against the warmongering enthusiasm of critics like Priscus, Theodosius' skillfully balanced foreign policy made good sense. He attempted to ensure the integrity of the northern frontier and the safety of the imperial capital while recognizing the advantages of maintaining a stable, if hostile, state beyond the Danube. Resource rich, the eastern Roman empire purchased the opportunities it needed to allow its armies to deal with serious security threats elsewhere.

Yet, at first sight, the Romans seem to have derived little obvious benefit from these payouts. After all, they did not prevent the Hun invasions in 434 and 441. It is unlikely, though, that anyone at court in Constantinople ever thought that peace could simply be purchased. Rather, these subsidies had more diffuse aims. On a day-to-day basis, they helped promote cross-border exchange. Some of the money paid to the Huns filtered back across the Danube to the benefit of Roman merchants. Continued small-scale commercial contact also permitted the unobtrusive transfer of information on the Huns' prosperity, their numbers, and the location of their settlements. Business trips abroad—like diplomatic missions—still remain one of the most plausible covers for espionage.

The transfer of cash across the border also offered a covert means of supporting dissident groups or individuals. Roman gold might have been used to fund a coup, replacing Attila with a more cooperative leadership. In many ways this was an attractive option. It certainly carried less risk than regime change by armed intervention. By itself, war is a crude and unpredictable weapon. In the unlikely event that sufficient manpower could ever have been found to launch a major Roman campaign across the Danube, Attila and his close comrades might have been removed after heavy fighting, but that could then have triggered the collapse of a defeated Hun empire. The resulting instability and civil unrest could have posed a serious security threat to the northern frontier and even to Constantinople. Sending in the troops is always a risky and expensive option. Indeed, there was a real chance that if a large Roman force had ever been sent against the Huns, it would only have succeeded in making a bad situation worse. To counter the dissolution of the Hun empire would have required an additional and costly long-term investment of military, administrative, and financial resources that was impossible without critically restricting the Roman empire's ability to react to the threats posed by Persia and the Vandals. Given the limited options available, Theodosius was right: Attila was more cheaply and effectively bought off than fought off.

For his part, while still demanding Roman subsidies, Attila moved to minimize their negative (as he saw it) consequences.

He was particularly concerned to prevent the formation of any opposition encouraged or financed from across the Danube. In 439 at Margum, he insisted that all payments be made to him or his brother Bleda personally. He closely monitored Hun dealings with Romans, repeatedly demanding the deportation of asylum seekers. After 447 some exiles refused to be repatriated. According to Priscus, many were executed by the Romans—unwilling to give Attila any grounds for breaking the peace treaty—"among them were some members of the Hun royal family who had refused to accept orders from Attila." More widely, Attila also moved to regulate trans-Danube commerce, dictating the location of trading posts. Markets were to be held only at specific sites: the fort of Constantia, on the left bank of the Danube opposite Margum, was designated in 439, the devastated city of Naissus in 447.

Despite these tough countermeasures, Attila recognized the benefits of being paid to keep the peace. (Theodosius would have been in much greater difficulty if he had faced a more conventional enemy who fought to conquer and hold territory.) Alongside his undoubted skill as a general and his claim to the divine favor of the war god, it was Attila's lavish reward of loyal supporters that guaranteed his own continued dominance. He depended on the steady flow of Roman gold across the Danube to underwrite his position at the apex of Hun society. Hence the seemingly endless round of sudden raids, lengthy diplomatic negotiations, and substantial payments that dominated the relationship between Huns and Romans in the first half of the fifth century. To the booty seized in war, Attila added an annual subsidy. It was to his advantage that the Huns should remain parasitic on their much wealthier imperial neighbor. While ruthlessly exploiting its weaknesses, it was not in Attila's long-term interests to hasten the decline and fall of the eastern Roman empire. He had too much to lose.

PART THREE

DINNER WITH ATTILA

CHAPTER THIRTEEN

MISSION IMPOSSIBLE

Five hundred years after Attila's attacks and the hurried rebuilding of the Theodosian Walls, Constantinople was still the capital of the eastern Roman empire (or Byzantium, to give it its Greek name). By the tenth century, the empire was no longer a superpower; it was no more than a local state surrounded on all sides by enemies. In defiance of political reality, the magnificently titled emperor Constantine VII Porphyrogenitus ("born in the purple") persisted in calling himself "lord of the whole Earth." In fact, Constantine controlled only the western half of Turkey, the Balkans, and the southern part of Italy. This was an imperial rump, a mere excuse for an empire. Much of the Mediterranean world once part of Christendom was now securely under Islamic rule.

Embattled emperors in Constantinople held fast to their Roman heritage. If they could no longer match ancient glories, they could ensure they were not forgotten. Constantine Porphyrogenitus commissioned a series of summaries of a vast amount of information taken from classical texts. For those who found libraries daunting places where (in the emperor's words) "the vast quantity of material induces fear and dismay," Constantine ordered a compilation of extracts taken from historical works. In selecting suitable passages, he instructed his editors "to break up that great mass of scholarship which is so ponderous and dull that just thinking about it is exhausting." In its place, Constantine's anthology claimed to offer "an overview . . . of all the most valuable lessons from history." Even so, readers were still confronted with fifty-three large volumes, each one dealing with a key theme: victories, letter writing, public speaking, brave deeds, hunting, conspiracies. From this enormous undertaking, only a handful of items remain. By chance, these precious relics have escaped the loss or destruction of most of the literature and history written in the ancient world.

One of Constantine's scrapbooks collected reports of embassies sent by the Romans and received from their allies and enemies. It is in this scissors-and-paste form that the most important ancient work on Attila and the Huns survives. Sandwiched between the often tedious accounts of endless diplomatic negotiations are the remnants of Priscus of Panium's *History of Attila*. Published at intervals between the mid-450s and early 480s, it dealt chiefly with contemporary events in the eastern Roman empire, focusing on the conflict with the Huns in the late 440s. The *History* was dismembered by Constantine's research assistants, who reduced its eight books to thirty-five fragments. A few long extracts offer a reasonably coherent account of a Roman embassy that met with Attila in summer 449 at his main residence on the Great Hungarian Plain. Priscus' report of his encounter with Attila attracted the attention of its tenth-century editors, and their fascination is easy to understand. This is not a secondhand narrative put together after long hours in a research library. Priscus was actually there. He offers his readers the only surviving eyewitness description of Attila and his court. No other history gets so close to the Huns. No other account makes it so tantalizingly possible for us to imagine what it might have been like to be there, too. What follows—with thanks to Constantine Porphyrogenitus and his editorial team—is Priscus' story.

Priscus was born around 420 in the town of Panium, on the northern shore of the Propontis, eighty miles down the coast from Constantinople. Like that of most people in the eastern Mediterranean, his first language was Greek; only a small minority knew Latin. Those engaged in official matters—bureaucrats, petitioners, litigants, lawyers, judges, courtiers, emperors—spoke Greek to each other, but almost all the written business of administration and the courts was conducted in Latin. After all, this was still the Roman empire. Like many ambitious Greek-speakers from well-off families, Priscus was taught Latin at school. This was language learning the hard way: the endless chanting of grammar and vocabulary, and the humiliation of corporal punishment that followed any hesitation or mistake. Most of the school day was spent studying the classics. The well educated could recite long passages of poetry by heart. Among their favorites were tragic speeches from Euripides (one of the great Athenian dramatists of the fifth century BC) and the quarrel between Achilles and Agamemnon that opens Homer's *Iliad*. Hard as it is for us to believe, spotting and swapping quotations from long-dead authors was regarded by many privileged Romans as one of the most enjoyable forms of polite dinner-party entertainment.

Priscus got out of Panium as soon as he could. From a provincial town where nothing much ever happened, he moved to Constantinople, where he continued his education in philosophy and rhetoric, the art of elegant and persuasive speaking and writing. As a student in the crowded wine bars of the capital, Priscus no doubt spent a great deal of time debating politics. How should the Hun threat be managed? Should the empire stand and fight, or was it a shrewder and longer-sighted strategy to pay Attila off? After completing his studies, Priscus decided to stay on in the city as a private tutor. It was perhaps through such a connection that, sometime in the early 440s, he met a young army officer called Maximinus. Maximinus was Constantinople born and bred. His wealthy relations might have been willing to help an up-and-coming teacher of rhetoric. This was precisely the kind of highbrow cultural activity that a prominent household with connections to the imperial court could be expected to support. Maximinus' parents probably encouraged the friendship. They may have regarded conversation with Priscus as a useful counter-balance to the time their son now spent away on tours of duty. It is unlikely that many dinners in the officers' mess ended with a round of witty quotations from Homer or Euripides.

In their mid-twenties, Priscus and Maximinus experienced the fear that the Huns could inspire. After the collapse of the Theodosian Walls, Maximinus may have been involved in the campaign to delay Attila's progress toward Constantinople. Mean-while, Priscus and his pupils probably cheered on the Greens and the Blues as they worked day and night to repair the earthquake damage. Both Priscus and Maximinus must also have shared the relief and joined in the celebrations when the Huns, skirting the imperial capital, turned north and marched back to the Danube. The peace negotiated by Anatolius and Nomus in late 447 was to be welcomed, even if Priscus would have preferred it to follow a crushing demonstration of Roman military superiority rather than an ongoing commitment to pay an annual subsidy to one of the empire's most destructive enemies.

In spring 449, a high-ranking Hun arrived in Constantinople. Edeco was a close companion of Attila's and one of his body-guards. He was accompanied by Orestes, a Roman who had been born and raised near the Sava River (on the border of modern Croatia and Serbia). Orestes' family estates fell within the ter-ritory along the Danube surrendered in 435 by Aetius in return for Attila and Bleda's support in France. Marooned outside the empire, Orestes had managed the imposition of Hun rule as well as he could. Perhaps in return for being allowed to keep his lands, he had offered his services to Attila as a confidential private secretary. His knowledge of Latin would be useful in furthering the Huns' diplomatic efforts in Ravenna and Constantinople.

At the Great Palace, lengthy ceremonial was set aside as Edeco was ushered into the throne room. Orestes was instructed to wait. In the capital no one paid attention to just another moderately well-off Roman from the provinces. Edeco was awestruck by the magnificence of the court. Some may have hoped that it would leave a definite and lasting impression of imperial power; others, more cynical, may have thought that the sight of so much wealth would only encourage the Huns to think again of attacking Constantinople. In the golden halls of the Great Palace, the battle-hardened Hun in his fur-lined cloak, leather jerkin, and trousers, must have looked out of place. Perhaps some of the courtiers in their beautifully patterned silken robes sneered as he passed. Official etiquette specifically prohibited the wearing of trousers in the emperor's presence. This was the uniform of a barbarian, not of someone who dared offer Theodosius II a letter and who clearly expected to talk terms.

But emperors do not negotiate—at least not in person. This was a formal meeting. As he approached the throne, Edeco prostrated himself: face down to the floor, eyes lowered, body tensed. Then, easing himself forward until his head was level with Theodosius' gem-encrusted shoes, he kissed the hem of the emperor's purple robe. Once Edeco had "adored the purple," as this ceremony was known, he retreated and stood at a respectful distance. At this point, it became clear that he did not know a word of either Greek or Latin. Silently one of the emperor's chief advisers came forward. Like Nomus before him, Flavius Martialis held the powerful court post of master of the offices. No petition was answered, no edict signed, no ambassador admitted, no honors conferred without his knowing about it.

Martialis signaled one of his subordinates to approach. Vigilas was an unimpressive sight, even in court dress. He is best pictured as a nervous man, perhaps always pulling at his robe and offering exaggerated compliments to all he met. Like many unused to the brittle world of high politics, he had misunderstood the purpose of flattery. Of course, the powerful expect to be flattered, but they also expect the distinctions of rank to be observed. Vigilas' mistake was to flatter everybody, and in many people's eyes that made him untrustworthy. Yet for the moment (after the emperor himself), Vigilas was the most important person in the throne room. Aside from Orestes, politely detained on Martialis' orders, he was the only Roman in the Great Palace who spoke Hunnic. How he had learned it was unclear. Most assumed the Huns had captured him as a boy on one of their raids across the Danube and that later he had managed to escape. Vigilas had exploited his only skill, offering his services as an interpreter to the eastern Roman government, most recently translating for Anatolius and Nomus at the peace talks in 447.

Attila's letter was read out by another of Martialis' bureaucratic underlings. It had probably been written by Orestes in his impeccable Latin. In formal exchanges, Attila was determined to present himself as Theodosius' equal. In this letter, he insisted that the emperor honor his recent undertakings. Despite sending at least four embassies to the imperial court in the last year—including one led by Edeco himself—he alleged that not all of the Hun refugees had been handed over. Nor, he complained, had the Romans withdrawn to the agreed frontier, five days' journey south of the Danube. Parts of the buffer zone were still being farmed, and the cross-border trading post at Naissus was not yet operational. Edeco expanded on these grievances. Standing defiantly in the middle of the Great Palace, the Hun envoy was an unsettling reminder of how close the Roman empire had come to disaster in the last ten years. As Vigilas' translation made clear, Attila insisted that high-ranking ambassadors be sent to explain why the treaty provisions had not yet been fully implemented. Unless these matters were speedily resolved, the

Huns might not keep the peace. Theodosius made no response to these belligerent threats. He did not move. This was a good diplomatic ploy; it both avoided confrontation and helped maintain the fiction that the godlike ruler of the Roman world was closer to heaven than to earth. The real negotiations took place elsewhere. Leaving Orestes waiting, Edeco was escorted through the palace to another splendid suite of rooms. Here he was greeted by Chrysaphius, the commander of the imperial bodyguard.

Edeco had never dealt with a eunuch before. There were none at Attila's court. In the great cities of the empire, they were rarely seen outside the wealthiest households. At first meeting, many found their appearance disturbing. Most eunuchs were tall and gangling with broad hips and prominent breasts. They seemed to sweat continuously. From a distance, their smooth skin had a shiny gloss like a young girl's; close up, under layers of artfully applied cosmetics, their wrinkled faces were like an old woman's. Eunuchs' crumpled features, in the words of one of their most spiteful detractors, "are like raisins and their bodies deformed, half male and half female." Flourishing in the secret world of the Great Palace, gliding through the shadows of its cool, marble colonnades, moving silently down its long, dark corridors, eunuchs lived, it was said, "like bats in a cave."

For all their strangeness—the cruel physiological consequence of castration before puberty—eunuchs were capable of acquiring great power. Many emperors preferred to trust advisers who could not be swayed by their own family interests. Eunuchs did not have wives or sons to think about; they depended for their position on the emperor alone. Proximity to the throne guaranteed their influence. Eunuchs could make or break an ambitious aristocrat. A quiet word might ensure the emperor's favor; malicious gossip might result in exile. It was rumored that Theodosius was too easily swayed by eunuchs who had looked after him since childhood. Certainly they were convenient scapegoats. Loyal Romans rarely criticized a living emperor openly; rather, they blamed unpopular policies on the jealousies and misinformation of those closest to him. Eunuchs were with the emperor while he ate, dressed, and bathed. At night they were locked into his bedroom and slept across the doors. In these private moments, it was suspected, Theodosius was most vulnerable to their malign insinuations. It was widely believed that things would be different if the emperor only knew what really went on behind his back in the seclusion of the Great Palace.

Chrysaphius was one of Theodosius' closest confidants. His meeting with the Hun envoy could not have taken place without the emperor's knowledge. Away from the stiff formalities of the throne room, it was now time to talk business. Slaves brought dainty pastries soaked in honey and cool sweet wine in delicate silver cups. Three distinct voices were clearly audible: Chrysaphius' fluting high-pitched tones were an ever-present reminder that he was a eunuch; Edeco's guttural Hunnic, that he was an enemy of the Romans; Vigilas' wheedling translations, that he was in this for whatever he could get. Vigilas again emphasized how much Edeco was impressed by the opulence of the Great Palace. Chrysaphius' small talk was probably all about chariot racing. He was a dedicated fan and generous backer of the Greens. In Priscus' account: "Vigilas—translating—said that Edeco admired the palace and regarded those who had such wealth as fortunate. Chrysaphius remarked that Edeco could also possess riches and rooms with golden ceilings if he were to set the interests of the Huns aside and work instead for the Romans."

Chrysaphius then asked Edeco how well he knew Attila. Edeco assured him that he was part of his inner circle. Feigning a professional interest as commander of the emperor's bodyguard, Chrysaphius pressed him for more details. How was Attila's retinue organized? How were his guards selected? What was the process of security clearance? Edeco replied that only the most trusted of Attila's friends were armed in his presence. A group of high-ranking men shared the responsibilities of a bodyguard according to a duty roster, and each knew in advance when it was his turn to protect Attila. Satisfied, Chrysaphius changed the subject. Looking up at the great gilded ceiling, the eunuch slowly closed his eyes and mused again on the advantages of wealth and how it might most easily be acquired. Vigilas made sure that nothing was lost in translation.

That evening Edeco and Vigilas were entertained alone in the eunuch's private residence. (Orestes was dispatched elsewhere on some pointless diplomatic errand.)

With Vigilas translating, they shook hands and exchanged oaths. The eunuch swore not to say anything to Edeco's detriment, but only to his great advantage. Edeco swore he would not reveal what was said to him even if he did not take it any further. Chrysaphius then said to Edeco that if he agreed to journey into Hun territory, kill Attila, and return to the Romans, he would enjoy a life of happiness and the greatest wealth. Edeco promised he would undertake the mission.

And so the deal was done. The details were worked out over dinner. The most pressing issue was how to secure the cooperation of Attila's bodyguard. Edeco reckoned that fifty pounds of gold would be sufficient to persuade them to join his cause. As a gesture of goodwill, Chrysaphius ordered the money to be fetched immediately. But Edeco advised he could not safely carry such a quantity of bullion back across the Danube. Attila was always suspicious of gifts received by Huns while on embassies to the Romans. Instead, it was agreed that Vigilas should accompany Edeco on his return journey to Attila's court. Through Vigilas, Edeco would then send instructions on how the gold was to be delivered.

Chrysaphius was all too aware of both the risks and the advantages of his scheme. If it failed, it might provoke revenge attacks.

If it succeeded, Attila might be replaced by a ruler more sympathetic to the Romans, and the northern frontier would again be secure. From within the Great Palace, the shrewd strategies of a eunuch would have removed one of the empire's greatest threats. In the war against Attila, there was no need of armies or a costly offensive. Astute diplomacy and well-directed bribery offered a better chance of achieving regime change. These pleasant thoughts in mind, Chrysaphius made his way to the most heavily guarded part of the palace and there discussed his plans with Theodosius. For those who have seen an emperor only in his throne room, or riding in a procession, or walking barefoot through the streets of the capital, it is difficult to envisage such a scene. How does the ruler of the Roman world behave in private? Chrysaphius perhaps interrupted a conversation about horses or hunting dogs or about some new entertainment in the hippodrome, or perhaps the pious emperor was at prayer.

Theodosius said very little. The plan to murder a hostile foreign leader presented him with no moral difficulty. In his view, an ethical foreign policy was one that best advanced the interests of the Roman empire. Even so, the emperor had no wish to be associated openly with Chrysaphius' conspiracy until it had achieved its objective. Nor did he request to be kept informed of progress. It was important to minimize the consequences of failure. If ever confronted by Attila's ambassadors, Theodosius would, of course, deny all knowledge of a plot. Sometimes an emperor does not want to know what really goes on behind his back. Then, if things do not work out, he can always blame the eunuchs.

Theodosius also consulted the master of the offices, Flavius Martialis. Martialis may have needed convincing that the project was worth backing. Surely Edeco had been won over too easily and too cheaply? He suggested that Vigilas' involvement would seem more plausible if it were associated with an official Roman embassy: as an interpreter he would have perfect cover. But this

was not a simple matter. Attila had insisted that he would negotiate only with an ambassador of the highest rank, and, given the
circumstances, no prominent courtier would be prepared to take
the risk. Of course, the Huns would offer the usual diplomatic
immunities that went with an embassy, but the long trek to the
Great Hungarian Plain presented too many opportunities for a
fatal accident. Martialis advised sending a young man, someone
not too far advanced in his career who would find an appoint-
ment as the emperor's envoy impossible to refuse. The difficulties
and dangers involved argued for a military man, rather than a
desk-bound bureaucrat.

The ambassador would carry a letter from Theodosius rejecting
Attila's suggestion that Roman noncompliance with the provisions of the treaty threatened to undermine peace and hinting
that it was the Huns' actions that called into question the agreed
withdrawal south of the Danube. According to Priscus, "Then
it was written, 'Anyone jeopardizing the treaty is not justified in
taking possession of Roman territory,' and, 'In addition to those
handed over so far, I am sending you seventeen refugees, and
there are no others.' These quotations are from the emperor's
letter."

The repatriation of seventeen more refugees was a clear gesture
of conciliation. (It was also a tacit admission that there was some
foundation to Attila's complaint that the empire was still harbor-
ing renegade Huns.) The letter would also make it clear that its
bearer came from a distinguished family and was among Theodosius' closest confidants. To avoid any preemptive objection to
his status, the ambassador would be given strict instructions to
insist on speaking to Attila in person and not to submit the letter in advance of a meeting. Chrysaphius suggested that a copy
be secretly shown to Edeco, so that he would have no reason to
question the emperor's motives in sending an embassy.

Once these details had been settled, Martialis carefully scanned
the army lists to identify a suitable candidate for the post of

ambassador. After some discreet inquiries, he recommended Maximinus. This was a good choice: an ambitious young man with a promising record and eager to serve the best interests of the empire. Maximinus was no doubt delighted—his merits had at last been noticed by the powerful in Constantinople. In the dark purple ink reserved exclusively for imperial use, the emperor had signed his formal letters of accreditation as an imperial envoy. Nothing at all was said of Chrysaphius' plot to assassinate Attila. Maximinus could be forgiven for thinking that his mission to the Huns was the beginning of what promised to be a brilliant diplomatic career.

CHAPTER FOURTEEN
CLOSE ENCOUNTERS

Maximinus left Constantinople in early summer 449. Traveling in the official party were Attila's envoy Edeco and his secretary Orestes, and the interpreter Vigilas. They were joined by Rusticius, a businessman who had his own private dealings with another of Attila's secretaries. He was a welcome addition because he had personal contacts with those close to Attila and was fluent in Hunnic. Maximinus perhaps thought this might prove useful if Vigilas turned out to be unreliable. It must have been a relief not to have to depend solely on Vigilas' translations. Priscus also joined the mission. "Maximinus by his entreaties persuaded me to accompany him on this embassy." It was not uncommon for those skilled in rhetoric to be part of an ambassador's staff. Maximinus' competence was on the battlefield rather than around the negotiating table. In his new civilian role, he may have felt the need for a mind more attuned to the advantages and pitfalls of subtle argumentation. He also seems to have been confident that his embassy would mark a significant moment in the Roman empire's relationship with the Huns. Perhaps he was eager that his achievements be properly recorded. Priscus could be relied upon to submit a well-judged report to the master of the offices, presenting Maximinus as a key player. If the emperor approved, then Priscus could write a more literary account of his best friend's diplomatic achievements.

Priscus had probably already published some of his set-piece lectures. Aside from friendship, what may have persuaded him to accept Maximinus' offer was the opportunity to collect first-hand data on the Huns. No other writer had ever had access to such information. The majority of Priscus' Greek-speaking contemporaries still based their views on Herodotus' account of *nomades*. Writing in Latin in the late 380s, Ammianus Marcellinus had made some advances in understanding the Huns, but he was not as reliable as was sometimes claimed. Priscus intended to go much further: aside from its literary merits (and Priscus prided himself on his stylish prose), his new account of the world beyond the Danube would be based on his own research in the field. That alone might be enough to make his *History of Attila*—only a working title at this early stage—a best-seller in Constantinople.

Thirteen days after leaving the capital, the travelers passed through Adrianople before reaching the burned-out shell of Serdica (modern Sofia, in Bulgaria). The three-hundred-mile journey along a well-built road brought stark reminders of the damage caused by the Huns two years earlier. Between Adrianople and Serdica were only ruins. Edeco was perhaps diplomatic enough not to boast of Attila's victories, or at least Rusticius and Vigilas were diplomatic enough not to translate. At Serdica, Maximinus decided to host a barbecue. Camp was pitched at a distance from the devastated city, now sheltering only a few shepherds who approached warily at the sight of Huns and Romans traveling together: was this a sign of a lasting peace on the northern frontier or a prelude to the surrender of even more of the empire's territory? Maximinus saw no reason to explain his mission. It was enough that these peasants acknowledged his status as an imperial ambassador and were prepared to sell him some of their sheep. Since leaving Constantinople, Maximinus and Edeco had communicated only when necessary. They had eaten apart, each with his own companions. Now Huns and Romans were sitting together around the embers of a campfire in that convivial mood which commonly follows an excellent dinner in the open air. Priscus took advantage of the occasion to study the Huns. There was much to be learned. Perhaps he was careful to note how Edeco preferred his steak. The standard view that Huns ate their meat half raw, or concealed it under their saddles, clearly required revision.

All seemed to be going well. As the wine, diluted with water in the traditional Roman manner, circulated freely, Maximinus proposed the emperor's health and continued good fortune. Edeco immediately interjected with his own toast to Attila. All had raised their cups when Vigilas was heard to comment "that it was not right to compare a god and a man, meaning by a man Attila and by a god Theodosius." Edeco was understandably offended. To the Huns, Attila's claim to be especially favored by the war god seemed as credible as Theodosius' belief in his closeness to Christ. After all, as Edeco might have said, had he really been spoiling for an argument, what better proof of Attila's divinely inspired destiny than the shattered walls of Serdica silhouetted behind them against a clear night sky? The evening turned sour. Maximinus hurriedly apologized. Perhaps it was obvious that Vigilas had drunk too much or that his remark was nothing more than a bad joke. Priscus attempted to move things along, his friendly conversation preventing Edeco's immediate withdrawal. What had seemed a successful meeting now stuttered to an unsatisfactory close. As the Huns prepared to return to their tents, Maximinus offered Edeco and Orestes rich presents of silk and pearls. Edeco seemed pleased, but said nothing. The whole incident, as Priscus realized much later, had been carefully stage-managed. The contrived public clash between Edeco and Vigilas had been intended to draw any suspicion away from their private arrangement. But not everyone was convinced that all was quite what it seemed. Before leaving, Orestes drew Maximinus aside.

He said that Maximinus was a wise and a very good man not to have acted in the same insulting manner as those at court, for they had invited Edeco to dinner on his own and had honored him with gifts. This remark meant nothing either to Maximinus or to me since we had no idea of what had happened, and so we asked Orestes repeatedly how and on what occasion he had been excluded and Edeco honored. But he withdrew without replying.

The following morning, Maximinus is likely to have expressed his disappointment to Vigilas. He probably took the view that sensitive diplomatic behavior could reasonably be expected from an experienced interpreter. Perhaps Maximinus was content to draw a line under the incident, if Vigilas could assure him that there would be no further lapses. Vigilas apologized: after all, the faked disagreement with Edeco had served its purpose. Maximinus then asked him to explain Orestes' remarks. Was it true that Edeco had been entertained on his own in the Great Palace and given gifts? This was Vigilas' first hint that Edeco's companions suspected that their embassy to Constantinople might have been compromised. In reply, Vigilas carefully avoided the specifics of what he suggested were no more than petulant comments. In his view, it would hardly be surprising if the difference between Orestes' status and Edeco's had been reflected in their reception at the imperial court, "since Orestes was a servant and private secretary to Attila, while Edeco, distinguished in war and a Hun, was by far his superior."

Nothing more was said on the subject. Confused and wary, all involved preferred to remain quiet. A few days later, while trying to find a place to pitch camp outside Naissus, the Romans were faced with a cheerless memorial to their failure to defend the Danube provinces. Near the walls—smashed by battering rams seven years earlier—the riverbank was still littered with the bones of the slain. That night it seemed best that Huns and Romans should eat apart. Leaving Naissus, they entered the buffer zone stipulated by Attila as part of the peace settlement of 447. For five days, they journeyed through territory that had once been part of the Roman empire. In a mostly deserted landscape, the wreckage of farm buildings and villages served as another bitter reminder of past prosperity. Perhaps here Priscus felt, even more strongly than at the time of the treaty negotiations, that Theodosius and his generals should have put up a fight. Surely, after more than four centuries of Roman rule, there could be no excuse for the deliberate abandonment of empire?

At last the travelers reached the Danube, probably somewhere near the ruins of Margum. Priscus is vague in giving directions and travel times. He clearly found the route difficult and disorienting. He disliked the twisting paths through the dark and overgrown woods. Sometimes, at least as far as he could judge by the sun, he seemed to be traveling west and then, as the narrow track corkscrewed again, back toward the east. Ferried across the Danube in dugouts hollowed from single tree trunks, Priscus must have felt that he had left civilization far behind. Constantinople was now more than three weeks away. It was a relief when messengers arrived to instruct them to attend a meeting with Attila the following day. Maximinus remained optimistic about the prospects for the embassy. After all, despite Orestes' cryptic complaints, he still knew nothing about Chrysaphius' assassination plot. To demonstrate that, even beyond the frontier, Roman hospitality was undiminished, Maximinus invited Attila's messengers to dine. Priscus is clear that the guests were well entertained. Regrettably, he gives no account of any after-dinner toasts. Perhaps this time Maximinus, practicing his diplomatic skills, decided they should quietly be omitted.

From the moment the Romans arrived, things went badly. Tents
that had been pitched on a grassy rise had to be moved since the
Huns insisted that no foreigner be allowed to overlook Attila's
camp. Edeco and Orestes soon returned from their own audience
with Attila. They were now accompanied by Scottas, reputed to
be one of Attila's most valued advisers and authorized to speak
with the Romans on his behalf. Scottas asked Maximinus what
he hoped to achieve by his embassy. Maximinus' reply was courteously evasive. He regarded the inquiry as abrupt in tone and
hostile in intent, but Scottas persisted, demanding a straight
response to a direct question. Maximinus, closely following the
instructions he had received in Constantinople, made it clear
that he had been ordered to deliver the emperor's letter to Attila
in person. Repeating his question, Scottas emphasized that he
asked it at Attila's specific request. "Surely," he remarked, "you
did not think that I would come to you just to interfere on my
own account?" Maximinus stuck to the rule of international law,
calmly—if rather pompously—observing, "It is not the convention for ambassadors to discuss the reasons for their mission with
third parties before they have even met those to whom they
have been sent." This, he noted, was a practice well known to
the Huns, and it had always been followed when they had sent
ambassadors to Constantinople. "We deserve to be treated in an
equal fashion; otherwise we will not divulge the purpose of our
embassy."

Scottas departed, his question still unanswered. Perhaps Maximinus was pleased with the result of this first encounter. He
had made his position clear and was confident that he would
soon speak to Attila. A little while later, Scottas returned and,
to Maximinus' embarrassment, summarized—without pause or
apology—the contents of the emperor's letter. He then requested
that the Romans leave Hun territory immediately unless they
had any other matters to discuss. Priscus and Maximinus were
at a loss: "we were unable to understand how decisions that the

emperor had made in secret had come to be known." Perhaps at
this point they should have realized that something was wrong.
Yet, to be fair, there was no reason why they should have suspected Vigilas (unlikely ever to have had access to such sensitive
state documents) or have associated this incident with Orestes'
baffling remarks at Serdica ten days earlier. The security breach,
they might well have reasoned, was most likely to have occurred
in the imperial capital. The culprit was perhaps to be found
among the officials working for Flavius Martialis. Such a surmise
would have been only half right. The letter had been shown to
Edeco in Constantinople—but by Chrysaphius. Of course, at
the time Chrysaphius was not to know that Edeco would later
double-cross him and share its contents with Attila.

Back beyond the Danube, Maximinus and Priscus were not
the only ones to have misunderstood the situation. Vigilas, too,
failed to grasp that Edeco had already betrayed him. He may
have told Orestes about the plot on the way to Serdica, or he may
have waited to tell Attila and Scottas. Priscus was never able to
establish the truth. "For Edeco had either made his promise to
Chrysaphius falsely, or he was afraid that Orestes might tell Attila
what he had said to us after dinner at Serdica and blame him for
speaking on his own to the emperor and the eunuch." Certainly
Vigilas assumed that everything was still running according to
plan. He had not been surprised that Scottas could quote from
Theodosius' letter. Edeco had been shown it precisely so that, if
questioned about any private meetings in the Great Palace, he
could claim that they were aimed at obtaining this confidential
information. What dismayed Vigilas was Maximinus' reaction.
He stood his ground, insisting on a meeting with Attila and refusing to confirm or deny Scottas' account of the emperor's letter.

As Priscus later realized, it was of vital importance to Vigilas
that the embassy go ahead, so that he and Edeco "might have
a pretext to discuss the plot against Attila and decide how to
transport the gold that Edeco had said he needed for distribu-

tion to those under his command." Hence Vigilas' frustration at Maximinus' intransigence. In Vigilas' view, it would have been better to fabricate some new topic for negotiation in order to secure an audience with Attila. Maximinus, who repudiated such falsehoods as beneath a Roman ambassador, could now see no way forward. He lay on the grass despondently. Perhaps he was watching the clouds go by and thinking how he would explain the failure of his mission when he returned to Constantinople.

Priscus—as he is proud to record—saved the day. With Rusticius as interpreter, he made his own approach to Scottas. It lacked subtlety (greater sophistication might perhaps have been expected from an experienced teacher of rhetoric): Scottas was offered gifts and asked to intercede with Attila. Priscus picks up his own story: "I said to Scottas that we had learned that his views carried weight with Attila, but what we had heard about him would not seem credible unless we had a demonstration of his power." Priscus was pleased with his tactics since Scottas, apparently all too eager to prove his influence, "immediately mounted his horse and galloped away to Attila's tent." Perhaps, if just for a fleeting moment, Priscus thought that dealing with the Huns was not so difficult after all. It had seemed childishly simple to play on Scottas' pride and get him to appeal to Attila to change his mind. But it was Priscus who had been fooled. It must already have occurred to Attila that if Maximinus knew his embassy had been compromised, then his insistence on an audience was an act of nearly suicidal recklessness. Given Maximinus' actions and those of his patronizing friend Priscus, it made more sense to assume that they still knew nothing about Chrysaphius' conspiracy. If so, this was a situation that could be turned to the Huns' advantage. Scottas was instructed to return to the Romans and invite them to Attila's tent.

The audience was a diplomatic disaster. Attila was surrounded by heavily armed guards. This was a reasonable precaution: after all, there was still a chance that Maximinus had been aware of Chrysaphius' conspiracy all along and that he was now prepared to risk his own life to strike a blow for the Roman empire, although somehow it seemed unlikely that the professorial Priscus would turn out to be a heroic man of action. Entering the tent, Maximinus and Priscus found Attila seated on a wooden chair. Maximinus presented Theodosius' letter with the flourish of a traditional Roman salutation: "The emperor prays that you and those dear to you are well." Attila replied that he wished the Romans precisely the same as he understood they now wished him. This cutting remark was completely lost on Maximinus. Only much later, when he learned of Chrysaphius' plot, did he understand its biting irony.

Priscus observed everything carefully. This was his first sight of a man who for many personified terror and destruction. He may have been expecting a barbarian monstrosity, a kind of nightmarish combination of Homer's one-eyed, man-eating Cyclops, and the crude, animal-like disfigurement typical of Herodotus' *nomades*. Perhaps to Priscus' surprise, nothing at all in Attila's appearance was immediately frightening: "he was short with a broad chest and a large head; his eyes were small, his beard sparse and flecked with gray, his nose flatish, and his complexion dark." Certainly Attila did not find the Romans who now stood uneasily before him particularly impressive. Ignoring Maximinus and Priscus, he turned to Vigilas and reminded him that it had been agreed at the peace talks two years earlier that no Roman embassies would be sent until all Hun refugees had been returned. Vigilas assured Attila that there were no more on Roman territory. Priscus continues, "Attila became angrier and grossly insulted him, shouting that, had he not known that it would violate the rights of ambassadors, he would impale him and leave him as carrion for the birds to punish him for the shameless effrontery of his claims." He instructed his secretaries to read out the names of those he alleged were still being sheltered by the Romans. Furious, he ordered Vigilas back to Constantinople, where he was to demand that Theodosius hand over any remaining fugitives. He was then to return and report the emperor's response. To add weight to Vigilas' mission, he would be accompanied by Eslas, one of the most experienced Hun ambassadors, who, fifteen years earlier, had negotiated with Theodosius on Rua's behalf. Maximinus and Priscus were to remain behind so that in due course they could receive a formal reply to the emperor's letter. Meanwhile, they were specifically directed not to attempt to ransom Roman prisoners of war or purchase any slaves or horses. The money they had brought with them from Constantinople they could use only to buy food.

Debriefing back at camp, Maximinus was at a loss to understand Attila's anger. Priscus rather lamely suggested that he might have been insulted by the report of Vigilas' objection to the toasts at Serdica. Vigilas could merely comment that at the peace talks in 447 Attila had been reasonable throughout. Vigilas' puzzlement at Attila's fury was genuine; after all, he was still convinced that the conspiracy was a secret. "For at the time," Priscus reported, "he did not think, as he confessed to us later, that either what had happened at Serdica or the details of the plot had been reported to Attila." That belief was strengthened by the arrival of Edeco. Taking Vigilas aside, he assured him that all was now in place and that on his return from Constantinople he should bring the gold to pay off Attila's bodyguard. Questioned by Maximinus about this conversation, Vigilas offered only a barefaced lie. He said Edeco had reported that Attila was angry because all the refugees had not been returned and—this a low blow—because it was obvious that he had not been sent an ambassador of any great experience or standing.

The Romans had been outwitted. Maximinus was still unaware of the plot. Despite the leaking of Theodosius' letter, he was determined to continue with the embassy. His best friend Priscus readily agreed. After all, he was under the smug impression that it had been his resourceful intervention with Scottas that had secured the interview with Attila. Vigilas still believed that Edeco intended to carry out the mission as arranged with Chrysaphius. From the Huns' point of view, things looked very different. Edeco had confessed everything he knew. Scottas' deliberately loutish questioning had been successful in confirming that Maximinus and Priscus knew nothing. Still unaware of Chrysaphius' schemes, the Roman envoys were willing to remain as guests of the Huns. Most importantly, Vigilas had taken the bait. He had been given a plausible reason for returning to Constantinople and had promised Edeco that he would bring back fifty pounds of gold. If he were then to be searched, Vigilas would have difficulty in explaining away such a large sum. With the ban on ransoming prisoners or purchasing slaves or horses, it was a great deal more than was necessary to buy food. This was a risk he was prepared to take. Only later did Priscus realize that this was part of Attila's trap "so that Vigilas should be caught easily and incriminate himself as he would have no excuse for bringing the gold." Vigilas had been cleverly set up. As far as Attila was concerned, the great game had now begun.

CHAPTER FIFTEEN

EATING WITH THE ENEMY

The next ten days were the most miserable part of the entire journey. There were no further meetings with Attila. Instead, as instructed by their Hun guides, Maximinus and Priscus made their way to his main residence on the north-western part of the Great Hungarian Plain. They probably traveled roughly parallel to the course of the Danube as it runs north for two hundred miles to the Great Danube Bend. In contrast to his precision within the empire, once beyond its frontiers Priscus' confused geography makes it difficult to map his route or locate Attila's residence with any certainty. To Priscus the landscape seemed a featureless expanse of open plain, broken only by marshes and rivers whose names he could barely pronounce. In this unfamiliar world without roads or cities—or even their ruins—he found it impossible to tell exactly where he was.

The going was tough. Rivers were crossed, as on the Danube, in large dugouts or, in marshy areas, on light rafts. As Maximinus and Priscus had by now used up most of the provisions they had brought with them, they obtained supplies from the villages through which they passed. "We were provided with plenty of food, millet instead of wheat and instead of wine . . . a drink made from barley." Eager not to seem ungracious, Priscus can be imagined smilingly eating the local produce, chewing his way through the hard bread made from hand-ground millet and trying the beer. The strong and sometimes sour ale made from malted barley was not a Hun import, but the continuation of a long Roman tradition of brewing. Beer was a frontier drink. Perhaps Priscus, as he hesitantly sipped a huge mug, hoped that no one would notice that, like most educated people in the Roman empire, he would have preferred a small white wine—mixed with water and sweetened with honey.

Without doubt, for Priscus the lowest point of the journey was the collapse of his tent in the middle of the night. During a storm, it had been caught in a violent gust of wind that also blew his baggage into a nearby creek. At such moments, Priscus encountered more of life beyond the frontier than he wished. With their campsite flooded, Priscus and Maximinus pressed on through the heavy rain to find shelter. In a nearby village, they were looked after by an aristocratic woman. Drenched and shivering as he was, Priscus admired her poise and dignified authority. She had once been, as he learned in conversation, one of Bleda's wives. The following day, after they had recovered their baggage and dried it in the sunshine, Priscus and Maximinus presented her with gifts, including three silver bowls, dates, and Indian pepper. From his close observation of their eating habits, Priscus already knew that spices and dried fruits were greatly prized as delicacies among the Huns.

These handsome offerings were also an apology in case such an evidently important woman had been offended. As part of her generous hospitality, she had offered her Roman guests Hun women as partners for the night. It was a difficult situation, particularly, as Priscus was informed, because such a courtesy was extended only to the highest-ranking Huns. Although they regarded the women as "good lookers" (to translate Priscus' praise precisely), the Romans had politely declined. With what reluctance Priscus does not reveal. Perhaps he and Maximinus preferred their own or each other's company; if they were married, perhaps they remembered their wives. Exhausted after the storm, they may not have been ready for a difficult cultural exchange that they would have to manage without the help of an interpreter. At all events, this was one firsthand experience of the Huns that Priscus decided to forgo. Perhaps he felt that sleeping with the enemy was taking the demands of fieldwork too far. Certainly nothing like this had ever happened to him in a library.

Priscus was impressed by his first sight of Attila's residence. The palace complex was sited on high ground in the middle of a large village. The main hall was a substantial wood-frame building with walls of carefully planed planks tightly fitted together. The whole structure rested on circular stone piles. The surrounding compound was screened by a tall wooden fence with towers at intervals along it. Some distance away, near the entrance to the village, Priscus noted a second cluster of buildings, similar in construction to Attila's, but not as imposing. This was the principal residence of Attila's closest comrade and adviser, Onegesius, who had no doubt already been briefed by his brother Scottas on the Roman assassination plot. Standing outside Onegesius' compound, Priscus and Maximinus had a good view of the crowd gathered to greet Attila. As he rode toward the village, young women rushed out to meet him. They lined up in groups of seven, while above their heads others held long white linen cloths. This was a carefully choreographed ceremony. Flanking the processional route under fluttering canopies, these women welcomed Attila with songs. Then Onegesius' wife presented him with food on a great silver platter and a cup of wine. It was later explained to Priscus that the offering and acceptance of food and drink was considered a great honor and a public affirmation of loyalty and friendship. There could be no doubting the significance that Attila placed on his relationship with Onegesius.

That evening Priscus and Maximinus were guests of Onege-

sius' wife and the most important members of his family. Onegesius himself was not at dinner, for he had been summoned to a
meeting with Attila. One urgent item for discussion was how
to deal with the Romans, who clearly expected an audience. To
make their point, they had made it known they would pitch their
tents near the palace. This was a situation that required careful
handling, especially since—as Onegesius was now made aware—
it was certain that Maximinus and Priscus still knew nothing
of the murder plot. It is likely that Onegesius advised that the
Roman ambassador's status should be respected. If Maximinus
were well treated, it would greatly strengthen Attila's position
when he finally had proof of Chrysaphius' conspiracy; and that,
of course, would have to wait until Vigilas had returned from
Constantinople with fifty pounds of gold.

For his part, Maximinus, reviewing his initial experience with
Attila and his companions, decided to do more than repeatedly
insist on a face-to-face meeting. He also needed the help of influential intermediaries. Priscus was probably quick to emphasize his
achievement in persuading Scottas to intercede on their behalf.
He was only too willing to try a second time. He had the advantage of being able to make informal approaches to leading Huns,
while Maximinus was constrained by his position and his instructions that he discuss official business only with Attila himself. To
his considerable satisfaction, Priscus was once again successful.
Early the following morning, shortly after receiving the gifts that
Priscus delivered in person to his compound, Onegesius made
his way across the village to the Romans' camp.

Rather than risk discussion on any substantive issue, Maximinus
preferred to rely on smooth talking. He observed that this was an
unparalleled opportunity for Onegesius to make his mark in history and that he could win lasting fame if he were willing to travel
to Constantinople and settle the disputes between Theodosius
and Attila. He would not only benefit as a statesman serving the
interests of his own nation; he would also gain personally, "since

you and your children would always be friends of the emperor and his family." In reply, Onegesius inquired, with just the slightest suggestion of sarcasm, what he would have to do to merit Theodosius' lasting friendship. Maximinus delivered another volley of platitudes. By leading a Hun embassy Onegesius would earn the thanks of the Roman emperor. He would easily dispose of any remaining disagreements by "examining their causes and resolving them under the terms of the peace accord."

Onegesius had heard enough. He made it clear that, even if he were to consent to act as an ambassador, he would do no more than repeat whatever he had been instructed to say by Attila. "Or do the Romans think that they can be so persistently persuasive that I would betray my lord, or would disregard my upbringing as a Hun, my wives and children, or would ever think that slavery with Attila could not be better than wealth with the Romans?" These were carefully chosen words; as far as Onegesius was concerned, to protect his own position he needed to stress his reluctance to negotiate with Theodosius. The risks of expressing even the slightest interest in such a mission were too great. After Edeco's entrapment, Attila would be wary of any prominent Hun who journeyed to Constantinople. Edeco had confessed all, but it must have occurred to Attila that someone cleverer and better paid might have kept his bargain with Chrysaphius. Aside from the matter of a Hun embassy—on which he had been unambiguously clear—Onegesius expressed himself willing to assist the Romans in their dealings with Attila. He suggested that he might discuss the issues involved with Priscus, rather than continue formal meetings with Maximinus. It was not to Onegesius' advantage to be in frequent private contact with the Roman ambassador.

The next day, Priscus continued his efforts to secure the goodwill of those close to Attila. He entered the palace compound unchallenged—by now he was well known to the guards—and made his way to the residence of one of Attila's most important wives. Erecan impressed Priscus; she was clearly a woman of sophistication and style. On being admitted to her presence, he found her reclining gracefully on a cushioned couch. She was surrounded by attendants and supervising a group of servant girls embroidering fine linen. The complex designs, which Priscus only glimpsed, probably incorporated many differently shaped and colored beads. Embroidery beads have been found in fifth-century female graves in eastern Europe and southern Russia. The meticulous report of a rescue dig carried out in 1991–93 near the center of Belgrade (ancient Singidunum) catalogued 764 beads from twenty-two graves dating from after the city's sack by the Huns in 441–42. The overwhelming majority were of glass, mainly blue, violet, red, and yellow; a small number were made from amber and coral. One tomb located within the old Roman fort contained 231 beads, 2 in amber and the rest in glass, mostly green and red, with a few larger examples in midnight blue with swirls of white. It is attractive to imagine that when Priscus first saw Erecan relaxing on her couch in her comfortable apartment she, too, was wearing a linen dress prettily decorated with colored glass beads. Perhaps these caught the light and shimmered as she rose slowly to greet her Roman guest.

Priscus does not recount any conversation he had with Erecan. He may have preferred a private visit without an interpreter. All seems to have gone well. Perhaps Priscus bowed graciously in what he hoped was a pleasing—but not too deferential—manner. Perhaps Erecan smiled encouragingly in return and indicated her pleasure at the presents Priscus had brought. In his account of the meeting—as of that with Onegesius early the preceding morning—Priscus passes quickly over these gifts, providing no description, not even a brief list. It may be that, given his strong objections to the annual subsidies paid by Theodosius' government, he was unwilling to call attention to his own part in adding to the total of Roman gold handed over to the Huns.

Priscus is likely to have presented Erecan with choice examples of the most costly jewelery from the best workshops in Constantinople. These superb pieces may have been similar to some of those discovered in 1797 and 1889 in two locations in the village of Şimleu Silvaniei, in western Romania. (Since Şimleu Silvaniei, then known as Szilágysomlyó, was part of the Austro-Hungarian empire, the finds were split between the Kunsthistorisches Museum in Vienna and the National Museum in Budapest.) The seventy-four items all in gold, many inlaid with precious stones—coins, shoulder brooches, pendants, rings, necklaces, and bowls—were not hidden by Huns. Because these various objects seem to have been accumulated over 150 years from the beginning of the fourth century (there are coins minted under Constantine) through to the mid–fifth century, it seems more likely that the two Şimleu Silvaniei hoards were part of a dynastic treasure belonging to a local ruler who now answered to Attila, but whose ancestors had been independent before the expansion of the Hun empire. The fourth-century coins (some surviving only as copies made by skilled Gothic craftsmen) reflect close contacts across the Danube and the efforts of Roman emperors from Constantine onward to win the support of the powerful beyond the frontier. Some of the late fourth- and early fifth-century jewelry was perhaps valuable loot taken in the destructive raids of the 430s or 440s and later distributed to loyal followers. Some pieces may originally have been Roman diplomatic gifts to prominent Huns.

The Şimleu Silvaniei treasure gives some idea of the jewelry that might have been worn by high-ranking women north of the Danube. One piece is outstanding and, judging from its quality, was made by a skilled goldsmith in Constantinople (see figure 22). Thirty small loops, set at regular intervals, are attached to a heavy, twisted chain seventy inches long. Hanging from these loops are fifty-one miniature objects, mostly workman's tools. The whole looks just like a modern charm bracelet, but, at twenty-five ounces of twenty-two-caret gold, executed on a much grander and more ostentatious scale. The "charms," each

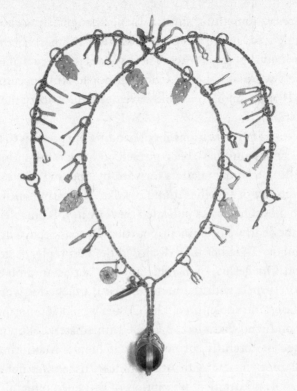

figure 22
Gold chain from the Şimleu Silvaniei treasure.

about an inch long, are delicately modeled. There is no need to
search for any deep meaning in this delightfully amusing collection: a blacksmith's hammer and anvil, shears and a ladder, a
chisel and pliers, a billhook and secateurs, an ax and a cudgel,
five stylized vine leaves, a curved handsaw and rasp, a sword,
a shield, and a naked man in a fishing boat holding the rudder
with both hands. How this chain was worn is not known: perhaps around the waist with a double drop at the front, or, as it is
long enough, over the shoulders crossing both chest and back. In
either arrangement, it would have been conspicuously elegant. It
is attractive to imagine that Priscus—on behalf of the emperor—

gave Erecan something similar, or no less chic. It is clear from
the Şimleu Silvaniei treasure that wealthy women north of the
Danube had expensive tastes. They wanted jewelery that equaled
the finest worn at court in Constantinople. Any successful gift
from a Roman embassy would have needed to satisfy their high
expectations.

Whatever his reservations about handing out presents to leading
Huns, Priscus must have been pleased with the results. Onegesius
was willing to move matters forward by opening discussion on
the possibility of a further round of talks. Repeating one of Attila's demands, Onegesius indicated that any new Roman embassy
should be led by an eminent courtier. Priscus reported this to
Maximinus. Together they discussed the best reply, deciding to
trade on Onegesius' own reluctance to act as an ambassador.
Priscus returned with the message that if Onegesius would not
go to Constantinople, then Theodosius would appoint his own
envoys and send them to the Huns. Immediately following this
exchange of carefully formulated statements, Maximinus was
granted an interview with Attila. Since Priscus was not admitted, there is no detailed description of this encounter, although
he does record that it was only a brief meeting. Maximinus was
handed the names of those whom Attila said he would regard as
acceptable ambassadors, a list that included Anatolius and Nomus,
who had negotiated the peace settlement in 447. Revealing an
increasing grasp of the subtleties of negotiation, Maximinus
replied that Attila was misguided in seeking to nominate particular individuals. To do so would only lead Theodosius to suspect
that they were no longer fully committed to the advancement of
Roman interests. Attila refused to continue the diplomatic sparring. He simply declared that if his wishes were not respected,
he would resort to war.

Despite his abrupt dismissal and Attila's curt statement, Maximinus was confident that he had made progress. He was sure that
an understanding could be reached. Even if Theodosius were

to send Anatolius and Nomus, it could always be made clear that this was his own considered choice and not the result of Attila's demands. For the moment, what mattered was to keep the channels of communication open. Maximinus was pleased when shortly afterwards he received an invitation to dine with Attila that evening. Priscus was also to attend as an honored guest. Maximinus was glad that he had stood his ground and not responded to threats of military action. In his view, the dinner invitation was a positive sign that he was not far away from a diplomatic breakthrough.

When Maximinus and Priscus arrived at the main hall in the middle of the palace compound, they were directed to stand at the threshold, where they were given a cup of wine before being shown to their places. For Priscus, this was the beginning of an experience that more than justified the hardships of his journey beyond the Danube. At last he could observe at first hand some of the customs and habits of the most powerful of the Huns, and from a privileged position as one of Attila's guests. But the accuracy of fieldwork is only as good as the memory of the researcher. Sometimes Priscus is unclear in his descriptions, sometimes inconsistent. To be fair, the surviving text, as well as being cut down, has in places been carelessly summarized by Constantine Porphyrogenitus' editorial team, but it is also evident that at times Priscus was struggling to recall the details of the evening.

One thing Priscus could not remember with any certainty was the seating plan. Attila was in the middle of the hall on a couch and to his right, in the place of highest honor, sat Onegesius. Down one side of the hall (to Onegesius' right) were seated high-ranking Huns, including two of Attila's sons. Or perhaps the elder—Priscus wasn't sure—was on the same couch as his father. The chairs to the left of Attila were occupied by other Hun notables; one of them, Berich, was able to speak some Latin. A little farther along sat Maximinus and Priscus. As a Roman ambassador at a state banquet, Maximinus might reasonably have expected to be much nearer to Attila and his senior advisers (see figure 23).

Priscus was also confused in his account of the rituals at the start of the evening. Attila was handed a wooden cup of wine by one of the attendants. He then took the cup and offered it to his guests in strict order of precedence. Each guest stood up and sipped the wine or drank the whole cup—Priscus could not remember which—and gave it back to the attendant. When, in

figure 23
Feast of Attila *(1870) fresco by Mór Than (1828–99). Priscus and Maximinus are seated front right. Priscus is shown bearded and holding a copy of his History, and Maximinus wears Roman military uniform. The young Ermac is next to Attila. It is clear from the details that Mór Than and his advisers were neither accurate nor attentive readers of Priscus.*

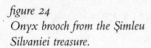

figure 24
Onyx brooch from the Şimleu
Silvaniei treasure.

turn, the guest honored by Attila had sat down, all the other guests raised their silver cups and drank together. After these greetings, tables were set up—again in order of precedence, beginning with Attila. There followed a lavish and well-prepared feast. The food was served on silver dishes and the wine offered to guests in gold and silver cups. After the first course, all rose and drank a full cup of wine to Attila's health. Next an equally splendid second course was served. Then all again stood and drained another full cup in a further salute to Attila. Perhaps Maximinus privately thought that the repeated toasting was a none too subtle response to Vigilas' own refusal in Serdica to honor Attila along with Theodosius. Needless to say, at Attila's feast no one proposed the health of the Roman emperor.

Priscus never forgot the scene. As darkness fell, the jewels worn by the Huns flashed in the flickering light of the pinewood torches that illuminated the hall. The second hoard from Şimleu Silvaniei contained a beautiful shoulder brooch for fastening a heavy cloak (see figure 24). Its oval-shaped body consists of a perfectly cleaved dark purple onyx stone three inches in diameter. The crosspiece is set with pale gray rock crystals and red garnets. (At the *strava* described in the prologue to this book, this brooch is imagined as part of Attila's funeral regalia.) The superb quality of the piece indicates that it, like the long charm chain, was made by a specialist jeweler within the Roman empire. Brooches similar in design were worn by emperors. A large silver plate, now in Madrid, is engraved with an idealized portrait of Theodosius I enthroned in all his glittering majesty. The emperor wears a cloak held in place on his right shoulder by a great oval brooch (see figure 25).

These imperial fashions were reproduced in workshops beyond the frontier. An oval brooch from the Pietroasa treasure is set with garnets and rock crystals under a perforated gold plate. This piece is less ambitious in its method of manufacture and uses poorer-quality stones than Roman originals, but it follows the same design. The Şimleu Silvaniei hoard also includes eight rectangular brooches that are likely to have been based closely on Roman models. For Priscus and Maximinus, all this must have come as something of a shock. Far beyond the Danube, they cannot have expected to find a hall full of Huns wearing jewelry that would not look out of place on the wealthiest courtiers in the Great Palace at Constantinople.

After dinner, two bards came and stood in front of Attila. Priscus continues with one of the most striking of his recollections: "They sang songs that they had composed, telling of Attila's victories and his deeds of valor in war. The guests at the feast gazed at them: some were delighted by the poetry, some were stirred by their memories of the wars, and others were moved to tears." Then the after-dinner amusements. First a madman whose unintelligible ravings provoked much laughter. (In this regard it must be emphasized that the Huns were not exceptional in their unsympathetic enjoyment of mental illness. The Romans were no more enlightened. Indeed, even in eighteenth-century London a visit to an insane asylum was regarded as a diverting afternoon's entertainment.) Next Zercon: the strange, stunted, stuttering favorite of Attila's dead elder brother, Bleda. Once on a whim, Bleda had given him the daughter of a high-ranking Hun in marriage. After Bleda's murder, Attila had sent Zercon to France as a somewhat ambiguous gift to Aetius. He had made his

figure 25
Missorium of Theodosius I (detail), silver plate
commemorating the tenth anniversary of Theodosius'
reign in 388.

way back to demand the return of his wife. "He came forward and by his appearance, his clothes, his voice and by the words he spoke, which were all muddled up (for he scrambled Latin, Hunnic, and Gothic), he put everyone in a good mood and caused them to laugh uncontrollably."

Everyone, that is, except Attila. Although seated some distance away from the Hun leader, Priscus had observed him carefully from the moment the evening began. He noted with interest that amid all the splendor of the feast, the silver tableware, and the fine food, Attila was served separately. For the first course, he had eaten only meat from a wooden plate and drunk wine from a wooden mug. His clothes were plain and did not gleam with gold or jewels. He remained aloof from the laughter that greeted Zercon. Only once did Priscus see Attila's attitude soften, when he was standing next to Ernac, his youngest son. He had drawn Ernac close and looked at him affectionately, "gazing at him with gentle eyes." Noticing that Priscus was watching them intently—while everyone else was enjoying Zercon's antics—Berich, the high-ranking Hun seated nearby, quietly explained (in Latin) that a soothsayer had once told Attila that the future of his empire depended on Ernac alone.

Wide-eyed Priscus treasured such moments. It was for these that he had agreed to accompany Maximinus on his embassy. By contrast, Maximinus had had enough. He knew when his status as an ambassador had not been properly respected. Perhaps his frustration showed. After all, he had put up with a low-ranking position at dinner. Seated on an uncomfortable chair some distance away from Attila and Onegesius, he had not been able to exchange a word with them all evening. In a long and boring ritual, he had been compelled to welcome every guest with a drink. He had toasted Attila's health three times and, worst of all, had been forced to listen to interminable and tuneless Hun songs in praise of their victories in war. Maximinus could see little point in staying if all that remained was to laugh at Zercon's incoherent ramblings. Priscus was probably reluctant to go; although he may have recognized that he had already drunk too much (and that this might blur his memory of some of the details of the evening). Yet there was a great deal more to be learned about the Huns and their leader. No doubt, Maximinus insisted that his friend accompany him back to their tents. Indeed, if Maximinus had not made it absolutely clear that it was now time to leave, Priscus might have stayed up all night drinking with the Huns and staring at Attila.

CHAPTER SIXTEEN
WHAT THE HISTORIAN SAW

The next morning Priscus' mind was still full of vivid images of the feast. As he tried to make sense of his experiences, and put them into some order that might be useful when he later came to writing his history, it became increasingly clear how misleading it was to describe the Huns as "barbarians"—as if that label explained anything. Certainly, for Priscus, some aspects of Hun society remained unappealing. He was unlikely, for example, ever to approve of polygamy. For Priscus, one wife was enough. Monogamy was an ancient practice that Christianity had sanctified as morally correct. Nor, no matter how broadminded he thought himself, could Priscus consider a people whose elite shunned cities as anything other than backward. Only the ignorant would turn away from the delights of urban living: the sunlit squares cooled by fountains, the hippodromes, the baths, the libraries, the theaters, the cathedrals, and the sophisticated societies that built and enjoyed them. Equally, although not a deeply committed Christian, Priscus, like most of his contemporaries, became uneasy when confronted by others' unshakable belief in gods whose existence he refused to recognize, except perhaps as evil demons and enemies of the true faith.

Like many classical historians—the intellectual heirs of Herodotus—Priscus could have listed the differences between the Christian Roman empire and these devil-worshipping lands. Their inhabitants could again have appeared grotesque, threatening, and primitive. For the educated in Constantinople—most without the inconvenience of ever having met a Hun—that might have seemed a plausible way of imposing order on a mass of miscellaneous and secondhand information about faraway peoples and places. The ten-day journey beyond the Danube had exposed the poverty of that approach. Priscus was determined that his account would be emphatically different. His *History of Attila* would offer readers something more challenging than another description of Hun society as the Roman world turned upside down.

One of the most remarkable things Priscus noticed when he first entered the village that clustered around Attila's palace was a stone-built bathhouse adjacent to Onegesius' compound. Its construction, Priscus learned, had posed severe problems, as the surrounding plain provided neither timber nor stone. The dressed blocks had been obtained by dismantling a building in a burned-out Roman town or on some abandoned great estate. The architect was a Roman prisoner of war captured at Sirmium, probably when that city had been destroyed in the campaign of 441–42. "The architect had hoped to gain his freedom as a reward for his ingenuity. But he was disappointed . . . for he was made a bath attendant and waited on Onegesius and his companions whenever they bathed."

Onegesius' building was a long way from any of the huge public baths that were among the most prominent structures in Roman town centers. The more important the city—or at least the greater its pretensions—the bigger the baths. These luxurious complexes, sometimes including shopping malls, performing arts centers, lecture halls, libraries, and museums, were visible expressions of prosperity and civic pride. Wealthy Romans reproduced miniature versions in their private houses. Some features were standard: a changing room (*apodyterium*), an unheated room (*frigidarium*) with a cold water basin, a warm room (*tepidarium*), and a hot room (*caladarium*) with a plunge pool. Top-of-the-range bath suites might also include a sauna (*sudatorium*, literally "sweat room"). The heat was provided by a wood-fired furnace. Hot air circulated through a hypocaust, a space under the tiled floors, which were raised two or three feet and supported on narrow brick pillars.

In Sirmium, part of a bath building was excavated in 1961 in a hurried two-week rescue dig ahead of the construction of a new hotel. The floor of the *caladarium* was raised on brick pillars two feet high. At one end was a semicircular plunge pool lined with waterproof white concrete. Directly behind, with separate access from outside the building, was a furnace, securely identified by a thick layer of charcoal. There is a strong possibility that this bath suite was associated with a large mansion whose foundations were discovered nearby. Acquainted with the layout of private baths in his hometown, the captive architect from Sirmium may have designed something similar for Onegesius. Priscus was right to be amazed at the result. On a treeless and stoneless plain, the construction and operation of even a modestly sized bathhouse were expensive undertakings. The very presence of such a building was an ostentatious proclamation by a leading Hun of his willingness to adopt a key Roman custom. Certainly it was more difficult to think of Onegesius and his companions as incomprehensibly barbaric if one could picture them vying to see who could stand the heat longest in the *caladarium* or splashing about in the plunge pool before bracing themselves for the invigorating shock of the cold water in the *frigidarium*. Perhaps Priscus wondered whether Onegesius ever invited Attila to bathe.

Onegesius' bathhouse was an identifiable fragment of Roman civilization north of the Danube. It was a solid point of contact between two very different cultures. In introducing the Huns, Priscus was determined to offer his readership a description of a society that, at least in part, they could understand. He set out to challenge earlier versions of the Huns as impenetrably foreign. Against Ammianus Marcellinus' claim that they were a people "without permanent settlements," who "like refugees . . . are always on the move with their wagons, in which they live," Priscus set his detailed description of Onegesius' and Attila's compounds. These were no temporary squatters' camps, an unsightly collection of sheepskin tents with wagons drawn up nearby. Rather, they created an impression of order and permanence. The design of Attila's palace followed architectural principles that any Roman would appreciate. It was well laid out and cleverly sited. Its superior status was made clear by its elevated position on a natural rise and by the towers set into its wooden circuit wall.

Priscus' encounter with Erecan directly contradicted Ammianus' statement that the "horrid clothes" of the Huns were woven for them "in their wagons by their wives." When Priscus had met her, Erecan was supervising embroidery on the finest linens. It is also clear from the comfortable decoration of her apartments that she was not accustomed to live in the back of a wagon. Nor is there the slightest suggestion in Priscus that there was anything unusual about the Huns' eating habits. He offers no corroboration of Ammianus' assertion that "they have no need of fire or pleasant-tasting foods, but eat the roots of uncultivated plants and the half-raw flesh of all sorts of animals." Priscus reports no bizarre culinary practices. If some Huns preferred beer to wine, then they were no more uncouth than many Romans who lived near the Danube frontier. High-ranking Huns clearly demanded that their meat be cooked and had a liking, in common with upper-class Romans, for spices and exotic dried fruits.

Of course, in all this Priscus is acutely sensitive to matters of scale. Attila's residence might be well planned and permanent, but it does not stand comparison with the splendor of the Great

Palace in Constantinople. One private bathhouse does not make for urban civilization. A few dates, some Indian pepper, and a well-done steak do not constitute haute cuisine. The Huns could never compete with the wealth and magnificence of Roman imperial culture. Yet, rather than following previous writers in underscoring the obvious contrasts between Huns and Romans, Priscus aimed to direct his readers' attention to a significant set of cultural coincidences (architecture, bathing habits, clothes, and food). After all, it doesn't take much to spot the differences, but it takes an open-minded and observant inquirer to isolate those precious moments when two worlds, if only briefly, can be seen to touch.

It is precisely this pattern of explanation that shapes Priscus' account of his evening with Attila. In many ways the feast fell far short of what might have been expected at a grand Roman dinner party. The setting was a long wooden hall decorated with tapestries and dimly lit by pine torches. It was not a purpose-built room embellished with the finest marbles and mosaics and brightly illuminated by oil lamps. An account of a lunch held in the 460s at a stately home near Nîmes, in southern France, records that the guests were first received in the library, where some admired the host's extensive collection of manuscripts, some amused themselves with board games, while others held a serious theological debate. When all had been made welcome, the party moved through to lunch. In the houses of the wealthy, the dining room was usually square with spacious alcoves on three sides. Each alcove held a semicircular couch on which the guests reclined. Only peasants sat on chairs. Each couch comfortably accommodated up to nine guests lying alongside each other (like the spokes of a wheel) facing low portable D-shaped tables on which the food was served. The seating plan directly reflected status, with the more important guests placed on the right-hand side of the couches. Dinner-party conversation was meant to be erudite and amusing, although no doubt not every guest managed to achieve such an exacting ideal. After the meal, dancing, music, or actors might provide further entertainment and provoke yet more edifying discussion.

The contrast with the arrangements for Attila's feast was plain: from the telltale use of chairs rather than couches to some of the after-dinner performances. There could be nothing further from the cultured trading of well-chosen quotations from classical literature than Zercon's pleading for the return of his wife in a meaningless jumble of languages. Yet rather than scoff at the Huns' failure to live up to Roman standards, Priscus offered some thoughtful parallels with more familiar conventions. Attila's feast may have lacked the sophistication of a Roman dinner party, but it had its own complex etiquette. Attila's guests may not have been greeted in a well-appointed reception room, but they were individually honored in an elaborate and courteous ceremony of welcome. They may (except for Attila himself) have been sat upright on chairs, but the seating plan was carefully worked out—and cleverly calculated to offend the Roman ambassador. The food was well prepared and beautifully presented on silver platters. The Huns drank wine out of gold and silver vessels, not beer out of earthenware mugs. The entertainment included not only Zercon but also a moving recital of Hun songs and poetry. Overall, the emphasis of the evening was on order and decorum. On this showing, the Huns could not simply be dismissed as a boorish bunch of *nomades*.

To be sure, Priscus did not doubt the merits of Roman civilization, but he was concerned to stress that its superiority could not be taken for granted. One morning while waiting outside Attila's compound, he was approached by a man wearing Hun clothes. Priscus was surprised to be addressed in Greek. "I returned the greeting and inquired who he was and where he came from. . . . In reply he asked why I was so eager to know. I said the fact that he spoke Greek was the reason for my curiosity." Priscus learned that the man was a wealthy trader from the frontier town of Viminacium, sacked in the Hun offensive of 441–42. Taken captive, he had been allocated to Onegesius as part of his share of the spoils from the campaign. He had then fought for the Huns and bought his freedom by giving his booty to his master. Now he had a Hun wife and children and boasted that, "as part of Onegesius' household, he had a better life than he had enjoyed previously."

The trader went on to offer a critique of Roman rule. The encounter, as reported by Priscus, is less of a conversation and more like an exercise set by a tutor of rhetoric. Even so, the staged debate again allows Priscus—here through the mouthpiece of a renegade Roman—to question some of the assumed differences between the two empires. The trader pointed to the Huns' skill in warfare. He pitied the citizens of the Roman empire, who untrained in the use of weapons "are put in even more danger by the cowardice of their generals who are unable to conduct a war properly." In addition, he alleged, they suffer high taxes and a poor system of justice in which the rich pay to secure an acquittal. "If the wrongdoer is rich, he does not pay the penalty for his offense, but if he is poor, and does not know how to deal with the matter, he suffers the penalty laid down by law."

Priscus replied in detail. From the start it is obvious that in this exchange he will have the upper hand—after all, this is his own story. For the most part, Priscus stresses the ideals of the Roman empire, rather than the everyday realities of its operation.

> "Those who founded the Roman state," I said, "were wise and good. . . . They laid down that those involved in farming and the cultivation of the land should provide for themselves and through taxation for those fighting on their behalf. . . . The founders appointed others to have as their concern

those who had been wronged, others to take charge of the cases of those who, because of their incapacity, were unable to represent themselves, and others to sit in judgment so the law might be upheld."

And so on for some time. (Priscus gave himself even more space in his original text. There are some obvious cuts by Constantine Porphyrogenitus' impatient editors.) Worn down by Priscus' rhetoric, or perhaps wishing that he had never started the argument, the trader finally agreed that "the laws were fair and the Roman state was good." But Priscus' victory was not clear-cut. The trader is allowed the last word: "Weeping he said . . . those in charge were wrecking the Roman state by not having the same thought for it as those in the past." Priscus offered no response. Unlike previous criticisms, it was not countered by a long-winded rebuttal. Priscus' uncharacteristic silence leaves open the possibility that, on this matter at least, he might have agreed.

In presenting Attila to his readers, Priscus pursued these themes even further. In his account of Attila's appearance, he turned his back on the long-standing tradition of describing *nomades* as more bestial than human. Attila did not look like a Roman, yet he was not so hideously ugly that, like Ammianus Marcellinus' Huns, he might be mistaken for a "two-legged beast or for [one of] those images crudely hewn from tree stumps that can be seen on the parapets of bridges." Nor did Priscus attribute to Attila any of the depravity or irrational behavior normally associated with the enemies of Rome (either in civil wars or in external conflicts) and, since Constantine, with non-Christians. Images of madness and immorality are commonplace in the histories of the fourth and fifth centuries. Indeed, after a while these seemingly inexhaustible catalogues of tyrants' personal failings dull through constant repetition. In 389 in a speech delivered in Rome before Theodosius I to celebrate the defeat of the usurper Magnus Maximus, the orator, claiming to have witnessed these events himself, abandoned any subtlety in order to drive his point home.

> We were the first to bear the brunt of the raging beast and his savagery was satisfied only with the blood of the innocent. . . . As drinking aggravates thirst in the sick, as flames are not dampened, but gain strength by the addition of kindling, so riches amassed through the impoverishment of the public excite the greed of the ravenous-minded . . . in pandering to his gullet and belly . . . he spends freely and carelessly. With an equal ease he accumulates and squanders. . . . To Maximus all ways of earning praise seemed fatuous. Rejecting that model of virtue that is innate even in the worst of men, he defined his greatest happiness in terms of acquiring possessions and doing harm.

This bravura tirade continues for another twelve printed pages or—since this is a speech—for at least another half an hour.

Priscus deliberately avoids these litanies of lurid claims, and, given the tone and content of the surviving fragments of his *History*, there is no reason to think that a lengthy section of abuse has been edited out. The notable absence of any sustained attack on Attila's character will have caught the attention of his readers. Some, knowing Priscus to be an accomplished rhetorician, might well have been looking forward to a virtuoso display of vituperation. It is highly unlikely that anyone actually expected Priscus to praise Attila. Yet, in his account of the feast, Priscus made a point of emphasizing Attila's moderation, frugality, and restraint. He wore no jewels; he did not find Zercon amusing; during dinner he was served only simple food and used a wooden plate and mug. "For us," Priscus noted, "there were lavishly prepared dishes presented on silver platters; for Attila there was nothing more than meat on a wooden plate. He showed himself moderate in other ways as well. For while gold and silver cups were handed to the men at the feast, his mug was of wood."

The educated knew how to read such signs. For nearly five centuries, ever since the first Roman emperor Augustus, behavior at banquets had been one of the moral measures of a ruler. Gluttony and excessive feasting were indications of a dangerously capricious monarch unfit to govern. It was at dinner that the most hated emperors of the first century had revealed their true natures. It was the disorderly seating at a sumptuous banquet that for many confirmed their suspicions of Caligula's incest with his sisters. According to the imperial biographer Suetonius, Nero held feasts that "lasted from noon to midnight, with frequent breaks for plunging into a warm pool or in the summertime into snow-cooled water." It was over dinner that Nero was first seduced by his mother, Agrippina. By contrast, the best Roman emperors were restrained and moderate. Augustus sometimes ate nothing or only a little plain food. Again according to Suetonius, "He was a frugal eater . . . and usually had simple fare. He was especially fond of coarse bread, whitebait, hand-made soft cheese, and green figs." For Eusebius, Constantine, the first Christian emperor, was the most virtuous ruler the empire had ever had. His dinners, too, were marked by moderation. A state banquet held in 326 to celebrate the twentieth anniversary of his rule was so restrained and orderly, and there were so many bishops as guests, that any onlooker "might have thought that he had imagined a vision of the kingdom of Christ."

It is against this rich backdrop of moralizing about the dining habits of Roman emperors that Priscus' readers would have placed his account of Attila. The absence of drunkenness, gluttony, and excess would have been most striking. Attila's behavior displayed a degree of moderation and restraint that could favorably be compared with that of the best of emperors. Remarkably, too, Priscus revealed Attila to be a subtle and effective diplomat, able to outwit the most powerful courtiers in Constantinople. The irony of Chrysaphius' plot is that it might have succeeded if Attila had been the stupidly cruel barbarian that the eunuch clearly assumed him to be. Indeed, Priscus was prepared to take these comparisons even further, suggesting that, in some respects, Attila achieved a higher standard of kingly virtue than Theodosius. In his criticism of the emperor's policy of subsidizing the Huns, Priscus implies that this is precisely the kind of cowardly action that might be expected from a ruler who squandered money on "absurd spectacles, unreasonable displays of liberality, pleasures and recklessly extravagant banquets that no right-thinking person would countenance even in prosperous times." The pointed contrast between Theodosius and Attila is too sharp to miss. On this view, Attila the Hun was a successful leader, not because he violated Roman moral codes or stood defiantly outside them, but because he fulfilled them. Judged by Roman standards, Attila was in some ways a more praiseworthy monarch than Theodosius. In Priscus' opinion, it was precisely Attila's frugality, moderation, and shrewdness as a ruler—rather than any uncontrolled savagery—that made him truly frightening.

In daring to reach these thought-provoking conclusions, Priscus' *History of Attila* is exceptional. It is rare in fourth- or fifth-century Roman literature to find an author willing to attempt some kind of balanced account of those who lived beyond the frontiers. Of course, in offering a less prejudiced picture of the Huns, Priscus was not intending to downplay the brutality of their Danube offensives. He did not seek to excuse Attila; rather, he aimed to show that the conflicts between Romans and Huns were more complex than clashes between good and evil, civilization and barbarism, virtue and tyranny. Black-and-white explanations of events, however attractive they may at first seem, are always likely to be wrong. This approach may not have been popular with all of Priscus' readers. For many Romans it was comfortable to think of the Huns as uncultured, uncivilized, and irredeemably foreign, and their leaders as treacherous, immoral, and wildly unstable. Priscus' *History* offered a more sophisticated description of the world beyond the Danube, and a deliberately more disturbing one. After all, it is always reassuring to think of our enemies as godless barbarians. It is troubling to learn that they might be more like us than we would ever care to admit.

CHAPTER SEVENTEEN

TRUTH AND DARE

From the moment he crossed the Danube, Maximinus was trapped in a pointless series of exchanges intended by Attila to give the impression that he knew nothing of the arrangements that had been made between Chrysaphius, Edeco, and Vigilas for the delivery of fifty pounds of gold. Attila hoped that Chrysaphius would be persuaded to proceed as planned. There was no reason for him to be suspicious either of the pretext for Vigilas' return to Constantinople or of the Huns' continued courteous treatment of the Roman envoys. Maximinus, still ignorant of the plot to assassinate Attila, was acutely aware both of his lack of progress and of his inability to understand the cause. Summer had nearly passed, and he had been away from Constantinople for over a month. Rather than attempt another fruitless round of discussions, Maximinus decided that it was time to return home.

Attila offered no objection to Maximinus' departure. By now, Vigilas should have arrived at the imperial court. Nothing further was to be gained by detaining the Roman ambassador more than another five days, sufficient to ensure that Vigilas had met privately with Chrysaphius. Meanwhile, there was every reason for Attila and Onegesius to keep up their show of tactful civility. On the same day he announced he was leaving, Maximinus at last received a formal reply to the letter from Theodosius he had handed to Attila at their first meeting. The reply was drafted by Onegesius in consultation with Attila's closest advisers and one of his Latin-speaking private secretaries. Nothing of what was said is known. Any further references have not survived the cuts made by Constantine Porphyrogenitus' editors. There may have been little for Priscus to report. With Vigilas soon to leave Constantinople, Onegesius may have advised against any strongly worded response. Perhaps he recommended that Attila's letter to Theodosius—like so many other bland diplomatic communiqués—simply substitute courtesy for content. Tough talking could wait until Vigilas had been stopped and searched, and confessed his part in Chrysaphius' conspiracy.

The round of dinner parties continued. Erecan invited Priscus and Maximinus to the house of her steward, Adamis, who managed all her property. Priscus briefly records another excellent meal with (in his admiring phrase) an impressive "spread of eatables." The Romans were again welcomed with an elaborate drinking ritual. All the Huns stood up and, in turn, offered a full cup of wine to their guests; they then embraced and kissed them and took back the cup. The next night, Priscus and Maximinus dined again with Attila. The feast took the same form as before. No doubt, the food was as fine and the gold and silver tableware as impressive. There was one significant difference: the Romans were seated nearer to Attila. Maximinus certainly welcomed this. He may have thought that it offered one last opportunity to resolve matters of mutual interest.

But Maximinus was again wrong-footed. Avoiding any reference to issues discussed in their previous meetings, Attila began a lengthy account of an alleged wrong suffered by Constantius, one of his confidential private secretaries. Constantius had originally come from Italy and was fluent in Latin. He had been sent as a gift by Aetius to serve on Attila's personal staff. (For Maximinus this must have been an unwelcome reminder that Attila continued to maintain close relations with powerful Roman generals who could not always be trusted by emperors.) Constantius, Attila claimed, while on an embassy to the imperial court, had struck a bargain with Theodosius, offering to promote peace with the Huns in return for the emperor's agreeing to arrange his marriage to a wealthy and well-connected woman in Constantinople. The undertaking had never been fulfilled, and the bride nominated by Theodosius had been seized—under what circumstances it was not clear—by the powerful general Flavius Zeno (responsible for the security of the empire's eastern frontier). She had then been married off to one of his senior officers. Attila demanded that Constantius should have his promised wife or be given another of similar standing. He instructed Maximinus to inform Theodosius of Zeno's intervention. Attila was sure that the emperor would act immediately to rectify the situation, "for it is not like a ruler to lie." Of course, if Theodosius was not strong enough on his own to control the actions of his subordinates, then he, Attila, was always ready to offer an alliance to enable the emperor to assert his full imperial authority.

Attila's allegations and his extraordinary offer to help Theodosius discipline a senior general tested Maximinus' diplomatic abilities to the limit. At times, he must have wondered whether the interpreter had made a mistake. Certainly Attila's mocking remarks were intended to discomfort his guest. After all, how should one respond when the leader of the Huns presents himself as a loyal ally of the Roman emperor? It was hardly a suggestion to be taken seriously, and yet to laugh might be insulting, or perhaps Attila meant it as a joke and not to laugh would be equally offensive. Maximinus may now have appreciated the advantages of being seated too far away from Attila to engage in conversation. As Priscus had found out at the first feast, it had been better—and much safer—just to stare.

Maximinus is best imagined as sitting with a fixed expression that he hoped was suitably ambiguous and listening attentively as Attila's tale of Constantius' disappointments unfolded. Perhaps, too, Attila should be thought of as having enjoyed the situation, taking the opportunity to point out some of Theodosius' weaknesses to a Roman ambassador who listened dutifully with his face set in a kind of rigid half smile. To be sure, it was not the first time the emperor had been accused of being unable to curb his powerful courtiers. In such situations, eunuchs were usually the first to be suspected. But, as Maximinus might later have remarked, it is one thing to hear that said quietly at a private dinner party in Constantinople, quite another when it is a matter for ridicule at a feast hosted by one of the empire's most dangerous enemies.

After this final, disagreeable encounter, Maximinus was glad to leave. As a parting gesture of goodwill, Attila ordered each of his closest companions to present him with a horse. Such generosity was again clearly intended to embarrass Maximinus, who selected only a few and returned the rest of the horses, explaining that his own modesty and dislike of lavish display prevented him from accepting such costly gifts. He hoped that the Huns would understand his natural restraint. In the virtuous game of competitive moderation, Maximinus was determined not to be outdone by Attila.

On their homeward journey, Priscus and Maximinus were accompanied by Berich, the Latin-speaking Hun who had sat near them at Attila's first feast. Then he had been helpful in explaining Hun etiquette and talking to Priscus about Attila. For the next few days, Berich's good humor continued, and the Romans enjoyed riding, eating, and conversing with him—"we thought him gracious and affable." But after they crossed the Danube, his demeanor changed abruptly. From then on, Berich was hostile, "treating us as though we were the enemy." He rudely took back the horse he had given to Maximinus, refused to speak, and took his meals alone. Challenged to explain this sudden shift in attitude, Berich would say only that he had heard, precisely how was unclear, that Maximinus had blamed the Romans' recent defeats on the failings of the generals Aspar and Ariobindus, who had both been relieved of their commands after the Hun offensive in 447. Berich rejected Maximinus' explanation outright: to claim that Aspar and Ariobindus had been incompetent was an insult to the military prowess of the Huns and the strategic brilliance of Attila.

Berich's exaggerated objection to Maximinus' remarks was only part of the problem. Like Onegesius before him, Berich feared that any report of an amicable association between him and the Romans, particularly once they were inside the empire, might be regarded by Attila as evidence of treachery. He may have felt himself especially vulnerable to such accusations because he spoke Latin. Any courtier wishing to entrap him would not even need an interpreter. Maximinus and Priscus—entirely unaware of these concerns—could only puzzle at Berich's behavior. Given his previous friendliness, his offensive rejection of everything Roman was strange and his excuses plainly inadequate. It must have seemed an unexpected irony that the closer Berich came to Constantinople, the more he chose to act like a stereotypical barbarian.

As they neared the capital, Priscus and Maximinus passed Eslas and Vigilas, who were starting out on their long journey back to the Great Hungarian Plain. This time, Vigilas was traveling with his son. The meeting with Chrysaphius had gone as Attila had hoped. The eunuch had found no reason to think that the assassination plot had been compromised, and Vigilas was given the fifty pounds of gold for delivery to Edeco. Nor can anything that Priscus and Maximinus had to say about their time at Attila's court have aroused Vigilas' suspicions. For the most part, they had been courteously treated and no attempt had been made to prevent them from returning to Constantinople. Confident that his mission had been a success and that Edeco had kept his side of the bargain, Vigilas continued on his way. His journey was uneventful. It was not until its final day that he walked straight into the trap carefully prepared for him. As he approached the village surrounding Attila's palace, he was arrested and searched. The fifty pounds of gold concealed in leather bags in his luggage was confiscated.

Brought before Attila, Vigilas was asked to explain why he was carrying so much money. His reply was predictable: some of the gold was to purchase food for himself and his servants as well as fodder for the horses and pack animals. The rest had been given to him by those in the empire who were eager that he should ransom their relatives still held captive by the Huns. Attila's response was curt and to the point: "You will not evade justice by your clever talk. Your excuses will not be good enough for you to escape punishment. The amount of money you have is more than enough to purchase provisions for yourself, your horses and pack animals, and to ransom prisoners of war, the very thing I banned you from doing when you came before me with Maximinus."

When Attila threatened to kill his son, Vigilas confessed everything, implicating Chrysaphius, Martialis, and Theodosius and confirming Edeco's and Orestes' earlier reports of a conspiracy. Perhaps at that moment Vigilas expected to be executed. Unmoved by his tears, Attila dismissed his desperate pleas for mercy. But Vigilas, yet again, had failed to read the situation correctly. He was in no danger of death. Instead, Attila imprisoned him and ordered his son to return to Constantinople. In the Great Palace, he was to insist on a meeting with Chrysaphius and on receiving a further fifty pounds of gold—the ransom Attila now demanded for his father.

Along with Vigilas' son, Attila sent two ambassadors, Orestes and Eslas. This was a nicely ambiguous choice. Chrysaphius would wonder how much each of them had known—and for how long. The Hun envoys were given specific instructions for the conduct of their audience with Theodosius. One of the leather bags in which Vigilas had hidden the gold was to be hung around

Orestes' neck. The bag was to be shown to both the emperor and Chrysaphius, who were to be asked directly whether they rec-ognized it. The envoys were to demand that the eunuch be sent across the Danube to explain his actions face-to-face with Attila. Eslas was then to observe that Theodosius was as nobly born as the Hun leader (itself a startling comparison), but while Attila had maintained his honor as a ruler, the emperor by his involvement in the assassination plot had reduced himself to the status of a slave. The claim was obviously exaggerated, and yet, like Attila's earlier jibe that Theodosius was unable to control his most pow-erful courtiers, it could not entirely be dismissed. Priscus hoped that it would again compel his readers to confront some difficult questions. At stake was the conventional and uncompromising contrast between virtuous Roman emperor and evil barbarian tyrant. Any who doubted the moral force of Attila's challenge to Theodosius had only to imagine Orestes standing silently in the glittering throne room of the Great Palace with an empty leather bag slung around his neck.

CHAPTER EIGHTEEN

END GAME

In cutting down Priscus' *History of Attila*, the members of Constantine Porphyrogenitus' editorial team had no sense of how to finish a good story. It is not at all to their credit that one of the passages they chose to discard was Priscus' account of the arrival of the Hun envoys in Constantinople in autumn 449. Regrettably, it is not known whether Orestes and Eslas ever played out their dramatic scene with the empty leather bag before the impassively enthroned Theodosius and his court. Sadly, it seems more likely that they never made it very far into the Great Palace. Perhaps, instead of confronting the emperor, they were seen by the master of the offices, Flavius Martialis, and their concerns dealt with in an entirely businesslike way. Nor is there any record of Maximinus' or Priscus' immediate reaction to the news that their embassy to Attila had been a dangerous blind. Priscus' anger can be assumed from the hatred for Chrysaphius that seeps through the surviving text of the *History of Attila* and was condensed by one of its later readers, the seventh-century monk and historian John of Antioch.

Theodosius, who ruled after his father, Arcadius, was unwarlike and lived a life of cowardice. He obtained peace by money and not by arms. Everything he did was under the supervision of eunuchs, and these eunuchs brought matters to such a ridiculous state that, in brief, they distracted Theodosius—just as children are distracted with playthings—and prevented him from achieving anything worth recording.

For Priscus, there was nothing praiseworthy in the way Theodosius or Chrysaphius had conducted themselves. Their attempt at regime change through assassination was as defective as their continued payment of subsidies, and that, in turn, was the result of a shameful failure by the emperor and his generals to defend the Danube provinces. In Priscus' view, his own advocacy of military action was not inconsistent with his revisionist portrayal of the Huns or with his claim that Attila possessed virtues traditionally associated with good Roman emperors. Priscus' time with the Huns had not made him any less patriotic. He had not "gone native." The Huns were still the enemy, and if an enemy is to be defeated, it must first be understood. (It is a mistake to think that greater comprehension necessarily leads to greater sympathy or closer cooperation. Effective warfare also depends on accurate intelligence.) A direct comparison with Attila further emphasized Theodosius' deficiencies. For Priscus, the merits of the Hun leader—as judged by Roman standards—were not an argument for a more friendly relationship. On the contrary, they suggested that Attila could be overcome by a properly virtuous Roman emperor.

Not all of Priscus' brash polemic against Theodosius and his advisers is persuasive. There were sound reasons for the military tactics adopted in 447. Given the security situation on three frontiers, it made good sense to pay subsidies rather than risk a major offensive that might lead to the dangerous fragmentation of the Hun empire. With a better understanding of Attila and the Huns, these strategies could no doubt have been more effectively pursued. Yet Priscus shows no interest in exploring these possibilities. He is not prepared to concede that Theodosius'

Danube policy could ever have produced positive results. Such conclusions are limited and unsatisfactory. They are a reminder that Priscus' strength as a historian lies in his description of the Huns, which is often perceptive and provocative, and not in his discussion of Roman foreign relations, which, tightly focused on a single frontier, is often hostile and blinkered. This he can be forgiven: after all, in attacking Theodosius and Chrysaphius, Priscus was understandably settling a score with those who were prepared to risk his life by using him as a front for an assassination attempt.

However loudly Priscus voiced his views on his return from the Danube, no one seems to have been listening, and he is very unlikely to have criticized Theodosius openly or to have offered his own favorable account of Attila's personal qualities. If Priscus expected Chrysaphius' position to be weakened by allegations that he had secretly masterminded a failed attempt to murder Attila, then he must have been disappointed. In Constantinople the news was greeted with well-practiced disbelief. Theodosius is likely to have made it clear that he had no knowledge whatsoever of any conspiracy. For many at court, the issue was clear: the whole story had been fabricated to embarrass the emperor and his advisers. Any claims to the contrary could be dismissed. After all, the Huns were still holding Vigilas captive. In the face of Attila's accusations, it was Chrysaphius' counterclaims that were believed. A disgusted Priscus bitterly concedes that the eunuch continued to enjoy "universal goodwill and support."

Denial was followed by cover-up. In early 450, the senior courtiers Anatolius and Nomus—the latter described by Priscus as a staunch supporter of Chrysaphius—were sent to discuss terms with Attila. (The same duo had successfully negotiated peace after the Hun invasion in 447.) The ambassadors' tactics were simple: "At first Attila negotiated arrogantly, but he was overwhelmed by the number of gifts and pacified by their conciliatory statements." Chrysaphius had ensured that Anatolius and Nomus had more than enough gold to buy off Attila and ransom Vigilas. There were to be no loose ends. Even Attila's complaint on behalf of his secretary Constantius was dealt with. The sorry tale of abduction and frustrated matrimony as told to Maximinus was probably false, but the Roman ambassadors preferred to provide a solution rather than provoke any further argument. Constantius was offered another bride, whose wealth and status were equivalent to that of the one he claimed Theodosius had originally promised. In return for these concessions, Attila affirmed his commitment to peace with, of course, the continued payment of subsidies. Perhaps to the surprise of the ambassadors, he was also willing to agree to a package of measures aimed at reducing diplomatic friction between the Huns and the eastern empire. Large numbers of prisoners of war were released without ransom, demands for the return of asylum seekers were dropped, all claims over Roman territory a five days' journey south of the Danube were withdrawn, and no further reference was made to the alleged conspiracy or the extradition of Chrysaphius.

Chrysaphius might reasonably have congratulated himself on surviving the crisis. Attila had been placated, and Anatolius and Nomus had secured peace on the northern frontier. Vigilas would not dare to return to Constantinople, Priscus had gone back to teaching rhetoric, and Maximinus had rejoined his regiment. At that time, too, it must have seemed to Priscus unlikely that his *History of Attila* would ever be published. He could not risk revealing Chrysaphius' involvement in the conspiracy to assassinate Attila or implicate the emperor. Maximinus would never agree to that. It would end their friendship and jeopardize their careers. As long as Theodosius was on the throne and the eunuch in power, the truth was better suppressed. It might instead be wiser to publish another collection of lectures on rhetoric. For the moment, working on a set of model orations appeared a safer prospect than writing history.

Within six months all that had changed. On 26 July 450, Theodosius, then in his late forties, suffered a serious spinal injury in a riding accident. He was carried back to the Great Palace and died in extreme pain two days later. Following long-established precedent, the new emperor, Marcian, rid himself of many of his predecessor's confidential advisers. It was rare for prominent eunuchs to survive such purges. Their loyalty was always suspect, and their removal a clear sign of the independence of the new regime. Eunuchs such as Chrysaphius simply knew too much, and after Theodosius' death there was no one to argue against his execution.

With Chrysaphius eliminated, Vigilas returned to Constantinople. Priscus was eager to meet the one man he knew was key to understanding the plot that had dogged Maximinus' mission. It was from Vigilas that Priscus finally learned the details of the meeting in the Great Palace between Edeco and Chrysaphius. Vigilas also explained Orestes' cryptic remarks at Serdica, as well as Scottas' rudeness and then sudden willingness to arrange an audience with Attila. For his own part, Vigilas admitted to having been taken in by Attila's anger over asylum seekers (he had not seen that it was a pretext to get him to return to Constantinople) and by Edeco's assurances that he could bribe Attila's bodyguard. No doubt, it was with grim amazement that Priscus realized that Attila must have known about the conspiracy right from the start. It was also clear that Vigilas' information would transform Priscus' *History*. Alongside his radically new account of the society and customs of the Huns, he planned to place a full account of Maximinus' embassy and of Chrysaphius' failed conspiracy. Thanks to Vigilas' eyewitness evidence, Theodosius and his advisers could now be exposed as outright liars.

Whatever his enthusiasm to get on with writing it, Priscus' *History* was again delayed. Marcian seems to have accepted that the embassy to Attila had been compromised from the start and that Maximinus had conducted himself as well as could be expected. He was again dispatched on diplomatic missions and invited Priscus to accompany him. In late 450 they journeyed together to Rome. A year later they set out from Constantinople, traveling first to Damascus, then overland to Alexandria, and down the Nile. Maximinus was responsible for negotiating with tribes threatening the security of southern Egypt. In late 452, soon after a peace treaty was ratified at Philae (just upriver from modern Aswan), Maximinus became seriously ill. He never recovered. In 453 Priscus returned alone to Constantinople, determined to commemorate his friend by completing his account of their experiences four years earlier at the court of Attila.

Priscus' *History of Attila*—the first part written in the mid-450s —met with immediate critical acclaim. Like most ancient books, it reached the majority of its contemporary audience through public readings, often given by the author himself. It was thought by its admirers to be "very learned" and "elegantly written." It soon became the most authoritative and widely quoted account of relations between the Roman empire and the Huns. The *History of Attila* launched Priscus on a successful literary career. He continued his project of writing contemporary history, publishing his work at intervals over the next twenty-five years. In addition, Priscus edited collections of his correspondence and his lectures. None of these has survived. They were no doubt also learned and elegantly written, but they are unlikely ever to have been as popular as his historical writing.

Aside from the critics' praise, which like any author he is sure to have enjoyed, Priscus hoped that his *History* was a fitting memorial to his best friend. He had attempted to show Maximinus as a loyal and honorable Roman—a trustworthy and straightforward soldier prepared to carry out his duty even in the most adverse circumstances. Regrettably, it is not known what Vigilas thought of Priscus' version of events. Given his importance in supplying so much crucial material, he might have wished for a more sympathetic portrayal. Too often he appeared as either deceitful or foolish. On the other hand, had it not been for Priscus' *History of Attila*, no one would ever have heard of Vigilas the interpreter.

Of course, that is what Chrysaphius had intended. It may safely be reckoned that the palace archives contained no record of any private meeting with Edeco or any payments to Vigilas. Chrysaphius had always assumed that if his schemes were ever to be compromised, Attila could be relied on to do the rest. An embarrassing failure in Roman foreign policy would disappear without trace. Once Edeco had confessed, Priscus, Maximinus, and Vigilas should have been butchered by a hot-blooded Hun seeking a swift revenge. If all had turned out as Chrysaphius expected—and Attila had behaved like a barbarian tyrant—then Priscus would never have survived to write his *History*. The truth should have been buried with him somewhere beyond the Danube.

PART FOUR

THE FAILURE OF EMPIRE

CHAPTER NINETEEN

HEARTS AND MINDS

I n summer 442 the once beautiful daughter of the Gothic ruler
Theodoric returned to her father. Her ears clipped and her
nose slit, she would never again be seen in public. No historian even recorded her name. This vicious punishment had been
carried out on the orders of Geiseric, leader of the Vandals, whose
teenage son Huneric had married Theodoric's daughter only a
short while before. Geiseric accused her of involvement in a plot
to poison him and sent her back—disgraced and disfigured—to
her father's court at Toulouse. This painful story is offered by
the sixth-century historian Jordanes in his *Origin and Acts of the
Goths* as an explanation for the hatred between Geiseric and
Theodoric. It is a sharp reminder that those peoples who now
occupied territory within the empire cannot be assumed to have
been natural allies. They fought among themselves as frequently
as they fought together against the Romans.

The deterioration in relations between the Goths and the Vandals was connected to Geiseric's attempts to strengthen his own
ties with the western Roman empire. In late 442 he announced
Huneric's engagement to Valentinian III's daughter Eudocia. At
the time she was just three years old. There was nothing unusual in
this arrangement. Twenty years earlier Eudocia's mother, Licinia
Eudoxia (the daughter of Theodosius II), had been promised to
Valentinian. Then Eudoxia had been two years old and her future

husband five. Huneric was free to make such a politically astute match only once his first wife had been banished. The suspicious affirmed her role in the conspiracy to remove Geiseric; the skeptical may have thought the timing rather too convenient. Geiseric himself had no regrets: if the mutilation of Theodoric's daughter had antagonized the Goths, it had been a price worth paying to clear the way for a dynastic connection between the Vandal ruling house and the Roman imperial family. For Jordanes, Geiseric's brutal international diplomacy was an indication of a strength of character (which in other circumstances might be admirable) and his determination to secure the permanence of Vandal rule in North Africa. "Geiseric was of medium height and limped as a result of a fall while out riding. He thought deeply, said little, and despised luxury. He had a violent temper and was single-mindedly acquisitive and remarkably farsighted. He was prepared to sow the seeds of discord and incite hatred in order to stir up others."

In promoting the special relationship between Carthage and Ravenna, Geiseric aimed to erase his past as an enemy of the Roman empire. He hoped to dissuade Theodosius and Valentinian from any further attempt at reconquest. Under the treaty agreed after the withdrawal of Roman troops from Sicily, Geiseric undertook to compensate the western imperial government for the loss of African tax revenue. Not all leading Vandals approved of these pro-Roman policies. The finalization of the peace settlement was followed by a major revolt. Internal opposition was brutally stamped out. Prosper of Aquitaine commented acidly in his *Chronicle* that Geiseric's suspicions meant that through torture and execution he "lost more men as a result of his own insecurity than if he had been defeated in war." For Valentinian, the rebellion underlined the importance of keeping Geiseric in power. It was clear that, if he were to fall, he might be replaced by a regime openly hostile to the empire.

It was also in Geiseric's interests to prevent an alliance between

Valentinian and Theodoric. As long as the main threat to imperial rule came from the Goths, even the most warlike of advisers in Ravenna would be reluctant to argue for a campaign in Africa. With this in mind, Geiseric made diplomatic contact with Attila, sending gifts and encouraging him to attack the Goths. Chaos in France would be to North Africa's advantage. The Romans would be compelled to fight Huns rather than Vandals. The success of Geiseric's scheme depended on Flavius Aetius. Sometime in the 440s, Aetius persuaded, or forced, Valentinian to confer the honorary rank of general on Attila. Of course, this does not mean that Attila ever commanded any Roman legions. At most, he received the substantial salary that went with the post. But as an honorary general Attila could formally be recognized as part of the imperial military establishment. However strange it must have seemed, Aetius could now claim Attila as his colleague. For Aetius, the public affirmation of his friendship with Attila was a useful insurance policy. Anyone who challenged him would have to risk the possibility of Hun intervention. Whether troops would be sent was always open to question—in 435, despite Aetius' bravado, the Huns had never turned up. Even so, no other Roman general could threaten to draw on military resources from outside the empire. Importantly, too, should Attila decide to advance westward on his own initiative, no other Roman general could hope to turn a Hun offensive to his own advantage.

Attila may have viewed his relationship with Aetius differently: a temporary convergence of mutual interest rather than a lasting friendship in which he would always safeguard Aetius' interests. Certainly Attila was not prepared consistently to support Aetius' efforts to maintain Roman rule in France. In 437, after the massacre of the Burgundians, Roman and Hun troops under Litorius had suppressed the Bagaudae. Despite the ferocity of the reprisals, Aetius had to deal with another rebellion a decade later. This was no peasants' revolt. At its core was a coalition of landowners—locals and those who had moved north to escape the permanent settlement of the Goths around Toulouse. Some of these economic migrants had managed to hang on to at least part of their wealth. The Bagaudae were concerned about their security and doubted whether allegiance to the empire offered any lasting guarantee of protection. Given this uncertainty, they preferred to rely on their own initiative and resources; but while they could offer some limited opposition to Roman rule, they could never muster sufficient manpower to defend themselves against any serious military threat. The Bagaudae could never withstand the Huns.

That same thought had occurred to those coordinating the unrest. In 448, after Aetius had crushed the latest uprising, a prominent member of the Bagaudae is reported to have fled to the Huns. This appeal for asylum should not be taken as any indication that Attila might have considered marching into France in support of a loose alliance of those disaffected with Roman rule. That said, as long as there was even a distant possibility of a Hun campaign in the West, it made good sense for the Bagaudae to establish direct contact with Attila. They could only benefit from a weakening of Aetius' much advertised relationship with the Huns. No doubt, too, Attila welcomed the opportunity to demonstrate his own independence. In sheltering a rebel leader hunted by Aetius, he made it clear that the Huns could not always be trusted to side with the empire.

How far Attila and Aetius had drifted apart was evident to Priscus in summer 449. As he and Maximinus approached the village that surrounded Attila's palace, they met up with another group of Roman ambassadors acting on behalf of Aetius and Valentinian. One of the purposes of this embassy was to resolve a long-running dispute. Eight years earlier, in the Danube offensive of 441–42, the Huns had sacked Sirmium. Before the siege, the city's bishop had given some golden bowls to one of Attila's secretaries, Constantius. (This is not the same man as the educated Italian sent by Aetius to serve on Attila's staff.) Constantius

promised that, should the city fall to the Huns, the bowls would
be sold and the funds used to ransom prisoners. With Sirmium in
flames and the bishop dead, he saw no reason to keep his word.
Two years later, while on business in Rome, he pawned the bowls
and received a good sum from the banker Silvanus. On his return
to Attila's service, Constantius was suspected of dishonesty and
executed. Meanwhile, as the pledge had not been redeemed,
Silvanus disposed of the bowls. Since they had once belonged
to the cathedral in Sirmium, he sold them on to priests. He had
not thought it proper that they should be melted down or used
as part of a grand dinner service. As far as Attila was concerned,
however, the bowls were his property—the legitimate spoils of
war from a conquered Roman city. Hun ambassadors sent to
Aetius and Valentinian insisted that Silvanus be handed over for
receiving stolen goods. It was alleged that he and Constantius
had been part of a scheme to defraud Attila by converting the
bowls to cash through a series of transactions they had intended
should not be traced.

Valentinian and Aetius refused Attila's request. In their view,
Silvanus had acted in good faith. However, they were prepared
to compromise. If, in Priscus' words, "Attila would not withdraw
his demand for the bowls, they would send gold as compensation
for them, but they would not extradite Silvanus, since they would
not hand over a man who had done nothing wrong." How this
stalemate was eventually resolved is not recorded. If Priscus knew,
his account has not survived the cuts of Constantine Porphyrogenitus' editors. In this case, the particular terms of any settlement
may not have been that important—except, of course, to Silvanus.
Like the convoluted complaint about the (Italian) Constantius'
marriage, which took up so much of Maximinus' time, what mattered was not the detail of the dispute but the pretext it gave Attila
to take offense. These were not intended to be issues that could
be resolved quickly or reasonably. Rather, they were barometers
of Attila's willingness to cooperate with the Roman empire.

Given the right conditions—and the absence of an assassination plot—Attila was always ready to negotiate. Anatolius and Nomus had found him attentive and reasonable. They had made good progress in 447 and again in 450 when Attila had agreed to substantial concessions to ease tensions along the Danube frontier. By contrast, in summer 449, with delegations from both the East and the West camped outside his palace gates, Attila avoided serious discussion by arguing over specific claims. Maximinus, his mission already undercut by Chrysaphius' conspiracy, made little progress in the face of Attila's insistence that he would negotiate only on issues of real importance with ambassadors of the highest rank. In the case of the western embassy, the deliberate sidetracking of the talks, so that they became mired in the trivial and time-consuming matter of Silvanus and the golden bowls, was a sure indication of the fragility of Attila's relationship with Aetius.

That something more serious was at stake is suggested by a conversation Priscus reports with Romulus, one of western envoys, while they were both waiting for Onegesius to return from a meeting with Attila. Then Romulus had expressed the view that the Huns' next campaign would take them farther east: "Attila is aiming at more than he has at present and to expand his empire further he wishes to attack the Persians." Romulus pointed out that Attila already knew what route he would take. Fifty years earlier, in 395, a Hun army had crossed the Caucasus Mountains between the Black and the Caspian Seas. Some units had terrorized the Roman empire, moving through Armenia and Cappadocia before being defeated by Eutropius; others had followed the Tigris River as far as Ctesiphon. In Romulus' depressing assessment, if the Huns decided to march east, the Persians "would be subdued and forced to pay tribute, as Attila has an armed force that no nation can resist."

In his prediction that the Huns were looking ahead to an eastern campaign, Romulus may have been offering an accurate account of Attila's intentions. Even so, it should be noted that Attila made no reference to these plans in his discussions with Maximinus, or the following year with Anatolius and Nomus, or—as far as is known—at any other time. Rather than a Hun invasion of Persia being part of Attila's grand strategy, it is equally plausible that it was part of Romulus' brief to suggest it to him. Carefully devised by Aetius, the presentation of such an apparently attractive proposition may have been the main objective of the western embassy. If so, it was an aim only half shared with Priscus. Knowing that his comments would be passed on to Theodosius and his advisers, Romulus would not have wanted it known in Constantinople that the government in Ravenna had encouraged Attila eastwards. In talking to Priscus, he would have found it more prudent to shift the blame and suggest that the idea was entirely Attila's own.

For Aetius, frustrated in the late 440s in his attempts to secure any credible assurance of assistance from the Huns, the advantages of dissuading Attila from intervening in a politically divided West were self-evident. The consequences of a Hun offensive were difficult to assess, and there was no guarantee, despite Geiseric's prompting, that the Huns would confine their attack to the Goths. Moreover, there was no certainty (as in their Balkan campaigns) that the Huns would return to the Great Hungarian Plain, and no knowing how they might seek to exploit their new links with the Bagaudae. If the Huns could not be relied upon to march west in support of the empire, it made good sense to push them even farther east. The suggestion of a Persian campaign was a daring attempt by an increasingly insecure Aetius to divert Attila's attention away from France. It was a final bid to make the Huns someone else's problem.

CHAPTER TWENTY

THE BRIDE OF ATTILA

Despite the best efforts of Aetius' envoys, Attila was not deflected from his disruptive interference in the West. He had been successful in creating a deliberate sense of doubt about his intentions. Would he, as Geiseric advocated, attack the Goths, or would he support dissident groups such as the Bagaudae? Would he respect his long-standing friendship with Aetius? Would Valentinian's grant of an honorary generalship be sufficient to ensure some lingering loyalty to the empire, or would Attila choose to fight alone, seizing any opportunities that might arise from the chaos of a Hun invasion? Whatever his ultimate strategy, Attila's plans were altered in early spring 450, following the unexpected arrival on the Great Hungarian Plain of the eunuch Hyacinthus. The eunuch, who had traveled in secret from Ravenna, was a curious choice for a diplomatic mission. Roman ambassadors were normally high-ranking administrators like Nomus or senior military officers like Anatolius and Romulus. It must have been extraordinary to see Hyacinthus in his flowing silks standing before Attila—even more so to hear his shrill, high-pitched voice as he announced that he came not from the emperor Valentinian but from his older sister, the imperial princess Justa Grata Honoria (see figure 26).

A few months earlier Honoria, then in her early thirties, had been forcibly engaged to the Italian aristocrat Flavius Bassus

figure 26
*Gold coin of Justa Grata Honoria, minted
in Ravenna, 430–45. Honoria wears a
diadem and necklace, and is blessed by the
hand of God above.*

Herculanus. Valentinian's choice was carefully made. He was
all too aware of his sister's ambitions; like their mother, Galla
Placidia, she wished to be the wife and mother of emperors. For
Valentinian, determined that his sister's marriage not undermine
his own position, Herculanus was a safe option: a respectable,
middle-aged landowner unwilling to lose his life or his estates
in a bid for imperial power. Herculanus could be relied upon to
keep Honoria in style in one of his magnificent country houses.
She would appear only infrequently at court.

No matter how uncompromising Valentinian's insistence on
marriage, Honoria had no intention of being paired off with
Herculanus. Her daring reply to her brother's increasingly brutal
behavior (as she saw it) was to send one of the few people she
could trust across the Danube. Honoria's proposition was simple:
in return for a substantial down payment in gold, and with more
promised to follow, she hoped to persuade Attila to intervene
on her behalf. As a token of good faith—and so Hyacinthus'
astonishing message might be believed—she also sent Attila a
signet ring. No doubt, Attila discussed Honoria's proposal with
his senior advisers. The cautious must have wondered whether
this was a trap to entice Attila to Ravenna. On the other hand,
if Honoria's predicament was genuine, it offered an unparalleled
opportunity to put pressure on Valentinian. Attila's response was
a brilliant piece of brinkmanship. Hyacinthus was instructed to
return to Ravenna and assure the princess that her marriage with
Herculanus would not take place. On one condition: Justa Grata

Honoria, daughter of Galla Placidia and sister of the western Roman emperor Valentinian III, was to become the next wife of Attila the Hun.

In seeking the Huns' assistance, Honoria had not acted rashly or foolishly. Nor is it likely, as Jordanes later claimed, that she was driven by a secret passion for Attila. Jordanes tended to explain actions he disapproved of as stemming from uncontrollable desires, especially in women. (At such moments it is worth remembering that Jordanes was a monk as well as a historian.) In fact, Honoria's bid to involve Attila in a family quarrel was a well-calculated attempt to strengthen her own dynastic position. Her situation had always been difficult. From her brother's point of view, she represented both a threat and an opportunity: a threat because of her ambition to ensure that her husband and children would be contenders for imperial power; an opportunity, since the prospect of marriage with a princess might help secure an alliance beneficial to the empire.

Honoria objected to being treated as a bargaining chip in her brother's schemes. Above all, she resented her confinement within the palace at Ravenna. Strict supervision of her movements was imposed starting in 429, when she turned twelve, the minimum age under Roman law at which a girl could be married. For Valentinian, the diplomatic value of his sister demanded that she remain a virgin until her wedding night. Honoria was also made an unwilling participant in their mother's renewal of her Christian faith. Sometime in the late 430s, Galla Placidia, then nearly fifty, decided on a life of prayer, fasting, and chastity. For her, two marriages, two dead husbands (one an emperor), and two adult children (one also an emperor) were enough.

Galla Placidia had spent two of the most difficult years of her life under Theodosius' protection in Constantinople. In early 423 she fled Ravenna and her half brother Honorius' accusations of treason. At Theodosius' court she first met Aelia Pulcheria, the emperor's older sister. In 413 Pulcheria, then aged fourteen,

had sidestepped marriage by taking a public vow of virginity
and persuading her younger sisters Arcadia and Marina to join
her. Pulcheria's influence at court rested not on her prospects
as a wife and mother but on her displays of piety and generous
encouragement of holy causes. In the admiring description of the
contemporary Christian historian Sozomen, the three saintly sisters were reported "to care greatly about the clergy and churches;
they are open-handed to strangers in need and to the poor. These
sisters generally take their walks together, and pass their days and
nights in each other's company, singing the praises of God. . . .
Although princesses, born and brought up in palaces, they avoid
pleasure and idleness, regarding them as unsuitable for those who
have dedicated themselves to virginity." As long as Pulcheria
occupied apartments in the Great Palace, she insisted that the
imperial household observe early morning prayers and fasting
on Wednesdays and Fridays. She was an unstinting supporter
of Christian orthodoxy and skilled at arguing subtle points of
doctrine. In the evenings she enjoyed reading religious tracts and
discussing edifying passages from Scripture.

During her later years at Ravenna, Galla Placidia, following
Aelia Pulcheria's example, founded churches and monasteries.
Like Pulcheria, too, Galla had an almost magnetic fascination
for Christian holy men. In 446 one of the most charismatic,
Germanus, bishop of Auxerre (eighty miles southeast of Paris),
visited Ravenna seeking to soften imperial hostility toward the
Bagaudae. Over the preceding twenty-five years, Germanus had
built up a formidable reputation as an ascetic, faith healer, and
wonder-worker. He hoped to avoid crowds of Christian well-
wishers by entering Ravenna after dark, but Galla ordered its citizens to maintain an all-night vigil. On his arrival, she sent him
a huge silver dish with a choice selection of beautifully prepared
dainties—all vegetarian, out of respect for the bishop's strict diet.
Germanus gave the food to his servants and ordered the dish to
be sold and the money distributed to Ravenna's poor. In return

he sent Galla a loaf of barley bread on a small wooden platter. She proclaimed herself delighted. That may have surprised Germanus: perhaps in offering such an ostentatiously humble gift, he had hoped to disturb Galla's apparently untroubled reconciliation of her piety with her wealth and imperial rank. If that had been Germanus' intention, he failed. Galla Placidia, always an astute politician, knew how to deal with such competitive displays of holiness. She had the barley bread preserved—it was later said miraculously to cure the sick—and the wooden platter mounted in a magnificent frame of solid gold.

It is unlikely that Honoria enjoyed such carefully calibrated exercises in public religiosity. She objected to being forced to share what she regarded as Galla's dreary daily round of compulsory devotion. Honoria blamed her gilded confinement on her brother, but she also recognized that she was responsible for making a bad situation even worse. As a teenager, she had been closely watched. There were always rumors that she had succeeded in smuggling some handsome youth past the palace guards. In fact, she had been much cleverer. Her lover was Eugenius, her own steward of estates who had every reason to visit the palace frequently on legitimate business. It should also be supposed that in this instance Honoria had allowed passion to outstrip ambition— Eugenius was hardly likely to be the father of emperors—or else, and to her subsequent regret, the seventeen-year-old princess had been seduced by one of her senior staff.

The affair was exposed when Honoria could no longer hide her pregnancy. On Valentinian's orders, Eugenius was immediately arrested and executed. Honoria was hurriedly shipped to Constantinople, where she was taken in by Pulcheria and her sisters. The unpleasant choice of such righteous company was no doubt deliberate. Honoria must have found the unwavering disapproval of the three imperial virgins difficult to bear. She was probably housed in the seclusion of their palace outside the Theodosian Walls near the Hebdomon. Here she gave birth. Despite her misery and suffering, it is unlikely that she received much sympathy. Honoria never saw her child. No historian recorded its name or its fate. The baby was probably secretly given away by Pulcheria. For all her piety, she knew precisely what dynastic politics required. As soon as Honoria was well enough to travel, she was returned to Ravenna under heavy guard. There her position was completely compromised. Now the mother of an illegitimate child, she was no longer the sought-after bride whose marriage might seal an alliance for the benefit of the empire. Honoria had also missed her opportunity—as Valentinian no doubt acidly observed—to follow Pulcheria's example and declare herself a lifelong virgin.

The problem of what to do with Honoria resurfaced with the approach of Eudocia's marriage to Huneric. It was probably intended that the ceremony take place in 451, when Eudocia turned twelve. Valentinian was determined that nothing should overshadow his daughter's wedding. He aimed to have his troublesome sister married off and out of Ravenna. Hence his obstinate demand that she accept Herculanus. Honoria objected that her future husband was unremarkable, unambitious, and unattractive. Despite his name, she complained, Herculanus was no Hercules. Faced with her implacable brother, who insisted that the marriage go ahead, Honoria appealed to Attila. What she had not predicted was his reply. It is unlikely, despite Jordanes' insinuations, that Honoria had ever imagined herself as one of Attila's wives. It is difficult to envisage her living contentedly amid the rolling grasslands of the Great Hungarian Plain, or joining Erecan in supervising embroidery in her comfortable wooden hall. Nor, for all her dislike of Galla's devotions, was Honoria ready to marry a non-Christian.

When news of Honoria's dealings with the Huns reached Ravenna, Valentinian was furious. Tortured before his execution, Hyacinthus confessed the details of Honoria's message to Attila. Concerned that protecting his sister might give the Huns a pretext for war, Valentinian ordered Honoria to pack her bags and make ready to join her new husband beyond the Danube. Honoria had never thought that it would come to this. Perhaps she begged to join a holy order and live out the rest of her life in cloistered chastity, or even to marry Herculanus. Nothing moved Valentinian. He no longer believed any of Honoria's promises. As far as he was concerned, her appeal to Attila had been a betrayal of the imperial family. This was too much for Galla Placidia. The bitter quarrel between her two children had now gone too far. She had not raised Valentinian to the imperial purple so that he could humiliate his sister. She also regarded her daughter's disgrace as poor diplomacy. There was a risk that Attila might view Honoria's expulsion from Ravenna as welcome evidence that the empire would seek to avoid conflict at all costs. If Attila took Honoria's punishment as a sign of weakness, Valentinian might risk encouraging the very attack he was attempting to avoid. Appeasement, as Galla might shrewdly have remarked to her son, does not always guarantee peace—sometimes it can hasten war.

In the end, Valentinian relented. He could stand up to his sister, but not to his mother. Honoria was handed over to Galla's care on condition that she marry Herculanus and live in the decent obscurity of the Italian countryside. It was one of Galla's last interventions on behalf of her children before her death in Rome, in November 450. Two years later, Valentinian conferred the high honorary office of consul on Herculanus. By then, it is to be hoped, Honoria had reconciled herself to a tedious existence with her ever-patient husband. She may even have come to appreciate the advantages of an entirely uneventful marriage.

CHAPTER TWENTY-ONE
TAKING SIDES

ttila refused to give up his claim to Honoria. As far as he was concerned, the gift of her signet ring and her plea for help were evidence of her willingness to assent to marriage. She was kept from following her desires only by the bullying of her oppressive brother and by the religious scruples of her interfering mother. In her heart—Attila claimed—Honoria still wished to be the wife of the leader of the Huns. It was to appeal on behalf of this princess in distress that an embassy was sent to Ravenna in autumn 450 to announce Attila's engagement. The ambassadors also insisted that Honoria, as the emperor's sister, be recognized as joint ruler of the western Roman empire. These demands were intended to be impossible for Valentinian to accept. No doubt, Attila was well aware that Honoria was now married to Herculanus. Equally, there is no good reason to think that he was ignorant of the basic constitutional constraints governing imperial succession: a woman could not rule the Roman empire. Certainly there had always been powerful women at court, particularly the wives, sisters, and mothers of emperors, but none of these had ever formally held imperial authority. Priscus, whose history of the early 450s survives in nine heavily edited fragments, briefly notes Valentinian's replies: "the western Romans responded that Honoria could not come to Attila in marriage, as she had been given to another man," and they affirmed what was well known, "that the right to rule the Roman empire was not granted to females, but to males." At the same time as these exchanges with Valentinian in Ravenna, Hun envoys arrived at the Great Palace in Constantinople. This embassy was also deliberately confrontational. Its aim was to challenge the new eastern Roman emperor, Marcian.

Few could have predicted Marcian's sudden rise to power. For a short while after Theodosius' riding accident in late July 450, a vicious contest must have seemed likely. There were no obvious successors: Theodosius' sisters were dedicated virgins; one daughter, Flaccilla, had died in childhood twenty years earlier; the other, Licinia Eudoxia, was the wife of Valentinian III. In good health in his late forties, Theodosius had not yet thought of sharing power. Strictly speaking, in the absence of any direct male heirs or an imperial colleague, Valentinian—as the surviving emperor—became ruler of both the West and the East, just as Theodosius had done briefly in 423, on the death of his uncle Honorius. But whatever Valentinian's ambitions, the threat of a Hun attack made it impossible for his dream of reuniting the Roman empire to be translated into political reality.

In Constantinople, a powerful coalition of interests moved swiftly to prevent a succession crisis. It was agreed to ignore Valentinian's claim and endorse Marcian, a retired junior military officer in his late fifties. He was, according to one brief and unenthusiastic account written a century later, "a tall man with lank gray hair and swollen feet." It was precisely Marcian's lack of distinction that made him such an attractive prospect. Like many compromise candidates, he enjoyed a wide range of support. His backers all believed that they could influence their man, or at least would not be threatened by his elevation. Among Marcian's strongest promoters were the senior generals Flavius Aspar and Flavius Zeno. For fifteen years, Marcian had served on Aspar's personal staff and been with him during the early 430s in the first campaign against the Vandals. For Aspar, unfairly stripped of his command by Theodosius in 447, supporting Marcian offered a way back to an influential position at court. To anyone who would listen, Aspar also claimed—whatever his differences with Theodosius—that he knew what the dead emperor would have wanted. In Aspar's own version of the imperial deathbed scene, the injured Theodosius had turned to Marcian and whispered, "It is clear that you must rule the empire after me."

Whatever Theodosius' wishes might have been, Zeno's backing was crucial. As commander of imperial troops on the eastern frontier, he had the military clout to make or break a new emperor. In the late 440s, Theodosius had become increasingly uncertain of Zeno's trustworthiness. He had apparently been responsible for thwarting the marriage deal struck between the emperor and Attila's secretary (the Italian) Constantius, although it is not clear how far Attila's story should be believed. Even so, Attila's suggestion to Maximinus that Zeno might be among those senior figures who could threaten the emperor revealed yet again his close knowledge of court politics. At the beginning of 450, Theodosius became convinced that Zeno was preparing to revolt. A few months before his unexpected death, he began covert preparations for a preemptive strike against military bases and units he suspected of disloyalty. Theodosius' fatal fall prevented what might have become a serious civil war. In agreeing to Marcian's elevation, Zeno seized the opportunity to dominate imperial policymaking without having to fight.

The key player in Marcian's rapid rise to power was the fifty-one-year-old virgin princess Pulcheria. She acted to prevent the eclipse of the Theodosian dynasty and, with it, the overshadowing of her own influence. Strikingly, she agreed to advance Marcian's cause by marrying him. On 25 August 450, shortly before their wedding, they appeared before troops at the Hebdomon. Screened by a wall of interlocking shields, Pulcheria presented Marcian with a diadem and a purple robe. This was the first time in the history of the Roman empire that the imperial insignia had

figure 27
Gold coin depicting the emperor Marcian (on the left), Pulcheria (on the right), and Christ, minted in Constantinople in 450.

been conferred by a woman. Not all accounts agree—for some, Pulcheria's role was perhaps too embarrassing to record. (In the future, in the absence of a senior emperor, the coronation would be performed by the bishop of Constantinople.) To the sound of cheers and the ringing clash of arms, the soldiers slowly raised their legionary standards in honor of the new emperor. Marcian, now swathed in purple, was greeted by a crowd chanting carefully rehearsed acclamations: "You conquer, you are pious, you are blessed! God has given you, God will protect you! Worshipping Christ you are always victorious! God will keep watch over the Christian empire!" Marcian agreed not to consummate his union with Pulcheria—there was to be no honeymoon and no marriage bed—a gold coin struck by the imperial mint in Constantinople to celebrate their wedding showed the happy couple shaking hands. Between them stood Christ, the wary guardian of Pulcheria's perpetual chastity (see figure 27). As always, there were doubters: high-society gossips sniggered that Pulcheria had at last succumbed to her passions, and all the more violently having been suddenly released thirty-seven years after her public vow of virginity.

The Hun delegation that arrived in the imperial capital shortly after Marcian was proclaimed emperor was intended to test the new imperial regime's commitment to the peace settlement renegotiated by Anatolius and Nomus eight months earlier. The ambassadors had only one demand: that "the tribute agreed by Theodosius" be handed over. They were met with a robust reply. As reported by Priscus, "The eastern Romans said that they would not undertake to pay the tribute agreed by Theodosius and that if Attila remained at peace they would give him gifts, but if he threatened war they would bring against him men and equipment no less powerful than his own." Marcian's response was not, as is often assumed, a reckless or negligent repudiation of Theodosius' Danube policy. It was not a refusal to pay. Rather, what was at stake was the diplomatic language that character- ized the relationship between the Roman and the Hun empires. No matter how disputed the policy of purchasing peace on the northern frontier had been, Theodosius had never accepted that the subsidies paid to the Huns could be described as "tribute." The Roman emperor was not subservient to Attila. The funds disbursed annually from the imperial treasury were "gifts" to a foreign ruler who held the rank of honorary general in the western imperial army.

In the face of Attila's demands, Marcian rejected any payment of tribute, but he did offer to continue sending gifts. His claim to be prepared to match force with force was not a petulant declara- tion of war but the first shot in what he assumed would be a new round of talks. It was timely, not ill advised, to press the point. The substantial concessions that Attila had been prepared to offer Anatolius and Nomus at the peace negotiations at the beginning of the year could now be seen as necessary measures intended to ensure stability on the Danube frontier ahead of a fresh Hun offensive in the West. If, as his growing interest in Honoria would seem to indicate, Attila was now set on campaigning in France or Italy, then he might be open to further negotiation. After all, like Roman emperors, he would wish to avoid fighting on two fronts at once.

Marcian's response, with its firm emphasis on correct diplo- matic terminology, was of no consequence. Attila had already decided to go to war. From that point of view, the sending of simultaneous embassies to Ravenna and Constantinople in autumn 450 had been a success. The envoys' provocative propositions had been predictably rebuffed. It was impossible for Honoria to marry twice or to share in imperial rule. No Roman emperor could ever countenance the payment of tribute to the Huns. By forcing Valentinian and Marcian to dismiss his demands, Attila had secured pretexts for war. According to Priscus, it only remained to be decided whether the Hun army should march east or west: "Attila was of two minds and entirely uncertain whom he should attack first, but it seemed best to him to prioritize the greater war and move against the West. There he would be fighting against not only the Romans but also the Goths . . . against the Romans to win Honoria and her wealth, and against the Goths to earn Geiseric's gratitude."

At the beginning of the following year, as Attila prepared for the campaign, he continued to send embassies to the West. In January or February 451, a Hun envoy in Ravenna repeated his demand: Honoria's right to a share in imperial power should be recognized by Valentinian, who was to hand over half of the western empire to her without delay. The envoy also claimed that Honoria had been betrothed to Attila before she had been forced to marry Herculanus. The proof was her signet ring. Hyacinthus had given it to Attila, and the Hun ambassador now presented it to Valentinian. No doubt, the emperor recognized the ring as his sister's, although, of course, he refused to accept that it could ever have been a token of matrimony. Perhaps, too, as war now seemed unavoidable, he regretted that he had not sent Honoria across the Danube. Whatever his private feelings, Valentinian had no alternative but again to reject the envoy's arguments. He is not likely to have been any more persuaded by a second embassy, which assured him that, in going to war, Attila aimed to attack the Goths in France and "as his disagreement was with Theodoric . . . not in any way to breach his friendly relations with the empire." The ambassador heading a third delegation, dispatched as the Hun army was on the march, did not bother with any diplomatic courtesies. He simply informed Valentinian, "Through me, Attila—my lord and your lord—has instructed you to prepare the palace for him."

This series of embassies had a serious point. Attila had nothing to lose by sending contradictory indications of his intentions; anything that caused even the slightest hesitation in Ravenna was to the Huns' advantage. In Jordanes' judgment, "Beneath his great savagery Attila was a subtle man, and fought with diplomacy before he went to war." Most importantly, Attila aimed to delay, and if possible prevent, an alliance between the Goths and the Romans. From that point of view, it was vital to emphasize the danger faced by Valentinian personally. Hence Attila's reiterated claims to be married to Honoria and his threat to occupy the imperial palace. The chance of a Hun offensive in northern Italy might make Valentinian reluctant to send reinforcements to France. Rather than risk troops in aggressively engaging an enemy northwest of the Alps, he might instead prefer to guard the mountain passes. Then, if the Goths were defeated, the Huns could be prevented from marching on Ravenna.

Aetius argued against any Roman retreat from France. Leaving Theodoric's Goths to fight alone was not worth the risk. If they were defeated, the empire would still have to deal with the Huns. Attila's campaign would not be confined to a surgical strike on the Goths. Large areas of France still loyal to the empire would also be devastated. Even if the Huns withdrew, it would still require a major military operation to restore imperial authority across a countryside wrecked by Attila's offensive. To be sure, there was a chance that the Goths would defeat the Huns. This too, Aetius argued, would mean the end of Roman

rule in France. Theodoric would certainly move to enlarge his
territory. Controlling the Goths would be much easier if the
Romans fought with them against the Huns. Some agreement
might be reached while Roman troops remained on the ground.
However things turned out, Valentinian could not simply stand
aside. In Aetius' view, it was not in the Romans' interest to see
either Attila or Theodoric victorious in France. Nor was there
much time left. By late March 451, the Hun army was already
on the move. If an alliance was to be made with the Goths, the
offer needed to be sent at once. Valentinian reluctantly agreed. In
truth, he had no choice. Whatever his view of the likely outcome
of a Hun invasion, he must also have been aware that Aetius,
whose loyalty was always in doubt, could act on his own initiative. This was the most dangerous scenario of all. Aetius might
join with the Goths, or even the Huns, and turn against the
empire. Valentinian's reign had begun twenty-five years earlier
with Aetius leading a Hun army into northern Italy. He had no
intention of its ending the same way.

The offer of an alliance with Theodoric was one of Valentinian's most significant policy decisions. It forced him to recognize the permanence of the Gothic state. He was compelled—as
he had been in his dealings with Geiseric—to concede that he
no longer controlled territory once securely part of the empire.
The Goths were invited to fight alongside the Romans against a
growing barbarian menace.

The emperor Valentinian to Theodoric, king of the Goths.
Bravest of nations, we are well advised to unite against this
universal despot who wishes to enslave the whole earth.
Attila requires no reason for battle, but thinks whatever he
does is justified. The measure of his ambition is his strength;
his arrogance is boundless; despising both law and religion,
he shows himself hostile even to the natural order of things.
He deserves everyone's hatred since he is undoubtedly the

common enemy of all. . . . Can you permit such arrogance
to go unpunished? Since you are a military power, face your
own troubles by joining together with us.

Something fundamental had changed. Valentinian's communiqué to Theodoric was phrased in the language of international
diplomacy between heads of state on equal terms, not in that
of a superior condescending to issue orders to an ill-disciplined
subordinate. The defense of France now depended as much on
Gothic goodwill as on Roman military might. For Valentinian,
to appeal to Theodoric for help as a valued friend and ally must
have seemed almost a defeat in itself. Only fear of Attila and
Aetius could together have overcome his imperial pride.

THE FOG OF WAR

Meanwhile, in Belgium, Servatius, bishop of Tongeren (near Maastricht, about fifty miles east of modern Brussels), returned from a pilgrimage to Italy. A few months earlier—despite his all-night vigils, fasting, and tears he had not received a satisfactory response to his appeal to the Almighty that the Huns be prevented from marching against the Roman empire. Dissatisfied, Servatius decided to take his cause to Rome and seek an authoritative answer from the shrine of St. Peter. After many days of fasting, he was finally granted a vision of the somewhat unsympathetic apostle:

> Why do you, most holy of men, disturb me? Behold! It has been unalterably decided in the counsels of the Lord that the Huns should invade France and that it should be devastated as if by a severe storm. Now follow these instructions: travel swiftly, put your house in good order, prepare your tomb, and make ready your burial shroud! Behold! Your spirit will have left your body so that your eyes will not see the evil deeds of the Huns in France. Thus the Lord our God has spoken.

Servatius did as he had been ordered. He traveled quickly home to Tongeren and made the necessary arrangements for his death.

Weeping, he informed his faithful fellow citizens that they would not see him again. He remained unmoved by their pleas: "Do not abandon us, holy father; do not forget us, holy shepherd." Turning his back on his congregation, Servatius journeyed eighty miles north to Utrecht, where, a short time later, he died of a fever. Through unquestioning obedience to his divine instructions, Saint Servatius ensured that by abandoning Tongeren he had saved it from the Huns, who passed one hundred miles to the south.

Not all cities were as blessed as Tongeren. Metz, ninety miles west of the Rhine frontier, was completely destroyed save for a chapel dedicated to Stephen, the first Christian martyr. This confirmed a vision of one devout Christian in the city who, before the Hun attack, had seen Stephen in heated conversation with the apostles Peter and Paul. These senior saints had turned down the martyr's request that Metz be saved: "For the sin of its people has increased, and the noise of their wickedness ascends to the presence of God; therefore this city shall be consumed with fire." As a concession, they agreed that Stephen's chapel should be spared. At Reims, ninety miles west of Metz, the looting and slaughter were only interrupted by its bishop, Nicasius. Along with his virgin sister, he was killed while reading from the Bible before the doors of the city's cathedral. While reciting Psalm 119, at the beginning of the twenty-fifth verse, *adhaesit pavimento anima mea*—"my soul clings to the dust"—Nicasius was decapitated. As his head rolled down the cathedral's steps, it was heard to complete the line, *vivifica me, Domine, secundum verbum tuum*—"give me life, Lord, according to your word." Saint Nicasius' talking head was sufficient to frighten the Huns into quitting the city (see figure 28).

Not all saints had to die for their cause. At Lutetia (now Paris) the young virgin Genovesa (or Geneviève) begged the population not to abandon the town. Through prayer and fasting its safety could be assured. The women were convinced and

figure 28
Martyrdom of Saint Nicasius, thirteenth-century relief sculpture, north portal of Reims Cathedral.

persuaded the men not to leave. Their faith in the virgin was affirmed when the town escaped the Huns. Only the mean-spirited would doubt Geneviève's achievement. Lutetia, it might be pointed out, was some distance away from Attila's route into central France. It was not a great prize like Metz or Reims; by the mid–fifth century it was a run-down settlement concentrated on a flood-prone island in the middle of the river Seine—the modern Île de la Cité, now dominated by the cathedral of Notre Dame. For all her holiness, Saint Geneviève cannot be said to have deflected Attila from one of his main objectives. The Huns were not marching on Paris.

By contrast, Lupus, bishop of Troyes (seventy miles due south of Reims), had to deal with the Huns as they prepared to attack his city. After prayer and fasting, he went out to face Attila himself. "Who are you?" asked Lupus fearlessly. Attila, in an apparently learned biblical reference, countered, "I am Attila, the whip of God." The penitent bishop's reply was heavy with his own

figure 29
Saint Lupus (Loup) confronts Attila at the gates of Troyes,
early sixteenth-century enameled panel by Nardon Pénicaud
from the reliquary of Saint Lupus in Troyes Cathedral.

sense of shame at his failure to keep his fellow citizens from sinning: "And I am Lupus, the destroyer of God's flock, and I have need of the whip of God." Saint Lupus' humility was sufficient to save the city. The gates were opened to admit the Huns, "but they were blinded by heaven and they passed straight through, in one gate and out by another, neither seeing nor harming anyone" (see figure 29).

In all these dramatic tales of steadfast holiness, Attila is absorbed into an entirely Christian world. He is, as he boasts to Lupus, *flagellum dei*, "the whip of God," the phrase most frequently associated with Attila in medieval and Renaissance literature. For many Christians—contemporaries as well as those who later celebrated these triumphant moments in saints' lives—the Huns' invasion

had been ordained by God as a punishment for the erring cities
of central France. Writing in the seventh century, the Spanish
philosopher and theologian Isidore of Seville argued that Attila's
attacks were part of God's plan for the correction of Christendom.
The Huns were the "rod of divine anger"—*virga furoris dei*—sent
to scourge the unrepentant and "force them to turn away from
the desires and errors of the age." Long ago the Old Testament
prophet Isaiah had threatened the sinful Israelites with the righteous fury of the Lord: "when the overwhelming whip passes
through, you will be trampled down by it." For many committed Christians, events in the fifth century continued to follow
an ancient pattern laid down in the Bible. History was divinely
inspired. The decisions of the Almighty might be revealed to
those holy few who could withstand the harsh regimen of fasting, prayer, and all-night vigils. But, as Servatius' encounter with
the apostle Peter suggests, these are matters of faith best left to
hungry bishops and chastising saints. Such visionary truths are
not the business of historians.

By mid-June 451 the Hun army had advanced as far as Orléans,
about 250 miles west of the Rhine. The city may have been
besieged. As with Metz, Reims, and Troyes, the account of
Attila's attack is part of a later, explicitly Christian tradition. At
Orléans it was the intercession of its bishop, Anianus, that was said
to have saved the city. He visited Aetius at Arles, over 300 miles
south, not far from the Mediterranean coast, and insisted that the
Roman and Gothic troops march north immediately. On the day
when Anianus knew his prayers would be answered, he sent his
congregation up to the ramparts: "Look out from the city walls
and see if God's mercy has yet come to our rescue." Nothing was
visible, and, as in all good stories, the faithful had to repeat their
actions, with ample time to doubt the holy power of their bishop.

As the dull thud of the Hun battering rams threatened to splinter the city's gates, Anianus exhorted the skeptics, "If you pray with conviction, God comes with speed." Only on the third climb from the cathedral to the walls did the sharp-eyed suddenly see a dust cloud on the horizon. Saint Anianus confidently proclaimed, "It is the help of the Lord."

The dust cloud was the Rómans and Goths on the move, and it may be that the arrival of the allies saved Orléans from destruction. Jordanes reports a different version, with no dramatic siege, no persistent bishop, and no timely dust cloud. After marching north, the Goths and Romans arrived at Orléans well ahead of the Huns and constructed an extensive network of ditches and earth barriers to protect the approaches to the city. When Attila arrived, "he was so discouraged by this turn of events and uncertain of his troops that he was afraid to begin any conflict." The Huns withdrew to the east, retreating a hundred miles across territory they had already pillaged. The allied forces probably shadowed them.

No account survives of the few days at the end of June 451 between the encounter at Orléans and the afternoon when the two armies faced each other. On one side stood the Romans under Aetius, together with the Goths under Theodoric and Thorismud, the eldest of his six sons. They were reinforced by units from the Burgundians and the Bagaudae. Both had an ambiguous relationship with the empire. In 437 the Huns in alliance with Aetius had butchered twenty thousand Burgundians. Six years later, the survivors, with Aetius' support, had been settled on Roman territory west of Geneva. The Bagaudae had also been ruthlessly suppressed in 437 by the Huns and again in 448 by Aetius. Then one of the rebel leaders had sought refuge with Attila. Nothing had come of this contact. Bitter memories of their violent destruction in 437 may have made many Bagaudae wary of risking an alliance with the Huns. They must have had similar reservations about Aetius. Perhaps in finally choosing sides it mattered to the Bagaudae, despite their deep distrust of imperial rule, that they should still be seen as Romans.

Fighting alongside the Huns were troops drawn from, in Jordanes' phrase, "the countless peoples and various nations that Attila had brought under his control." Most important were the Goths, the descendants of those who, seventy-five years earlier, had remained north of the Danube. Some had moved into parts of the former Roman provinces of Pannonia and Valeria. (In the mid-430s Aetius had agreed not to dispute Hun control over this territory in return for Attila and Bleda's help in France.) The Goths in this frontier region were led by Valamer, Thiudimer, and Vidimer. These three brothers were especially favored by Attila, who treated them as close comrades and valued advisers. Valamer was said by Jordanes to be "steadfast in keeping secrets, subtle in speech, and skilled in deception." The prominent presence of these three brothers is a reminder that the conflict in central France was not just about Huns and Romans or the rancorous end to a lifelong friendship between Aetius and Attila. It was also about the divisions that separated two groups of Goths with sharply opposing histories.

According to Jordanes, the two armies clashed on the Catalaunian Plains. This is not a specific location but part of the Champagne region in France, a rough triangle bounded by Reims, Châlons-en-Champagne (known until 1998 as Châlons-sur-Marne), and Troyes. Jordanes also offers an alternative name for the battlefield, the *locus Mauriacus*, which has often been identified with the similar-sounding Méry-sur-Seine, a small town about twenty miles northwest of Troyes. Sometimes correspondences between ancient and modern place-names can be helpful (as in Londinium to London), sometimes not (as in Lutetia to Paris). Without other evidence, it is impossible to tell whether the apparent connection between *Mauriacus* and Méry is meaningful or just a misleading coincidence. In the end, despite the understandable pride of local historians, all that can be said with certainty is that the "Battle of the Catalaunian Plains" took place somewhere amid the green fields and gently rolling hills of Champagne.

The battle began in the early afternoon. The first struggle was for possession of a ridge at the top of a steep slope. To follow Jordanes' account: "Hun forces seized the right side, the Romans, Goths, and their allies the left, and then the fight began to occupy the crest." The Roman advance was led by Aetius, supported by Goths under Theodoric and his son Thorismud. "Attila sent his men to take the top of the rise, but was beaten to it by Thorismud and Aetius, whose troops, in their attempts to reach the crest, gained the higher ground and, with the advantage of their position on the ridge, were able easily to dislodge the Huns as they came up." As the Hun army was pushed back down the slope, Attila rallied his troops with a speech. What might seem to modern tastes a rather strange interruption to the action would have been expected by Jordanes' readers. This was an important literary fiction. There are usually speeches in the accounts of battles by the great classical authors. Certainly no one would have assumed that Jordanes had access to Attila's actual words, or that Attila had stopped fighting to deliver an oration. It was up to the historian to imagine what ought to have been said. Meanwhile, the narrative was put on hold—just long enough to allow time for Attila to speak.

Huns, here you stand after victories over many nations and after conquering the world. . . . For what is war to you but a way of life? What is more satisfying for a brave man than to seek revenge with his own hand? Nature imposes on us this heavy duty: to glut our souls with vengeance. Let us attack the enemy keenly, for those who press on with the battle are always bolder. . . . Let the wounded claim in recompense the death of his opponent; let those who are unharmed, glory in the slaughter of the enemy. . . . I shall throw the first spear at the foe. If any man can stand unmoved while Attila fights, then he must already be dead.

Inspired by Attila's speech—only about a sixth of the text is quoted above—the Huns engaged the enemy even more fiercely. That, at least, is Jordanes' explanation. Whatever the cause, they surged dangerously across the flat ground in front of the ridge. "Hand to hand they fought, and the battle was fierce, convulsed, dreadful, unrelenting—like none ever recorded in times past." A stream running through the middle of the battlefield gushed red, flooded with gore. In the midst of this bloody chaos, Theodoric was killed. Some reported that while urging on his troops he had been thrown from his horse and trampled to death. Jordanes preferred the more grimly symbolic alternative: that he had been transfixed by a spear thrown by a leading Goth loyal to the Huns. Fighting ceased only at nightfall. In the confusion Thorismud strayed into the Hun lines. He was rescued by his own men, but not before he had been pulled from his horse and attacked. Aetius, stumbling directionless in the dark, failed to find the Roman camp and spent the night sheltering with his Gothic allies. The following morning, as the summer mist burned slowly off the plain, the shattered corpses of the slain were visible piled high across the battlefield. Both sides had suffered significant losses. Most frightening for Aetius and Thorismud was the stillness. The Huns had withdrawn behind the protective screen of their wagons, silently waiting to see what Attila would do.

"Attila was like a lion brought low by hunting spears that paces back and forth in front of his den and dares not spring but does not cease to terrify those around him by his roaring." In the middle of the circle of wagons, Attila ordered saddles to be piled high. Here he proclaimed that, if need be, he would fight to the death. Attila the Hun would never be taken alive, but throw himself onto a funeral pyre of burning saddles "so that the overlord of so many peoples should not be taken by his enemies." For all of Attila's destructive hostility toward the Roman empire, the Hun leader's courage demands admiration. For Jordanes, there is no doubt that Attila was the most valiant warrior on the Catalaunian Plains. The contrast with Aetius is clear. Jordanes offers no dramatic scene in which his courage is on display. Attila is the only commander to be given a rousing speech. Theodoric, without saying a word, is killed; Attila roars majestically like a lion at bay while Thorismud and Aetius, dazed and disoriented after the battle, cannot even find the way back to their own camps.

Despite Attila's challenges, Aetius and Thorismud decided against any further fighting. Instead, they resolved to starve the Huns and their allies into surrender by blockading their camp. Theodoric's body was recovered from the battlefield and buried nearby. Thorismud led the mourners, publicly asserting his own position as the new leader of the Goths in France. Only in death is Theodoric finally praised by Jordanes: "The Goths honored him with songs and carried him away in full view of the Huns. . . . Tears were shed—but only those fitting for brave men. For this was death, but the Huns can testify that it was a glorious one."

The morning of the next day, the second after the battle, Hun scouts reported that Thorismud's Goths had broken camp and were marching swiftly south. This was one of the oldest tricks in ancient warfare. (It had once fooled the Trojans: leaving the wooden horse behind, the Greek army had sailed out of sight just over the horizon.) Attila suspected that the Goths' maneuver was a ploy to draw him out into open ground. The Huns stayed alert but under strict orders not to break cover. After a tense delay, scouts reported that the Romans were also preparing to leave. Again it is likely that the Huns remained behind their wagons until they had confirmation that both Thorismud's and Aetius' troops were well clear of the battlefield and moving in different directions. There was now no time to be wasted. Attila gave the order to march east with all speed back to the Rhine. He aimed to reach the safety of his own territory as quickly as possible.

For Jordanes, the sudden withdrawal of coalition forces from the Catalaunian Plains was a disgrace. Bristling with monkish disapproval, he observed tartly that "human frailty" too often prevents leaders from seizing "the opportunity to perform great deeds." In this instance, the frailty was Thorismud's and his weakness was to listen to Aetius, who had raised doubts about the security of his position as Theodoric's heir. Aetius advised Thorismud to return to Toulouse and prevent any of his five younger brothers from seizing power. He warned that delay might mean fighting a difficult civil war. "Thorismud—motivated by what he perceived to be his own interests—accepted Aetius' advice without grasping its ambiguity." Many historians have followed Jordanes' suggestion that Aetius deliberately misled Thorismud, his duplicity the result of his long-standing friendship with Attila. Aetius deliberately threw the Battle of the Catalaunian Plains— the Huns, so the argument goes, could easily have been wiped out on the first day—and then engineered a plausible excuse to get rid of the Goths. The seventh-century Burgundian chronicler Fredegar claimed that Aetius had played a clever double game. The night after the battle, he went secretly to Attila's camp. There he expressed his regret that he had not joined with the Huns to defeat the Goths. He also warned Attila that Gothic reinforcements would arrive the following day. In return for 10,000 solidi (140 pounds of gold), he agreed to persuade Thorismud to withdraw. According to Fredegar, Aetius then went to Thorismud's camp to warn him that Hun reinforcements would soon arrive. In return for a further 10,000 solidi, he agreed to persuade Attila to retreat and advised Thorismud to return without delay to Toulouse.

That such stories should have been told of Aetius is hardly surprising; after all, he had cheated in single combat against his rival Boniface, twice led Huns against Ravenna, and paraded his friendship with Attila, for whom he had secured an honorary generalship. That said, there is always the possibility that Aetius actually gave Thorismud good advice or that Thorismud reached the same conclusion on his own. Certainly he was right to be concerned about the succession. In 453, only two years after the encounter on the Catalaunian Plains, he was assassinated in the palace at Toulouse by two of his brothers; the elder, Theodoric (named after his father), immediately took his place. Of course, it might be argued that Thorismud would have been in a stronger position had he waited to return in triumph after defeating Attila. Yet victory was by no means assured, and it was certain that Attila would never surrender. On the first afternoon of the battle, the two armies were fairly evenly matched. There were large numbers of Goths on both sides, and the Huns' tactics—the flights of arrows, the cavalry charges, the lassos, and the sword fighting at close quarters—cannot have come as any surprise to either Aetius or Theodoric. Aetius had spent his teenage years beyond the Danube, and the Huns had fought alongside Romans and against Theodoric's Goths in France only twelve years earlier. What made the difference was Aetius and Thorismud's early success in taking the ridge that dominated the battlefield. If hostilities resumed, there was no certainty that the Goths and Romans would hold the high ground. Whatever the outcome, losses on both sides would again be heavy. As with most battles in the ancient world, casualties are not easy to quantify. Jordanes offers the impossible figure of 165,000 dead in one afternoon. Prosper of Aquitaine is more honest in admitting that "the number of the slain could not be calculated." On balance, both Aetius and Thorismud may have decided that it was more important to preserve the combat strength of their troops. Thorismud did not wish to arrive in Toulouse with an exhausted army that could not enforce his authority as the new leader of the Goths.

Undoubtedly, the withdrawal of coalition forces from the Catalaunian Plains was to Aetius' advantage. According to Jordanes, "He feared that if the Huns were annihilated by the Goths, then the Roman empire would be overwhelmed." Aetius had always suspected that victory would prompt a renewed attempt by the

Goths to expand their territory. At least he now commanded a Roman army in France that could counter their ambitions. Most importantly, Aetius also recognized the dangers of wiping out Attila and his loyal supporters. Confronting the problem of regime change had been part of Theodosius' strategic thinking in the 440s. Even if sufficient manpower had been available, there would have been strong arguments against a campaign north of the Danube. Attila might well have been eliminated, but without his leadership the Hun empire could have dissolved into civil war. For Theodosius, an effective military response to the Huns was never a possibility; for Aetius, it was a real option. Despite the difficulties, he could choose to hold his position on the Catalaunian Plains.

This is a risk analysis that has no need of elaborate conspiracy theories. Despite the undoubted glory of destroying Attila and the Huns, Aetius was aware that victory might mean little more than the replacement of one threat with another. If Attila's empire collapsed, then in the violent competition for control that followed, there might again be pressure from the displaced and the defeated to move across the frontier. Aetius doubted that he had sufficient military manpower both to prevent a mass movement of refugees into the Roman empire and to deal with the Goths in southwestern France. The Battle of the Catalaunian Plains had been sufficiently damaging to force an immediate Hun withdrawal. There was nothing to be gained, and too much to be lost, by risking another engagement. It is to Aetius' credit that he grasped a key paradox: the preservation of Roman rule in France depended on the survival of Attila and the Huns. The flaw in Aetius' strategic thinking was the security of Italy.

CHAPTER TWENTY-THREE
THE LAST RETREAT

The experienced general Apollonius was widely regarded as one of the bravest men in the eastern Roman empire. In late 451, less than six months after the Battle of the Catalaunian Plains, he was sent across the Danube by Marcian to open negotiations with Attila, who had renewed his demands for the payment of "tribute." Apollonius took with him only the customary diplomatic gifts. Like Maximinus and Priscus in 449, he probably carried silks, spices, pearls, fashionable jewelry, and some gold. For Attila this was not enough. Through one of his close advisers, perhaps Onegesius, he made it clear that because the Roman envoy had not come with any tribute, there would be no meeting and no talks. Instead, Apollonius was instructed to hand over all the gifts he had brought. If he refused, his safety while in Hun territory could no longer be guaranteed.

Apollonius' reply to Onegesius was uncompromising, and his supporters insisted that he would have been no less forthright in front of Attila himself. He tersely remarked, "It is not right for the Huns to demand what they can receive as gifts or take as spoils." Perhaps Onegesius grasped this (almost) pithy one-liner. In his *History*, Priscus offers a helpful explanation: "Apollonius meant by this that if the Huns welcomed him as an ambassador, then what he had brought would be given to them as gifts, but if they killed him, then what he had brought would be taken from him as spoils." Priscus does not report Attila's response, noting only that Apollonius traveled back to Constantinople without achieving anything. Nor is there any further mention of the gifts. If Apollonius left them behind, this was perhaps best forgotten. Priscus did not want to tarnish a glowing tale of Roman courage (almost) in the face of Attila the Hun.

Relations between Attila and the eastern Roman empire had steadily deteriorated in the two years since the diplomatic row over the payment of "tribute." Whatever Marcian's initial intentions, once it was certain that the Huns were marching west, he decided to stop the transfer of Roman gold across the Danube. But there is no indication that he took any military advantage of Attila's offensive fourteen hundred miles away in France. Not until August and September 451 was there any increase in activity along the northern frontier. Details of these operations are sketchy and known only from the official minutes of a conference of five hundred bishops from across the eastern empire. This church council met at Chalcedon, directly opposite Constantinople on the eastern shore of the Bosphorus. The meeting was delayed until October to allow the emperor to take command of troops in the Balkans. In September, Marcian wrote to a preliminary gathering of the bishops at Nicaea, in northwestern Turkey, asking them to pray "that our enemies may yield to us, that peace may be secured throughout the world, and that the Roman state may continue untroubled." It is not known how extensive the campaign was or how great the threat; even the identity of the enemies is unclear. This lack of detail may not be accidental. Perhaps, while repelling some small-scale raids, Marcian took the opportunity for a show of strength on the Roman side of the frontier. No doubt, the bishops would have celebrated loud and long if the emperor had actually led a successful expedition across the Danube.

Despite these provocative gestures, it is unlikely that Marcian was spoiling for war. For all Apollonius' tough talk, the purpose of his embassy had been to open negotiations on the contested issue of subsidies. The campaign along the Danube had been safely undertaken in the knowledge that, only a few weeks earlier, Attila's army had been forced out of France. Above all, Marcian still had to take into account the same strategic constraints that had limited Theodosius' response to the Huns in the 430s and 440s: the Vandal occupation of North Africa and the security of the eastern frontier. It is equally unlikely that Attila was prepared to risk another major conflict. His army had sustained substantial losses in France. Previous Hun attacks across the Danube had been carefully timed to take advantage of competing Roman military commitments—or, in 447, the earthquake that had so severely damaged Constantinople. Importantly, too, the Huns had now lost the psychological advantage that had once made them seem such terrifying enemies. On the Catalaunian Plains, Aetius and Theodoric had demonstrated that the Huns could be defeated. Whatever Attila's plans, there was no reason to call off his diplomatic offensive. He continued, as his abrasive treatment of Apollonius demonstrated, to insist that the eastern empire keep to the terms of the peace settlement negotiated by Anatolius and Nomus in early 450. Well-advertised hostility toward Marcian also had a wider purpose. As Jordanes remarked of Attila's tactics, "shrewd and cunning, he threatened in one direction and moved his troops in another."

In spring 452, nine months after the Battle of the Catalaunian Plains, seasoned Hun watchers at court in Ravenna and Constantinople agreed that there was no immediate threat. Attila was unlikely to march against Marcian or attempt another strike against Aetius in France. The real danger would come the following year, after the Huns had recovered from their losses. Until then, the army would probably remain on the Great Hungarian Plain, while the Goths and other contingents were stood down. This strategic assessment was only half right. Although unwilling to chance another major engagement with Roman forces,

Attila was, according to one contemporary observer, "furious about the unexpected disaster he had suffered in France." He was determined not to react as if he had been defeated. The Hun army was mobilized in summer 452 and, as correctly predicted by Roman military analysts, made no move toward either France or the Balkans. Instead, in a lightning strike, it marched unopposed 350 miles southwest through Hungary and Slovenia and straight into Italy. Attila had at last made good his threat that he would come to claim Honoria as his bride.

Attila had carefully considered the risks. He is likely to have calculated that by invading Italy he would not have to take on the combined forces of the Romans and the Goths. Valentinian may have been coerced into an alliance the preceding year to preserve imperial interests in France, but it was another, and much more dangerous, step to invite Thorismud to send an army to Italy. There was the strong possibility too that, even if Valentinian was desperate enough to seek help, Thorismud, still fearing the ambition of his younger brothers, would refuse to leave France. Aetius might also be unwilling to march back over the Alps, aware that the return of Roman units would allow the Goths to expand their territory unopposed. Some even doubted the strength of Aetius' commitment to Italy. According to Prosper of Aquitaine, after he had failed to block Attila's advance, Aetius was suspected of planning a complete withdrawal, including the evacuation of Valentinian and the imperial court. In Prosper's hostile view, Aetius agreed to even a limited deployment of troops in Italy only "out of a sense of shame."

Attila's first objective was the wealthy and well-defended city of Aquileia. Situated at the head of the Adriatic, it was a vital trading link between central Europe and the Mediterranean. Aquileia's harbor itself has long since silted up, but the docks—

figure 30
Jonah and the whale, early fourth-century floor mosaic
from the Basilica Patriarcale Aquileia.

now marooned inland—are well preserved. Here merchant ships loaded their cargoes in front of a long row of stone-built warehouses. Here it is possible to imagine the noise: the creaking of wooden cranes, the rattle of crates stacked on the quayside, and the swearing of stevedores hard-worked in the summer heat. The town is still dominated by its magnificent basilica. This great church has the largest early Christian mosaic floor in Europe: about 12,000 square feet in all, an area not far short of four tennis courts. The most beautiful of the mosaics were laid at the beginning of the fourth century, around the time Constantine became the first Roman emperor to convert to Christianity. One large panel shows the story of Jonah and the whale, a good choice for a port city (see figure 30). Even so, the craftsmen

who designed the floor had clearly never seen a whale. A long
snake-like creature with a surprised expression, looking more like
some sort of seagoing dragon, disgorges a naked Jonah feet first,
while his companions on a very Roman-looking boat drag him
aboard. Nearby, in another boat—and entirely ignoring Jonah's
difficulties—naked cupids play at being fishermen.

At first sight, these two images are difficult to reconcile. To
our eyes, playful putti enjoying an afternoon's fishing seem to
have no place next to a serious story from the Old Testament. For
contemporaries, the conjunction of these scenes was reassuring.
It confirmed a fragile alliance between an old classical heritage
and a new faith. Like witty quotations from Homer, Euripides,
or Virgil exchanged at smart dinner parties, the well educated
in the Roman empire celebrated the possibilities of connecting
a non-Christian past with a Christian present. It was important
that Old Testament figures and laughing cupids could occupy the
same space and be seen as part of the same world. Christianity in
the Roman empire attracted converts because it was more than
a religion for just the poor or underprivileged. It had room for
the socially superior along with their intellectual pretensions and
their wealth. Leading members of the Christian community in
Aquileia who donated money for the building of the basilica were
publicly commemorated. Their portraits were carefully worked
into the mosaics on the floor. Their smug, complacent stares still
challenge the inquisitive gaze of modern tourists. Nor were these
self-satisfied Christians embarrassed to advertise their benefac-
tions. The precise extent of their generosity is still plainly visible.
A matter-of-fact inscription, again worked into the floor, records
that "as a gift to God" the wealthy Januarius was responsible for
financing "880 square feet" of mosaic. In Aquileia there were no
anonymous donors.

It is this prosperous and devout world—as in so many other cities across the empire—that was wrecked by Attila and the Huns.
Aquileia did not fall as quickly as some of the fortified cities south

of the Danube. The prolonged siege was an unwelcome delay for an army that relied on speed for its success and on plunder for its supplies. According to the sixth-century historian Procopius, Attila was considering bypassing the city when his attention was caught by an abandoned stork's nest on one of its towers. Attila observed that the stork had recently flown off with its young. Procopius, clearly no bird-watcher, explains, "the fledglings, as they were not yet quite ready to fly, sometimes shared their parent's flight, and at times rode on his back." Attila took this remarkable sight as a favorable omen. If the stork and its family were fleeing Aquileia, it must be a sign of forthcoming destruction. "Look at the birds; they can see the future and are leaving the city because it will perish, abandoning its defenses because they will be destroyed by the danger that now threatens . . . for birds can foresee events, and out of fear of what is to come they change their behavior."

Attila—or at least the stork—was right. The Huns resumed the attack, and the walls were soon undermined. The tower that the stork had deserted was said to have been the first to collapse. The Huns gutted Aquileia, massacring the inhabitants and setting the city ablaze. Paradoxically, the scale of the devastation ensured the town's preservation as a modern archaeological site. The floor of the basilica is still scarred by scorch marks. Here, as the whole building collapsed, burning roof timbers covered the mosaics in a protective layer of ash. Local tradition holds that those who survived abandoned the ruins and settled sixty miles along the coast on the shores of a sheltered lagoon. It may then be one of the curious accidents of history that, by destroying Aquileia, Attila the Hun was responsible for the founding of Venice.

Leaving Aquileia behind, the Huns advanced westward along the edge of the Po valley, sacking Pavia and then Milan. The loss of life in these cities may not have been so severe. There is some indication that Aetius had already implemented a policy of systematic withdrawal toward the Alps and, ultimately, the safety of France. This can be seen as a prudent defensive strategy, rather than as proof of Prosper's damning claim that Aetius wished to abandon Italy. If the evidence of an anonymous sermon preserved among the works of Maximus, the fifth-century bishop of Turin, is reliable, the Hun army pillaged Milan—"what once seemed to be ours was despoiled by looting or was destroyed by the sword and consumed by fire"—but many of its citizens had already left, easily outdistancing the Huns, who now moved slowly, their wagons heavy with booty.

Milan was a great prize. It had been the capital of the western Roman empire from 382 to 402, until Alaric's invasion had forced Honorius to move to Ravenna. Although much more compact than either Rome or Constantinople, Milan was still a splendid imperial city with an imposing palace, a hippodrome, a monumental bath complex, and grand colonnades, one extending a mile beyond its main gate. The city's prosperity was evident in the mansions of the powerful; its piety—or so its citizens claimed—in the beauty of its churches. Some of these, like S. Lorenzo and S. Nazaro, survive imprisoned within later medieval and Renaissance rebuildings. Nothing of the imperial palace remains. It was somewhere in its golden halls that high-ranking Huns gathered after securing the city. It is regrettable that Priscus' account of this evening with Attila is lost. Only a few lines that probably come from the *History of Attila* are included in the entry under "Milan" in the *Souda*, a bulky and often unreliable tenth-century encyclopaedia whose compilation had perhaps been inspired by Constantine Porphyrogenitus' vast editorial projects. "When Attila saw a painting of Roman emperors sitting on golden thrones and Huns lying dead at their feet, he sought out an artist and ordered him to paint Attila upon a throne and the Roman emperors with sacks on their shoulders pouring out gold at his feet."

Priscus' readers would have immediately recognized the image. Tribute-bearing barbarians were part of the standard representa-

figure 31
Barbarini Ivory (13½ x 11½ inches), carved in
Constantinople in the sixth century.

tion of Roman victory. The magnificently carved Barberini Ivory
(now in the Louvre) shows a sixth-century emperor fully armed
and on horseback. Above, in celestial clouds and surrounded by
angels, a serene Christ offers an approving blessing; below, the
leaders of vanquished peoples, some bent almost double, stagger
under the weight of their offered wealth (see figure 31). It was this
striking image of imperial power that Attila instructed the painter
in Milan to reverse. It is difficult to believe that, in the full text of
his *History*, Priscus would have let such an extraordinary moment
pass without comment. Even in his own imagination, Attila the
Hun wished to look like a triumphant Roman emperor.

While the Huns advanced across northern Italy, Valentinian
remained in Rome. This was neither an act of cowardice nor a

grand dramatic gesture. Valentinian's actions made good sense and may have been carefully coordinated with Aetius' steady westward withdrawal. The same strategy had been used seven hundred years earlier after the Roman army had been wiped out at the Battle of Cannae by the Carthaginians under Hannibal. Following the advice of Fabius Maximus—admiringly named Cunctator, "the Delayer"—the Romans had avoided pitched battles. Instead, they burned their crops and retreated to fortified cities. Slowly starved by this scorched earth policy, Hannibal's army abandoned the campaign. Valentinian may have had a similar idea. Under the late summer sun, he hoped to drive a hungry enemy into retreat. Only the boldest—or most pedantic—of his courtiers would have reminded the emperor that it had taken fifteen years to force Hannibal out of Italy.

Attila was also aware of the risks of striking south. For the moment, the Hun army stayed north of the Apennines and by late summer 452 had moved eighty miles southeast of Milan to Mantua. Just outside the city, near the river Mincio, Attila received an embassy sent by Valentinian from Rome. The delegation was headed by the pope, Leo I. This is one of the great encounters in history. Regrettably, no eyewitness report survives. Constantine Porphyrogenitus' editors failed to include this embassy in their collection of excerpts from Priscus' *History*. Prosper of Aquitaine's brief account reminded his Christian readers that the pope "trusted in the help of God, who he knew never neglects the labors of the devout." Faced with the sternness of Leo's gaze and the magnificence of his gold-embroidered pontifical robes, Attila fell silent. Later tradition added to the scene a mysterious old man, perhaps Saint Peter himself, who protected Leo and threatened Attila with a drawn sword. The confrontation is most dramatically imagined in one of the brilliant frescoes painted by Raphael between 1512 and 1514 for the papal apartments in the Vatican (see figure 32). Here Leo, followed by two cardinals, rides a snow-white mule. Pope Leo X, who carefully supervised

figure 32
The Meeting of Leo the Great and Attila *(1512–14), fresco by Raphael.*

Raphael's designs, ensured that his own aristocratic profile provided the model for his predecessor. Attila's ash-colored charger is caught just in the moment before it rears in fear at the sudden appearance of both Saint Peter and Saint Paul, who hover menacingly above the pope's head, brandishing swords. Thanks to Leo's intervention, the city of Rome—which in a miraculous disregard for Italian geography fills the background of Raphael's fresco—will not be sacked by the Huns.

There are other explanations for Attila's willingness to withdraw from northern Italy. It is not unreasonable to speculate that Valentinian had supplied the embassy with gifts and gold to be presented to Attila, perhaps in belated recognition of his claim on Honoria. If he would not hand over his sister, Valentinian might still have been prepared to offer a dowry. It is also likely that the

Huns were already facing difficulties in provisioning their army. In the preceding year, harvests had failed in many parts of Italy, and the crops were little better in 452. In addition, in some rural districts a malarial plague had broken out. By now, too, news had probably reached Attila of Marcian's renewed offensive, this time across the Danube frontier: the first and only occasion that Roman forces fought the Huns outside the empire. The operation was far from a full-scale invasion, but Marcian's limited success exposed the dangers Attila faced in moving the Hun army west without a firm guarantee of security along the Danube.

Attila's Italian campaign cannot be regarded as a failure either because the Huns did not reach Rome or because they finally negotiated a withdrawal. As they had done at the conclusion of their two offensives in the Danube provinces in the 440s, they returned to the Great Hungarian Plain with their wagons piled high with plunder. For Valentinian, the invasion of Italy had been a stark demonstration of his own political and military weakness. In 451 he had been forced to recognize that the Goths could never be dislodged from France; in 452 it was evident that the Roman army was unable to protect Italy. Attila's brief and bloody intervention had decisively shifted the balance of power in the West. It was clear that the Roman imperial government could now neither control nor defend the empire.

Many in Constantinople must have wondered whether Marcian's daring dash across the Danube had been worth it. It had helped force the Huns to quit Italy, but it might also have provoked Attila into attacking the East. As he had done for each of the last three years, Attila continued to issue threats. In late 452 he sent another embassy to inform Marcian that he was planning a campaign the following year that would "devastate the provinces because the promises made by the previous emperor, Theodosius, have not been kept." This time "the fate of his enemies would be even crueler than usual."

At the beginning of 453, Attila decided to take another wife (how many he had is not known). His new bride, Ildico, was said by Roman writers to be a woman of outstanding beauty. After the wedding, Attila feasted late into the night. The next morning, he did not appear. When his anxious bodyguard finally broke down the doors of the bridal chamber, they found Ildico weeping hysterically over her husband's lifeless body. There was no wound, and it seemed that Attila had hemorrhaged through the nose during the night. While he lay on his bed in a stupor, the thick, dark blood had drained into his throat and he had choked in his sleep. Some suspected Ildico of murder; others believed that the death was just what it appeared—an extraordinary accident. For the abstemious monk Jordanes, judgmental to the very end, Attila's inglorious demise was a warning against the dangers of binge drinking: "Thus did drunkenness put a disgraceful end to a famous war leader."

The news traveled quickly to Constantinople. At court all waited to see how Marcian would react. The emperor was equal to the moment, calmly informing his advisers that he had already known of Attila's death. Two nights earlier he had been unable to sleep, and his troubled thoughts had turned to the defense of the Danube provinces. Then he became aware of an angel standing beside his bed. This heavenly messenger silently showed the emperor a broken bow. God, as the pious Pulcheria was no doubt quick to point out, had at last answered the prayers of the Roman empire. There is no account of Valentinian's reaction in Ravenna. Amid all the rejoicing that followed, the emperor must have been aware of the extraordinary twist of fate that decreed Attila should not have been slain in battle or flung himself on a burning heap of saddles. Aetius was later to allege, in a strange reprise of Chrysaphius' assassination plot, that he had bribed the commander of Attila's bodyguard to commit the murder, but it is doubtful whether anyone believed him. Whatever the truth, no Roman could claim the credit for Attila's death. He had died after feasting with his fellow Huns in their new homeland on the Great Hungarian Plain. It must, then, have been with a curious mix of emotions that the emperor reported the news of this fatal marriage night to his sister Honoria. The bare facts probably sufficed: Attila the Hun, one of the most feared enemies in the history of the Roman empire, collapsed drunk in bed and died of a nosebleed.

CHAPTER TWENTY-FOUR
ENDINGS

Aetius' fears were proved right: after Attila's death the Hun empire fell apart. Three of his sons—Ellac, Dengizich, and (the youngest) Ernac—fought among themselves, their rivalry disrupting the careful balance of oppression and reward so skillfully maintained by their father. The immediate result was the breakup of the army as those once loyal to Attila now supported one of his sons. Jordanes was quick to point out the political and moral lessons. "A struggle for overall control broke out among Attila's heirs—for the minds of young men are often inflamed by an ambition for power. Each was driven by a rash desire to rule, and together they destroyed their father's empire. Thus kingdoms are often burdened with a superfluity rather than a shortage of successors."

Disunity among the Huns was exploited by their subjects. Subsequent cooperation between the brothers came too late to prevent a major revolt. The crucial battle was fought in 454 on the banks of the Nedao, an unidentified river probably somewhere in modern Slovenia. The Huns were overwhelmed by a new confederation of peoples once part of their empire. Ellac was slain, and the victors claimed thirty thousand Hun casualties. These severe losses came less than two years after Attila's death. For Jordanes this was a satisfyingly swift reversal of fortune. "And so the Huns were halted—a people to whom it was once thought the whole world would yield. So destructive a thing is division that the Huns, who were so terrifying when their strength was united, were now brought down separately."

After their defeat at the Nedao, Dengizich and Ernac marched south to threaten Goths settled along the middle Danube and in the former Roman provinces of Pannonia and Valeria. Again according to Jordanes, these Goths successfully fought off the Huns "who came at them as though they were seeking to recapture runaway slaves." A decade later, troops under Dengizich were turned back as they attempted to reestablish control along the Danube west of the ruined Roman city of Singidunum. The Goths' leaders—the brothers Valamer, Thiudimer, and Vidimer—had considerable experience of Hun battle tactics. At the Catalaunian Plains, they had been close comrades of Attila.

Not all groups fought to regain their independence. Farther east along the Danube (outside territory controlled by the three brothers), some Goths took the opportunity to cross into the Roman empire. Throughout the 450s and 460s, a number of separate groups—in all about fifty thousand men, women, and children—were resettled in Thrace (roughly modern Bulgaria) on condition that they recognized the authority of the emperor and supplied recruits for the army. Some of the problems of a century earlier were avoided. There were no mass movements of refugees and no internment camps; fertile farmland was quickly found, and the Goths' leaders held high-ranking posts in the army and at court. The eastern imperial government at last seemed committed to establishing an effective cordon of migrant settlements between Constantinople and the northern frontier.

Instability along the Danube intensified with Dengizich's and Ernac's attempts to reassert Hun dominance. In 468, ahead of a major campaign, they sent ambassadors to Constantinople to offer a peace treaty and the establishment of a frontier trading post. The emperor Leo, who had taken the throne after Marcian's death in 457, dismissed the embassy without seriously considering its proposals. Dengizich and Ernac disagreed over their response. Ernac argued that his limited military strength was already fully engaged in protecting the greatly reduced Hun territories north of the Danube. He could not risk war on another front. After this warning, no historian ever mentions Ernac again. Twenty years earlier at dinner, Priscus had witnessed the affection shown by Attila toward his youngest son: "he drew him close . . . and gazed at him with gentle eyes." At the time, Berich explained that a soothsayer had predicted that the survival of Attila's empire would depend on Ernac alone. Certainly he had failed to live up to his promise.

Dengizich, despising his brother as a coward, decided to lead his own troops against the Roman empire. He sent another embassy to the Great Palace to demand both land and money. Leo offered to allow the Huns into Thrace on the same conditions as the Goths: in exchange for resettlement, they should recognize the authority of the emperor. Dengizich refused and crossed the Danube. The Hun army was quickly overwhelmed by Roman forces under Anagast, the son of Arnegisclus, who at the Utus River had come closer than any of Theodosius' generals to defeating Attila. Dengizich's body was pulled from the rout and his severed head paraded through the streets of the imperial capital. Stuck on the end of a long wooden pole, it was displayed above the Xylokerkos (the modern Belgrad Kapısı), one of gates in the Theodosian Walls that had been restored after the earthquake in 447. Then Constantinople had been threatened with destruction by Attila; those who remembered the dangerous days when the city was without its defenses now came to jeer at the rotting head of his son.

With the defeat of Dengizich, the Roman empire was finally freed from the threat of invasion by the Huns, who had been forced back as far east as the Black Sea, where only a century before they had first appeared in Europe. But the Huns' retreat did not restore order along the Danube. The Goths under Valamer,

Thiudimer, and Vidimer had to defend themselves against the expansionary ambitions of other peoples previously held in check by the Huns. An effective response was hindered by Valamer's death in battle and the growing rivalry between his two brothers. According to Jordanes, the Goths also suffered shortages of both food and clothing. Faced with these new pressures, those loyal to Vidimer elected to march west, first into Italy and then to join the Goths in France, while in 473 Thiudimer—carefully assessing the risks of defending Pannonia alone—decided to take his followers across the frontier and into the eastern Roman empire.

The imperial government in Constantinople was unable to concentrate enough military force to deal conclusively with this sudden movement of fifty thousand people. Attempts to encourage those Goths already settled in Thrace to block the advance of the newcomers failed; peace was assured only through the payment of subsidies and the provision of land for both groups together. In 484 their joint leader Theodoric, the son of Thiudimir, was appointed to a consulship. That high honor is an indication that the eastern empire was prepared to attempt some degree of reconciliation. This time there was to be no Adrianople. Instead, the objective was to contain the Goths and prevent them from establishing a secure state on the model of Alaric's successors in France or the Vandals in North Africa. Sheltered behind the walls of Constantinople, the imperial army was sufficiently threatening to ensure a military and diplomatic deadlock.

Rather than fight for land in the Balkans, Theodoric in 488 marched his Goths west into Italy. The pattern was familiar: in the 390s Alaric had also been pushed west. Twice in one hundred years, the East was unable to eliminate Goths, but coerced them into moving on. Similarly, in securing peace with Attila on the Danube in the 440s, Theodosius had been well aware that the likely consequence would be to increase Hun pressure on the Rhine. In the end, the continued ability of the eastern empire to shunt its military problems westward was a vindication of Constantine's decision 160 years earlier to abandon Rome and establish his new capital on the Bosphorus. Not only was the East wealthier, but the division in the empire meant that after Valens the imperial government in Constantinople was ultimately prepared to put its own interests first. Repeated—and unsuccessful—attempts to dislodge the Vandals from North Africa were not matched by any similar commitment to the security of Roman rule in France or Italy. In the fifth century, the East ensured its own survival by sacrificing the West. The tough truth is that one of the chief reasons for the fall of the Roman empire in the West was the continued success of the Roman empire in the East.

The western Roman empire, as Aetius clearly saw, had fewer options. A balancing strategy between Romans, Goths, and Huns in France, which had led to the decision at the Catalaunian Plains to let Attila go, was wrecked within a year by the invasion of Italy. This exposed the limits of any alliance with the Goths and the difficulty of establishing even a workable arrangement to coordinate the defense of just a handful of Roman provinces. Aetius' failure to defeat the Huns—either in France or in northern Italy—undermined his own position. Ironically, too, the death of Attila removed any possibility, no matter how remote, that Aetius might again be able to rely on the Huns to fight on his behalf.

In 454 Aetius fell victim to a group of Italian courtiers led by the wealthy landowner Petronius Maximus. They were convinced that Aetius had little interest in defending Rome or Ravenna and claimed that under pressure he would even have been prepared to surrender Italy to save France. Valentinian seems to have been persuaded that Aetius was aiming at imperial power. Some blamed the emperor's suspicions on his closest advisers. It was said that the eunuch Heraclius had convinced him that Aetius planned to have him killed. Valentinian's violent reaction to the allegation must have surprised even Petronius and his supporters. John of Antioch, drawing on his reading of Priscus' *History*, offers the fullest account of Aetius' last visit to the imperial palace in Rome.

As Aetius was explaining the imperial budget and calculating the revenues raised through taxation, Valentinian suddenly leapt from the throne with a yell, shouting that he could no longer be insulted by such disloyalty. The emperor claimed that Aetius wished to deprive him of his power by blaming the empire's troubles on him. . . . Valentinian drew his sword from its scabbard and along with Heraclius—who had come prepared with a cleaver concealed under his cloak—rushed at him. Together they continued to hit Aetius about the head until they had killed him.

Attila had never been so foolish. The murder of his brother Bleda secured him sole rule; the murder of Aetius lost Valentinian an empire. In response to the emperor's claim that he had been wise to remove a potential usurper, one courtier remarked boldly that he had succeeded only in harming himself: "the one thing I understand perfectly is that you have behaved like a man who cuts off his right hand with his left." Valentinian did not survive long. Six months later, while out riding with only a small retinue, he was ambushed and, along with Heraclius, killed by two former members of Aetius' bodyguard. It was rumored that the assassins had been bribed by Petronius Maximus. Certainly he was quick to take advantage of Valentinian's death: the next day he seized the imperial throne and shortly afterward compelled the emperor's widow Eudoxia to marry him.

The bloody elimination of Aetius was a self-indulgent moment of dynastic politics that Valentinian could ill afford. His own murder shortly thereafter marks the beginning of the final phase of Roman imperial rule in western Europe. Without Aetius and Valentinian, there was no longer any chance of maintaining the empire intact. Nor would this arrangement have been to the advantage of the Goths in France: unless their own security was directly threatened, it was in their interests to see the Roman empire fall. They offered no assistance when Attila invaded Italy in 452. Three years later, they refused to send help when a Vandal fleet attacked Rome. Petronius, whose reign lasted only seventy-seven days, was killed in panic by his own troops and his corpse dumped in the river Tiber. The next morning, the Vandals sacked the city. The disruption in Italy caused by the removal of Aetius and Valentinian allowed Geiseric to achieve what Attila had only hoped for. Again Pope Leo intervened, persuading the Vandals to refrain from setting the city on fire and slaughtering its citizens. Instead, for two weeks Geiseric's troops systematically stripped the old imperial capital of its accumulated riches. Tradition has it that the Jewish holy treasures from the Temple in Jerusalem (the great seven-branched candlestick, silver trumpets, and the scrolls of the law), which four centuries earlier had been paraded in triumph through the streets of Rome, were now carried off to North Africa. For Geiseric, the greatest prize was Valentinian's daughter Eudocia. Dragged back to Carthage, she was made to honor her childhood engagement and forcibly married to Geiseric's son Huneric.

The western Roman empire collapsed fitfully across the next twenty years. The disintegration of a superstate develops its own momentum as the powerful—those able to command troops and resources—become less willing to risk them in distant campaigns. The death of Aetius, the fragmentation of the Hun empire, and the renewed Vandal threat to Italy allowed the Goths to expand without encountering any serious opposition. In the late 450s, they invaded and held most of eastern and southern Spain; in France, Narbonne was brought under Gothic control in 462 and Arles and Marseille in 476. Twenty years after the Battle of the

Catalaunian Plains, the Gothic kingdom in the West extended from the Loire valley to the Strait of Gibraltar. Any advance farther northward was blocked by the Franks. Originally concentrated east of the Rhine and subject to the Huns, they had moved across the old Roman frontier after Attila's death. There was no army to stand in the way of their landgrab. Like Theodoric's Goths in the Balkans, the Franks may have been pushed into the empire by expansionary pressure from other peoples in northern Europe now freed from Hun rule. It had been precisely such instability that Aetius had warned against. The tightening of the Franks' hold over territory once part of the Roman empire was followed by aggressive moves south. In 507, under their king Clovis, they defeated the Goths and sacked Toulouse. The Goths retreated across the Pyrenees to Spain, leaving Clovis and his successors—the Merovingian dynasty—to rule a new kingdom in France.

The history of Italy in the second half of the fifth century is also marked by the erosion of long-standing political and economic ties with the rest of the Mediterranean. Initially isolation was strongly resisted as the combined military resources of the eastern and western empires were directed against the Vandals. That made good strategic and economic sense. For the East, the Vandals still posed a threat to the security of Egypt. For the West, there was a better prospect of reestablishing Roman rule in North Africa than in northern Europe. War in France brought with it the risk that one enemy would simply be replaced by another. If the Goths were defeated, the Roman army would face the Franks. Yet the Vandals were too firmly entrenched in Africa to be dislodged without a long and bloody campaign. Both Roman attempts were utter failures. In 460 newly refitted troop transports were captured even before they had crossed the Mediterranean. In 468 initial progress on land was forfeited when the Roman fleet anchored off Carthage was destroyed by Vandal fire ships. After these defeats, Italian politics turned in on themselves. A series of short-lived rulers attempted, and failed, to secure the support of powerful generals. In 476 the last Roman emperor was deposed in a bloodless coup. Romulus Augustulus, his name a pathetic recollection of Rome's legendary founder and its first emperor, was pensioned off and permitted to live in retirement on a comfortable country estate. It was a measure of Romulus' unimportance that he was not even thought worthy of assassination. The Roman emperor was now an irrelevance. At the very end, the western empire did not fall. It was simply declared redundant.

Odoacer, Romulus' replacement, might reasonably be called the first king of Italy. With strong military backing, his rule lasted over a decade, but he could not withstand the invasion of the Goths in the late 480s. These were the same Goths who had been pushed into Roman territory following the collapse of the Hun empire. Unable to establish themselves securely in the Balkans, they had in 488 moved west under Theodoric. In March 493, Odoacer ended a three-year siege of Ravenna by agreeing to share power. Ten days after surrendering, he was killed at a banquet by Theodoric, who remarked, after he had skillfully sliced his rival in half in full view of his guests, that Odoacer "did not seem to have any bones in his body." Over the next thirty years, as he steadily consolidated his rule, Theodoric provided security and prosperity for the local population and encouraged their integration with the invading Goths. His achievement was to manage the transformation of Italy from being the center of a fractured Roman empire to a successful and independent Gothic kingdom.

Throughout these dramatic shifts in political control, there are clear signs of an accommodation between Roman landowners and these new centers of authority. In the early 460s, Sidonius Apollinaris, who owned estates in central France, praised the virtues of the Gothic king Theodoric II. This is the Theodoric who had taken the throne in Toulouse in 453 after murdering his brother Thorismud. Sidonius was eager to point out the extent to which Theodoric conformed to traditional Roman ideals of good kingship. "The judgment of God and the designs of nature have together endowed him with the most pleasing combination of qualities." He is impressive in appearance, prompt and fair-minded in the administration of justice, modest in demeanor, and careful to restrain his temper. He allocates the proper amount of time to his work, his devotions, his leisure, and his sleep. After lunch and a brief rest, he enjoys playing board games. All is summed up by Theodoric's dinner parties. Reclining comfortably on couches, his guests are served fine food and wine, but in elegant moderation. "When you join him at dinner . . . there is no great tarnished heap of old, discolored silver set down by exhausted servants on sagging tables. The weight here is in the conversation, for nothing is said on these occasions unless it is serious." This was a Gothic king with whom a Roman aristocrat could do business. Here was a ruler who understood perfectly the courtesies of courtly life. Sidonius sometimes found it politic to lose an afternoon game of backgammon. "On such occasions, if I have a request to make, I am happy to be beaten, for I allow my pieces to be taken in order to win my cause." No doubt, too, at times Theodoric chose to play along.

Throughout his description of Theodoric, Sidonius turns his back on classical images of the barbarian. There is nothing outlandish in Theodoric's appearance; he is not deficient in morality or self-discipline; he is not irrational or lawless in his behavior. The firm distinction between Romans and barbarians so well exploited by Ammianus Marcellinus 150 years earlier had lost much of its force. Its sharp distinctions had already been doubted by Priscus in his *History of Attila*. Sidonius, Priscus' contemporary, deliberately blurred any careful categorization of the differences between Romans and those barbarians now permanently settled within the empire. The Goths could no longer be thought of as outsiders. They were to be allowed to merge into a world that could still be portrayed in very Roman terms.

This deliberate emphasis on continuity was not a denial of reality in the face of a collapsing imperial state; rather, it was an attempt to make sense of that transition in traditional ways. The educated elite in the West was remarkably successful in waging these cultural wars. It was a significant victory that their new rulers—even if not as perfect as Sidonius claimed—were prepared to accept Roman forms of rule. Among the Franks, Roman law was enforced, and well-educated aristocrats continued to write first-rate Latin poetry. In Ravenna, after his defeat of Odoacer, Theodoric followed Roman protocols in his administration. His imposing palaces mirrored the magnificent architecture of Constantinople. Those orators who praised him remarked on his wisdom, self-control, moderation, and piety: "Your stature is such that by its height it proclaims one who rules . . . your eyes are fresh with a lasting serenity. It is inappropriate for anyone to boast—yet the advantage that other rulers gain through wearing a diadem is achieved by my king through his God-given nature." As a Christian ruler, Theodoric continued to assert the special relationship between his kingdom and its heavenly model. In the golden mosaics of the churches in Ravenna, Theodoric appeared opposite Christ, both shining in majesty like Roman emperors. These continuities eased some of the painful consequences of the decline of the western Roman empire. They helped ensure that many wealthy families in Italy and France prominent under the emperor Valentinian continued to exercise influence with his kingly successors. But the attractive sheen of Roman-ness that makes the courts of Clovis and Theodoric so seemingly familiar should not mask the sheer scale of political change in the fifth century. It is a striking register of the dissolution of Roman authority that within ninety years of Alaric's halfhearted sack of Rome, the western empire had fragmented into separate kingdoms and the Eternal City been properly pillaged by the Vandals.

Of course, Attila cannot be held responsible for all this. He cannot in any straightforward way be blamed for the fall of the Roman empire in the West. Nor could he have foreseen it. That said, it could not have happened without him and without his unexpected death. Without the threat of the Huns' intervention, Galla Placidia might have eliminated Aetius in the early 430s. Without the Hun offensives in the 430s and 440s, it might have been possible for the empire to have defeated the Vandals before they consolidated their hold on North Africa. Without Attila's western campaign, Valentinian would never have been forced into an alliance with the Goths in France and Aetius would never have let both the Goths and the Huns go at the Catalaunian Plains. Without the sudden appearance of the Huns in the 370s, Fritigern's Tervingi would never have been propelled across the Danube. Without the collapse of the Hun empire less than a century later, the Franks would not have moved across the Rhine and Theodoric's Goths would not have been pushed into the Balkans in the 470s and west into Italy a decade later. And so on.

In any attempt to understand the past, the what-ifs can always be endlessly multiplied. What is certain is that the Huns' sudden attacks on France and Italy in the early 450s hastened the end of the western Roman empire. In deciding to invade France, rather than campaign across the Danube, Attila forced Valentinian to recognize the Goths settled around Toulouse as partners in an alliance against the Huns. This was a risky venture brilliantly managed by Aetius, who drove the Huns back across the Rhine without significantly weakening Attila's hold over his own empire. That fragile equilibrium lasted less than a year. The reasons for the Huns' invasion of Italy are unclear: an opportunistic raid while the bulk of the Roman army was in France, or a quickly executed revenge for the stalemate on the Catalaunian Plains, or a dramatic attempt to seize Honoria. The consequences were to expose the difficulty of maintaining imperial authority in France while ensuring the security of Italy. It was that problem which fatally divided Aetius and Valentinian. After their deaths, the western Roman empire never recovered its balance. Its rulers were unable to prevent the expansion of the Goths or the invasion of the Franks now released from Hun domination. They failed to reconquer North Africa, or protect Rome from Vandal raids, or defend Italy against Odoacer or Theodoric's Goths. The Huns' intervention in France, and then swiftly afterward in Italy, was the catalyst that set this complex chain of events in motion. The Roman empire in the West disappeared within a generation of Attila's death. The new kingdoms that seized control marked a significant shift in the pattern of European power. In the end, a Mediterranean empire that had lasted for five centuries was replaced by separate states. A grand imperial narrative fractured into a set of divergent national histories. After Attila, the Hun empire left no trace, while the fragments of the western Roman empire—now shattered into France, Spain, and Italy—formed the foundation of a recognizably medieval Europe.

REPUTATIONS

On 27 July 1900, at the naval dockyard in the North Sea port of Bremerhaven, Kaiser Wilhelm II addressed German troops who were to be sent to China to help the British suppress the Boxer Rebellion (see figure 33). This nationalist uprising had broken out in protest at the occupation of Chinese territory by the colonial powers. Europeans in Peking were besieged, and the German ambassador had been assassinated. The kaiser was determined to send an uncompromising message to the rest of the world.

> You must know, my men, that you are about to meet a crafty, well-armed, cruel foe. Meet him and beat him; give him no quarter; take no prisoners. Kill him when he falls into your hands. Even as, a thousand years ago, the Huns under King Attila made such a name for themselves as still resounds in fable and legend, so may the name of Germans resound through Chinese history a thousand years from now, so that no Chinaman, no matter whether his eyes be slit or not, will dare to look a German in the face.

There is a self-evident irony that one of the most powerful equations between Germans and Huns should have been made by the kaiser himself. The German chancellor, Prince Bernhard von

figure 33
Kaiser Wilhelm II addresses German troops at Bremerhaven, 27 July 1900.

Bülow, was appalled. He later described the kaiser's outburst as "the worst speech of the period and perhaps the most harmful that Wilhelm II ever made." Bülow did his best to suppress the text, circulating a censored copy to the press. His efforts were in vain; a reporter out of sight on a roof overlooking the dockyard took down the speech in shorthand and telegraphed a translation to major newspapers in Britain and the United States.

At Bremerhaven the kaiser had not so much fabricated a new German Attila as misjudged his audience. He had been inexcusably unaware that his speech would attract international attention. He had thought of himself as speaking only to his fellow countrymen. It is significant that on this occasion Wilhelm chose to refer to Attila by his German name, King Etzel. Etzel is the wise king of the *Nibelungenlied*, a medieval romance that brought together a series of much older courtly tales. This collection of overlapping narratives—again refashioned—formed the basis of

figure 34
Entry of King Etzel with Kreimheld into Vienna *(1909–10), painting by*
Albin Egger-Lienz (1868–1926) as a design for banqueting rooms of the Rathaus
in Vienna. The scene is imagined from the Nibelungenlied *Aventiure 22.*

Richard Wagner's cycle of operas, *Der Ring des Nibelungen*. One
tale in the *Nibelungenlied* tells of Siegfried's widow, Kriemhild,
and her marriage to Etzel, king of the Huns (see figure 34). Etzel
is a courteous and civilized monarch who celebrates the marriage with festivities lasting seventeen days. On the eighteenth,
Hagen, Siegfried's murderer, arrives with sixty men. Etzel wel-
comes them; but Hagen has come not to enjoy his hospitality but
to take Siegfried's sword back from Kriemhild. Without warning,
Hagen's warriors attack the wedding guests. In the words of the
Nibelungenlied, "Etzel's men strongly defended themselves, but
the visitors moved through the king's hall from one end to the
other, slashing with their bright swords."

Even amid the bloodshed, Etzel remains calm. Finally, Kriemhild attacks Hagen with Siegfried's sword. Hagen is decapitated,
but not before he has fatally stabbed Kriemhild. They fall together:
"There lay the bodies of all who were doomed to die. The noble
lady was cut to pieces; Etzel began to weep and greatly lamented
both his kinsmen and his vassals." In this tale Etzel/Attila is the

victim, rather than the perpetrator, of seemingly senseless violence, and it is his court that is wrecked. While it is true that this
tale offers a different view of Attila and the Huns, even so—as
Bülow might have pointed out to the kaiser—it still has slaughter
as its centerpiece. It is difficult to think that this story might successfully authorize Wilhelm's vision of Etzel/Attila as the savior
of European civilization.

Certainly the English-speaking world would have rejected
King Etzel out of hand. Most well-educated people in the late
nineteenth century formed their view of Attila from the famous
character sketch offered a century earlier by Edward Gibbon in
his *The History of the Decline and Fall of the Roman Empire*. For
Gibbon, Attila was one of the causes of that fall. He had wantonly
smashed Roman civilization wherever he had found it: "The
haughty step and demeanour of the king of the Huns expressed
the consciousness of his superiority above the rest of mankind."
The Huns themselves—"the Scythian shepherds," in Gibbon's
contemptuous phrase—were "uniformly actuated by a savage and
destructive spirit." This was not a heroic story; Attila was not a
noble savage uncorrupted by civilization. Rather, in Gibbon's
view, the Huns had thrown themselves mercilessly against an
empire that was already rotten at the core. Theodosius II was one
of a succession of rulers who "had abandoned the church to bishops, the state to eunuchs, and the provinces to the Barbarians."
Valentinian III was "feeble and dissolute," "without reason or
courage." These "incapable princes" no longer cared to maintain
civic virtue or military discipline. Gibbon concluded that even
the early elimination of Attila would not have saved the Roman
empire. "If all the Barbarian conquerors had been annihilated in
the same hour, their total destruction would not have restored
the empire of the West." For Gibbon, Attila was a warning from
history. States that failed to secure freedom and liberty for their
citizens would inevitably decline and fall.

Victorian morality found Gibbon's homilies on degeneracy

and the perils of prosperity very much to its taste. The destructive power of Attila the Hun served as a permanent reminder that civilization would always have to be defended and the great imperial powers to be on their guard. For Victorian readers, Gibbon's analysis was further refined by Thomas Hodgkin. Hodgkin is now unread, but in the 1880s his eight-volume history *Italy and Her Invaders* was widely regarded as offering a more balanced account of the end of the Roman empire than *The Decline and Fall*. The second volume, published in 1880, dealt at length with Attila. Hodgkin's account differs strikingly from Gibbon's in its emphasis on the Mongolian origin of the Huns. Victorian ethnography insisted on a close link between many of the peoples who had invaded Europe since the collapse of the Roman empire. Hodgkin argued strongly for a racial connection between the Tartars (under Genghis Khan and Tamberlane), the Huns, the Bulgars, the Magyars, and the Ottoman Turks. The Huns were another example of "a multitude of dull barbarians, mighty in destruction, powerless in construction, who have done nothing for the cause of civilization or human progress, and who, even where they have adopted some of the varnish of modern customs, have remained essentially and incurably barbarous to the present day."

Looking back to the beginning of the nineteenth century, Hodgkin reflected on the near-destruction of Europe by Napoleon. Here was a latter-day Attila, although not, as Hodgkin was all too predictably eager to point out, from a racial point of view. There were vast "differences between the uncultured intellect of the Tartar chieftain, and the highly-developed brain of the great Italian-Frenchman who played with battalions as with chessmen." But in his aim to destroy Europe, in his "insatiable pride, in the arrogance which beat down the holders of ancient thrones . . . in all these points no one so well as Napoleon explains to us the character and career of Attila." England had survived

Napoleon and established a worldwide empire. One of the main purposes of Hodgkin's historical project was to ask, "Will England fall as Rome fell?" He returned a qualified answer, arguing that a balance of power between the Old World and the New World would prevent any one state from being consumed by an "overweening arrogance which is unendurable by God and Man." He also believed that a strong Anglican Church would ensure a high standard of morality in public life. But the fall of Rome and the destructive success of the Huns offered a salutary lesson. Hodgkin advocated democracy as the best defense against despotism. He was particularly concerned that contemporary politicians in Europe and the United States might abuse the prosperity of the nations they governed. "Will the great Democracies of the Twentieth Century resist the temptation to use political power as a means of material self-enrichment?" Success itself might mark the beginning of a new cycle of decline and fall. A wealthy and complacent populace would allow the construction of "palaces in which British or American despots . . . will guide mighty empires to ruin, amidst the acclamations of flatterers." And like the Roman empire, these modern superstates would fall easy prey to some new Attila.

Attila and the Huns have remained powerful symbols of the threats that face European civilization and might again cause its fall. For Gibbon, Attila exploited the Roman empire's failure to maintain the integrity of its political institutions. For Hodgkin, he represented the dangerous forces of oriental barbarism ranged against a virtuous and democratic Christendom. The sense that there might be a fundamental and irreconcilable antagonism between the nomadic Huns and the settled peoples of Europe was deep-rooted. It is a basic pattern that has been repeated again and again. For British soldiers in World War I, the Germans were the Hun—a comparison ironically authorized by the kaiser himself. In 1914 Rudyard Kipling captured the national mood.

For all we have and are,
For all our children's fate,
Stand up and take the war.
The Hun is at the gate!
Our world has passed away,
In wontonness o'erthrown.
There is nothing left to-day
But steel and fire and stone!

Again the theme was the preservation of civilization against the barbarous destruction of "a crazed and driven foe." The sentiment was both inspiring and uncompromising. Thomas Hodgkin would have approved. Edward Gibbon, who was more wary of such unrestrained patriotism, would have been slower to applaud.

There is but one task for all—
One life for each to give.
Who stands if Freedom fall?
Who dies if England live?

More recent versions of Attila have offered variations on this theme. In 1954 the Hollywood epic *Sign of the Pagan*, with Jack Palance in its title role, returned to the orientalist fears of the nineteenth century. This was a film that would have appealed to Senator McCarthy; Attila (here conceived as a cross between Ming the Merciless and Mao Zedong) galloped with Mongol-style hordes across central Asia to attack a decadent Roman empire. This was an unambiguous warning of the grim consequences of moral weakness. Middle America must not make the same mistakes as the Romans; to do so was to risk decline and fall. The Huns were to be both feared and despised. They had no regard for private property, for the sanctity of the family, for Christian values, or for personal cleanliness. These were signs of an anti-American barbarity. Attila's advance on Europe was one Long March against civilization. The Huns were clearly proto-communists on horseback.

There are many Attilas. He can be viewed through the powerful lens of First World War propaganda, or through the distasteful conclusions of Victorian historical racism, or through the communist scare of 1950s America, or through the romantic stories of the *Nibelungenlied,* or through Gibbon's *Decline and Fall* and his memorable tableau of ignorant Scythian shepherds smashing a once great European civilization. In truth, Attila does not merit any of these reputations. He is not always what we expect—or perhaps not always what we would like him to be. Attila was not part of a yellow peril; he was not on a single-minded mission to destroy the Roman empire; he was not a prototype for medieval chivalry; he was not a forerunner of either Napoleon or Mao Zedong.

To reject these images of Attila is not for a moment to downplay the damaging impact of the Huns on the Roman empire. They crossed the Danube in 422, 434, 441–42, and again in 447; in 450–51 they invaded France and in 452 northern Italy. No other enemy faced by the Romans had ever breached the frontiers of both the eastern and the western empires in the short space of a decade. In both East and West the Huns burned undefended farms and villages to the ground and sacked a long list of cities (some strongly fortified): Sirmium, Singidunum, Margum, Viminacium, Naissus, Serdica, Ratiaria, Philippopolis, Arcadi-opolis, Marcianople, Metz, Reims, Aquileia, Pavia, and Milan. The brutality of these attacks should not be doubted. A terror-stricken population faced, in the monk Jerome's striking phrase, "the wolves of the North." Even for the most sympathetic, it is difficult not to be desensitized by the dull repetition of stories of

the Huns' ruthlessness. Not every incident has the memorable
force of the extermination of twenty thousand Burgundians or
Priscus' grim account of the bleached bones of the slain strewn
along the riverbank outside the broken walls of Naissus. To echo
Jerome (himself echoing Virgil), "Not even if I had a hundred
tongues and a hundred mouths and a voice of iron could I recite
the names of all these disasters."

If the Huns' cruelty is not to be diminished, it must be put in
context. The Huns were not the only threat faced by the Roman
empire in the fifth century, and not the only enemy to sack its
cities. Italy was pillaged by Goths and Vandals, France by Goths,
Burgundians, and Bagaudae, the Balkans by Goths, and North
Africa by the Vandals. These, too, were bloody and disruptive
incursions, and unlike the Huns, who withdrew beyond the frontier after each campaign, the Goths and Vandals fought to establish themselves on Roman territory. The Huns never succeeded
in sacking Rome; the Goths pillaged the city in 410 and the
Vandals in 455. In direct encounters with the Roman army, the
Hun record is not particularly impressive. Against Arnegisclus at
the Utus River, they sustained heavy casualties. The Battle of the
Catalaunian Plains was at best a stalemate. By contrast, Geiseric
and the Vandals seized North Africa by force and repulsed a series
of Roman expeditions. At Adrianople, Fritigern and the Goths
wiped out twenty thousand legionaries in one afternoon. Attila
registered no such achievement. His strategic brilliance lay not
in fighting the Romans but in seeking to avoid any large-scale
confrontation.

Arguably, too, the dislocation associated with the disintegration of the empire in the West was eclipsed by the sheer brutality
that had accompanied its formation. The most violent force in
the ancient Mediterranean world was the Roman empire. In the
annexation of France five centuries before Attila, Julius Caesar's
troops had massacred one million people in battles and reprisals
and enslaved a further million. In human and economic terms,

Caesar's imperial achievement was not to be equaled in the scale of its destruction until the Spanish invasion of the Americas. A consistent policy of merciless oppression is one of the keys to the Roman empire's success. In AD 60 the local population of Iceni in southeastern Britain revolted. Roman counterattacks swiftly imposed control. Tens of thousands of Britons were killed in battle; Roman casualties numbered barely four hundred. In an early example of ethnic cleansing, the Roman army continued to target the Iceni until all opposition was eliminated. Boudica, one of the Iceni leaders, took her own life. Her attempt to expel the Romans from Britain had been a miserable and costly failure.

Of course, such cruelty had a point. It was repeatedly presented as a necessary and unavoidable part of Rome's fulfillment of its divinely sanctioned mission to conquer the independent peoples of Europe, North Africa, and the Middle East.

> *Roman, remember through your empire to rule*
> *Earth's peoples—for your arts are to be these:*
> *To pacify, to impose the rule of law,*
> *To spare the vanquished, and war down the proud.*

On this view, the pain and suffering of subjugation was a fair price to pay for the peace and prosperity that came with empire. By contrast, for their actions the Huns seemingly offered no moral or religious justification, however thin or unconvincing. They sought neither to find a new homeland on Roman territory nor to glorify themselves as heroic freedom fighters warring down a harsh imperial regime. The Huns appear more brutal precisely because they had no known motive for their raids beyond the acquisition of booty and captives. Or at least because not a single line of Hun poetry survives to contradict that powerful image presented by their Roman enemies.

Alongside Attila's reputation for ruthless destruction should be set his success as an empire builder. No coherent story can be told of the consolidation of Hun dominance over peoples from the Urals to the Rhine; there are only occasional fragments that hint at the scale of this enterprise and its possible justification: the discovery of the Pannonhalma, Pietroasa, and Şimleu Silvaniei treasures, the presence on the Catalaunian Plains of troops from (to quote Jordanes) "the countless peoples and various nations that Attila had brought under his control," the prominence of the Gothic leaders Valamer, Thiudimer, and Vidimer, and Attila's claims to have been favored by the war god. The Hun empire did not survive Attila's sudden death. It quickly broke apart when fought over by his sons. Even so, and if only fleetingly, Attila harnessed the social and economic transformation of the Huns on the Great Hungarian Plain. By systematically exploiting a network of tributary states, the Huns became the dominant power in northern Europe. This remarkable achievement has received very little attention—perhaps because it does not fit comfortably with conventional images of either Attila or the Huns.

But it was celebrated in Renaissance Hungary, whose rulers and their historians sought to create a national history for an emerging state by reaching back beyond the Magyar conquests of the ninth and tenth centuries to imagine the foundation of Hungary by the Huns. Attila's new champion was the Hungarian king Matthias Corvinus, who in the fifteenth century annexed large parts of Austria, Slovakia, and Poland, establishing his capital in Vienna. Corvinus claimed Attila as his ancestor. In this version of the past, most fully set out in János Thuróczi's *Chronica de gestis Hungarorum* (published in 1488), Attila—like Corvinus—was a skillful general and an enlightened monarch. Both enjoyed sophisticated philosophical debate. Corvinus was pleased to be known as "a second Attila." In this king's successes, enthused Thuróczi, "fate revives the ancient glory of the Huns that shone in brilliance during the time of Attila."

Attila had to wait a millennium before he was first portrayed as a European nation builder rather than a destructive outsider. By contrast, the transformation of the Goths took less than a century. In the 370s and again after Alaric's sack of Rome in 410, Roman writers had regarded the Goths as the ultimate barbarian menace, yet in the 460s Sidonius Apollinaris offered a strikingly different picture of the civilized courtesies at the court of Theodoric II. Whatever the history of their hard-fought opposition to the empire, the Goths had converted to Christianity, settled permanently in France, and now received the enthusiastic praises of Roman aristocrats eager to reach an accommodation with their new rulers. In the end, the Romans had sided with the Goths, who could no longer be seen simply as barbarian outsiders. The Huns had none of these advantages. Perhaps if the pattern of alliances established by Aetius in the 430s—when Huns fought alongside Romans against Goths—had been successfully maintained, then the Huns might have been treated differently by Roman writers. Instead, in electing to attack both the eastern and the western empires, Attila confirmed his reputation as a pitiless savage whose malevolent presence in a Christian world could be explained only by God's righteous anger against the sinful cities of the Roman empire. Attila stood condemned as both nomad and devil. To recall the powerful words of a seventh-century Christian apocalyptic vision: "The Huns will move faster than the winds, more rapidly than storm clouds and their war cries will be like the roaring of a lion. Terror at their coming will cover the whole earth like the floodwaters in the days of Noah."

These exaggerated images, of either ruthless barbarity or enlightened nationalism, are a stark reminder of the problems surrounding any final assessment of Attila and the Huns. Any satisfactory judgment is unlikely to be so clear-cut. Hence the importance of Priscus of Panium. In summer 449 Priscus set off to meet a bloodthirsty barbarian hell-bent on wrecking the Roman empire. The reality, as he discovered, was disturbingly different. The Huns could not easily be dismissed as *nomades* who had nothing in common with the elegance of classical culture. Attila turned out to be surprisingly civilized and a dangerously shrewd player of international politics. His attacks on Roman cities were not pointless acts of destruction. They were part of a careful strategy to force an already overcommitted empire to pay for protection rather than fight. In Priscus' story, it was Theodosius II and his advisers—prepared to use diplomatic immunity as a cover for a poorly planned assassination plot—who appeared morally questionable.

Of course, Priscus never doubted Attila's hostility toward the Roman empire. His intention was neither to excuse nor to justify. Rather, by exploring the complexities of that conflict, his *History of Attila* aimed to move its readers beyond crude stereotypes of Huns and Romans. Priscus opens the door on a different understanding of the Roman empire in the fourth and fifth centuries. This book has enthusiastically followed his lead. As Priscus would be among the first to affirm, history should continually seek to challenge our assumptions. It should prompt us to look differently at the world and make us less self-assured about our own ideals and beliefs. What makes great empires endure or collapse? How do governments defend their actions? What causes the breakup of a leviathan superstate? When is it right to go to war, or purchase peace, or pay off an enemy? What justifies the label "barbarian" or constitutes a convincing claim to "civilization"? These are issues of enduring importance. They are not abstract questions best left to the ivory tower discussion of graduate seminars in classics; rather, they involve intensely personal dramas that demand that we confront the motives and the reputations of those who seek to preserve empires and of those who aim to bring about their destruction. It is always perilous to suppose that the past is over and done with or that it can ever safely be disconnected from the pressing concerns of the present. At the end of a history of Attila and the Huns, we should gently be encouraged to think about more than the decline and fall of the Roman empire.

NOTES AND FURTHER READING

The last serious, full-length historical study of Attila and the Huns in English was published sixty years ago: Edward Thompson, *The Huns* (Oxford, 1948), revised with an afterword by Peter Heather in 1996. In January 1969 the great Austrian scholar Otto Maenchen-Helfen handed in a manuscript to the University of California Press just a few days before his death. Much of the work was not yet in its final form; under the exemplary editorial supervision of Max Knight, all that was publishable was included in Maenchen-Helfen, *The World of the Huns: Studies in Their History and Culture* (Berkeley, Calif., 1973). Aside from Maenchen-Helfen, the most important recent contributions to Hun archaeology are István Bóna, *Das Hunnenreich* (Budapest, 1991), which offers a comprehensive overview of the material, but is confusingly, and often irritatingly, arranged, and the thorough and meticulously detailed study by Bodo Anke, *Studien zur Reiternomadischen Kultur des 4. bis 5. Jahrhunderts*, 2 vols. (Weissbach, 1998). Four shorter discussions are also useful introductions: Michael Whitby in Averil Cameron, Bryan Ward-Perkins, and Michael Whitby, eds., *The Cambridge Ancient History*, vol. 14, *Late Antiquity: Empire and Successors, A.D. 425–600* (Cambridge, 2000), 704–12; Hugh Kennedy, *Mongols, Huns and Vikings* (London, 2002), 22–55; Herwig Wolfram, *The Roman Empire and Its Germanic Peoples*, (Berkeley, Calif., 1997); 123–44; and Denis Sinor, "The Hun Period," in Sinor, ed., *The Cambridge History of Early Inner Asia* (Cambridge, 1990), 177–205. Two exhibitions on the Huns—at the Musée de Normandie in Caen, June–October 1990, and at the Historischen Museum der Pfalz in Speyer, June 2007–January 2008—have resulted in valuable catalogues: Jean-Yves Marin, ed., *Attila, les influences danubiennes dans l'ouest de l'Europe au Ve siècle* (Caen, 1990), and *Attila und die Hunnen* (Stuttgart, 2007).

Full and detailed coverage of the third to fifth centuries AD (a period conventionally known as "late Antiquity" or "the later Roman empire") is provided by *The Cambridge Ancient History* (= *CAH*): Alan Bowman, Averil Cameron, and Peter Garnsey, eds., vol. 12, *The Crisis of Empire, A.D. 193–337*, 2nd ed. (Cambridge, 2005); Averil Cameron and Peter Garnsey, eds., vol. 13, *The Late Empire, A.D. 337–425* (Cambridge, 1998), and vol. 14, *Late Antiquity.* Three older works remain indispensable: Ernst Stein, *Histoire du Bas-Empire: De l'État romain à l'État byzantin (284–476)* (Paris, 1959, originally published in German in 1928); Émilienne Demougeot, *La formation de l'Europe et les invasions barbares, de l'avènement de Dioclétien au début du VIe siècle*, 2 vols. (Paris, 1979) and A. H. M. Jones, *The Later Roman Empire 284–602: A Social, Economic, and Administrative Survey*, 3 vols. (Oxford, 1964). For a comprehensive collection of the evidence for the biographies and career patterns of all known fifth-century civil and military post holders, professionals (doctors, poets, rhetors), and their families, see John Martindale, *The Prosopography of the Later Roman Empire*, vol. 2, *A.D. 395–527* (Cambridge, 1980). This is one of the most impressive examples of fundamental scholarship undertaken in the last generation.

All translations from Greek and Latin texts are my own. At the end of these notes, there is a consolidated list of the most frequently cited late-antique authors, with a guide to modern translations.

CHAPTER ONE: FIRST CONTACT

Ammianus 31.3–9 is the most important account of events from the advent of the Huns west of the Black Sea to the revolt of the Goths under Fritigern. The most helpful modern accounts are Noel Lenski, *Failure of Empire: Valens and the Roman State in the Fourth Century A.D.* (Berkeley, Calif., 2002), 320–34; Peter Heather, *Goths and Romans 332–489* (Oxford, 1991), 122–47, reworked in *The Goths* (Oxford, 1996), 97–104 and 130–34, and *The Fall of the Roman Empire: A New History* (London, 2005), 151–53 and 158–67; Herwig Wolfram, *History of the Goths* (Berkeley, Calif., 1988), 64–75 and 117–24; Guy Halsall, *Barbarian Migrations and the Roman West, 376–568* (Cambridge, 2007), 165–78; Michael Kulikowski, *Rome's Gothic Wars* (Cambridge, 2007), 123–37; and Maenchen-Helfen, *Huns*, 26–28. Valens' insistence that the Tervingi convert to Christianity is reported in Socrates 7.33.4 with Heather, *Goths and Romans*, 127–28; but see Noel Lenski, "The Gothic Civil War and the Date of the Gothic Conversion," *Greek, Roman and Byzantine Studies* 36 (1995): 51–87, and *Failure of Empire*, 320–21 and 347–48, suggesting that Fritigern may have converted in response to Valens' earlier support of his insurgency against Athanaric. Peter Heather defends Lupicinus (with deepening sympathy) in *Goths and Romans*, 133, *Goths*, 131, and *Fall*, 165–66. The transformation of the Roman empire from Augustus to Constantine is beautifully evoked in Peter Brown, *The Making of Late Antiquity* (Cambridge, Mass., 1978). For innovative studies of the problems faced at the frontiers of empire, see Dick Whittaker, *Frontiers of the Roman Empire: A Social and Economic Study* (Baltimore, 1994), and Benjamin Isaac, *The Limits of Empire: The Roman Army in the East*, 2nd ed. (Oxford, 1992). Christopher Kelly, *Ruling the Later Roman Empire* (Cambridge, Mass., 2004), explores the transformation in the way the Mediterranean world was governed and the impact and extent of imperial power. The division of the empire and its causes are thoughtfully considered by Émilienne Demougeot, *De l'unité à la division de l'Empire romain, 395–410: Essai sur le gouvernement impérial* (Paris, 1951); on the administrative and legal aspects, see Malcolm Errington, *Roman Imperial Policy from Julian to Theodosius* (Chapel Hill, 2006), 79–110. The first Christian emperor, Constantine (ruled 306–37), is a pivotal figure. Averil Cameron, *CAH* 12: 90–109, and Noel Lenski, ed., *The Cambridge Companion to the Age of Constantine* (Cambridge, 2006), offer excellent introductions; for a more detailed consideration of his political and religious aims, see Raymond van Dam, *The Roman Revolution of Constantine* (Cambridge, 2007). The best description of Constantinople in English is Richard Krautheimer, *Three Christian Capitals: Topography and Politics* (Berkeley, Calif., 1983), 41–67. Key to understanding the city are Gilbert Dagron, *Naissance d'une capitale: Constantinople et ses institutions de 330 à 451*, 2nd ed. (Paris, 1984), and Raymond Janin, *Constantinople byzantine: Développement urbain et répertoire topographique*, 2nd ed. (Paris, 1964). In Istanbul the commemorative porphyry column that marked the center of Constantine's Forum still stands (not far from the Grand Bazaar); the pleasant park, known as At Meydanı, next to the Sultan Ahmet (or Blue) Mosque, marks out the area of the hippodrome. The remains of the Milion are visible, now marooned in the middle of a traffic island at the northern end of At Meydanı, just beyond the ugly cast-iron fountain presented by Kaiser Wilhelm II to Sultan Abdül Hamit II. The main narrative for the lead-up to Adrianople and the battle itself is Ammianus 31.11–13; see too Socrates 4.38 (jeering in the hippodrome at 4.38.4); Zosimus 4.21–24.2 (body on the road at 4.21.2–3). The most considered account of Adrianople, its causes and consequences, is Lenski, *Failure of Empire*, 334–67, usefully read alongside Heather, *Fall*, 167–81; Kulikowski, *Rome's Gothic*

Wars, 137–43; Halsall, *Barbarian Migrations*, 178–80; and Wolfram, *Goths*, 117–31. Themistius' dark remark is from *Oration* 16.206d. For the imperial mausoleum in Constantinople, see the remarkable description in Eusebius, *Life of Constantine* 4.58–60, and Cyril Mango, "Constantine's Mausoleum and the Translation of Relics," *Byzantinische Zeitschrift* 83 (1990): 51–62, at 54–58 (= *Studies on Constantinople*, Variorum reprints 394 [Aldershot, 1993], no. 5). The highest hill in Istanbul is now dominated by the Fatih Mosque. Nothing remains of the mausoleum.

CHAPTER TWO: THE AXIS OF EVIL

Ammianus 31.2.1–12 for his description of the Huns with important discussions in John Matthews, *The Roman Empire of Ammianus* (London, 1989), 332–42, and Thomas Wiedemann, "Between Men and Beasts: Barbarians in Ammianus Marcellinus," in I. S. Moxon, John Smart, and Tony Woodman, eds., *Past Perspectives: Studies in Greek and Roman Historical Writing* (Cambridge, 1986), 189–201. Classical views of "the barbarian" are treated comprehensively by Yves Dauge, *Le barbare: Recherches sur la conception romaine de la barbarie et de la civilisation* (Brussels, 1981), 330–52 (on Ammianus), 413–66 (on barbarian character traits), 604–9 (on comparisons to animals), and 620–34 (on barbarian social structures). For thoughtful approaches to the material, see Peter Heather, "The Barbarian in Late Antiquity: Image, Reality, and Transformation," in Richard Miles, ed., *Constructing Identities in Late Antiquity* (London, 1999), 234–58; Brent Shaw, " 'Eaters of Flesh, Drinkers of Milk': The Ancient Mediterranean Ideology of the Pastoral Nomad," *Ancient Society* 13/14 (1982–83): 5–31 (= *Rulers, Nomads, and Christians in Roman North Africa*, Variorum reprints 497 [Aldershot, 1995], no. 6); and especially Alain Chauvot, *Opinions romaines face aux barbares au IVe siècle ap. J.-C.* (Paris, 1998). For the Roman imperial mission, see Virgil, *Aeneid* 6.851–53; Caesar's description of Ariovistus is from his *Gallic Wars* (de bello Gallico 1.31.12–33.5) with Dauge, *Le barbare*, 415–16. Trajan's Column is described scene by scene in Lino Rossi, *Trajan's Column and the Dacian Wars* (London, 1971), 130–212. For barbarians dragged by the hair, see Annalina Caló Levi, *Barbarians on Roman Imperial Coins and Sculpture* (New York, 1952), 25–26; for barbarians on the Arch of Constantine, see Chauvot, *Opinions*, 83–86; for triumphant gaming boards, see Max Ihm, "Römische Spieltafeln," in *Bonner Studien: Aufsätze aus der Altertumswissenschaft Reinhard Kekulé* (Berlin, 1890), 223–39, quoting 238, no. 49. *On Military Matters* 17 (de Rebus Bellicis, ed. Andrea Giardina [Milan, 1989] for the description of the oxen-powered warship and 6.1 for concerns about a growing barbarian menace. For translation and discussion, see Edward Thompson, *A Roman Reformer and Inventor* (Oxford, 1952), and Mark Hassell, ed., *Aspects of the De Rebus Bellicis: Papers Presented to Professor E. A. Thompson* (Oxford, 1979). Themistius' deliberately divisive characterization of the Goths is from *Oration* 10.133; for the peace settlement between Valens and Athanaric in 369, see Lenski, *Failure of Empire*, 132–37; Ammianus 31.4.9 for the volcanic image of the Tervingi. Tacitus, *Germania* 22.1, on drunkenness; 18–19 on the sanctity of marriage (ed. Michael Winterbottom, in Winterbottom and Robert Ogilvie, *Cornelii Taciti: Opera Minora* [Oxford, 1975]). James Rives (Oxford, 1999) provides a translation and outstanding commentary. François Hartog, *The Mirror of Herodotus: The Representation of the Other in the Writing of History* (Berkeley, Calif., 1988) (French rev. ed., Paris, 2001), pt. 1, and Paul Cartledge, *The Greeks: A Portrait of Self and Others*, 2nd ed. (Oxford, 2002), 51–77, are both brilliant explorations of Herodotus' Greek-centered worldview. Herodotus, *Histories* 4.46–47, 59–82, and 110–17, describes the Scythians; 4.16–36 and 100–9, the strange peoples who live on the steppes beyond; 3.99, the Padaei. Homer, *Odyssey* 9, narrates the Greeks' confrontation with Polyphemus.

CHAPTER THREE: A BACKWARD STEPPE

Hun customs and social organization—especially as presented by Roman historians—are best understood within the wider physical and economic constraints imposed by life on the Eurasian steppes. See the essays in Wolfgang Weissleder, ed., *The Nomadic Alternative: Modes and Models of Interaction in the African-Asian Deserts and Steppes* (The Hague, 1978); Antal Bartha, "The Typology of Nomadic Empires," in *Popoli delle Steppe: Unni, Avari, Ungari*, Settimane di studio del Centro italiano di studi sull'alto Medioevo 35, 2 vols. (Spoleto, 1988), 1: 151–79; and the impressively wide-ranging comparative study by Anatoly Khazanov, *Nomads and the Outside World*, 2nd ed. (Madison, Wisc., 1994) (first published in Russian in 1983). The archaeological evidence for cranial deformation is carefully surveyed in Anke, *Reiternomadischen Kultur*, 1: 124–36, and Luc Buchet, "La déformation crânienne en Gaule et dans les régions limitrophes pendant le haut Moyen Age son origine—sa valeur historique," *Archéologie médiévale* 18 (1988): 55–71. The "practical" aspects—of what is here presented as a process of beautification—are attractively illustrated by Maria Teschler-Nicola and Philipp Mitteröcher, "Von künstlicher Kopfformung," in *Attila und die Hunnen*, 270–81. The incidence of cranial deformation in Europe in the fourth and fifth centuries offers solid evidence of the intrusion of a steppe practice. Its association with the Huns is more problematic. Joachim Werner, *Beiträge zur Archäologie des Attila-Reiches* (Munich, 1956), 5–18, was overly hasty in arguing that it was an index of the Huns' steady advance from the Black Sea to France. There are four main complications. First, it is clear that cranial deformation is widespread among steppe nomads; it may well have been practiced by the Huns, but certainly not exclusively. Second, cranial deformation was already established north of the Black Sea in the first and second centuries, well before the westward migration of the Huns. It is known, for example, among the Alans who came into violent contact with the Huns in the fourth century and in the 360s fought as their allies against the Goths (Ammianus 31.3.1). Cranial deformation in Europe may, then, be an indication of the intrusive presence of Alans as plausibly as Huns or (most likely) indistinguishably both. Third, it is not clear how common cranial deformation was among the Huns. If it was intended to mark out an elite group or was viewed as beautiful, then Attila, his wives, relatives, and advisers might be thought to be likely candidates. The eyewitness description of Attila and his high-ranking retinue by the Roman historian Priscus of Panium never mentions anything as striking as cranial deformation (see above, chap. 14, p. 171). Fourth, the practice continued in Europe well beyond the fifth century and the dissolution of the Hun empire, an indication that—if it had ever been—it was now unlikely to be a trait that had any direct associations with Hun culture or conquest. The Mongol prohibition on the washing of clothes is cited in Paul Ratchnevsky, *Genghis Khan: His Life and Legacy* (Oxford, 1991), 193. The observations on raw meat by Hans Schiltberger are from his own account of his travels, Valentin Langmantel, ed., *Hans Schiltbergers Reisebuch* (Tübingen, 1885), chap. 37 (trans. J. Buchan Telfer, *The Bondage and Travels of Johann Schiltberger, a Native of Bavaria, in Europe, Asia, and Africa, 1396–1427* [London, 1879], 48). Finds of Hun cauldrons are listed in Anke, *Reiternomadischen Kultur*, 1: 48–55, adding to the surveys in Maenchen-Helfen, *Huns*, 306–18, and Bóna, *Hunnenreich*, 240–42 and 275 (for Törtel-Czakóhalom). The rock drawings from Minusinsk were published by M. A. Dévlet in *Sovetskaia Arkheologiia* 3 (1965): 124–42, at 128–29, figs. 3–6. Khazanov, *Nomads and the Outside World*, 15–84, provides a fascinating account of the pastoral economy of nomads and the limitations imposed by the ecology of the Eurasian steppes. For a detailed discussion of the Hun horse, see Maenchen-Helfen, *Huns*, 203–14; Vegetius' description is from his *Handbook on Equine Medicine* (*Mulomedicina*

2.Prologue and 3.6.5, ed. Ernest Lommatzsch [Leipzig, 1903]). The information on Hun bows in Maenchen-Helfen, *Huns*, 221–32, is expanded and updated in Anke, *Reiternomadischen Kultur*, 1: 55–65. The effectiveness of the Egyptian composite bow is discussed by Wallace McLeod, "The Range of the Ancient Bow," *Phoenix* 19 (1965): 1–14, and *Composite Bows from the Tomb of Tutankhamun* (Oxford, 1970), 37. Taibugha's remarks on bow manufacture are quoted from his *Essential Archery for Beginners*, translated in John Latham and William Paterson, *Saracen Archery: An English Version and Exposition of a Mameluke Work on Archery* (London, 1970), 8. On Hun battle tactics, see the useful observations in Thompson, *Huns*, 58–60, with Ammianus 31.2.9 on the use of the lasso. The problem faced by nomads disposing of a surplus in an undiversified economy is part of a wider pattern of regular contact between nomads and settled communities elaborated in Khazanov, *Nomads and the Outside World*, 202–12. See Ammianus 31.2.1 for his speculation on the origin of the Huns. For excellent introductions to the Xiongnu, see Ying-shih Yü, "The Hsiung-nu," in Sinor, ed., *Cambridge History of Early Inner Asia*, 118–49, and "Han Foreign Relations," in Denis Twitchett and Michael Loewe, eds., *The Cambridge History of China*, vol. 1, *The Ch'in and Han Empires, 221 B.C.–A.D. 220* (Cambridge, 1986), 377–462, at 383–421. The arguments in favor of a connection between Huns and Xiongnu were efficiently summarized and effectively rebutted by Otto Maenchen-Helfen, "Huns and Hsiung-nu," *Byzantion* 17 (1944–45): 222–43, quoting 243 on the Ordos bronzes, and *Huns*, 367–75; see, too, the levelheaded conclusions of Ursula Brosseder, "Zur Archäologie der Xiongnu," in *Attila und die Hunnen*, 62–73. For the excavations at Ivolga, see Antonina Davydova, "The Ivolga Gorodishche (A Monument of the Hiung-nu Culture in the Trans-Baikal Region)," *Acta Archaeologica Academiae Scientiarum Hungaricae* 20 (1968): 209–45, and *Ivolginskii arkheologicheskii kompleks II: Ivolginskii mogil'nik* (The Ivolga archaeological complex II: The Ivolga cemetery) (St. Petersburg, 1996).

CHAPTER FOUR: ROMANS AND BARBARIANS

The history of the Goths from Adrianople to their settlement in France in 418 is reviewed in Wolfram, *Goths*, 117–71; Demougeot, *La formation de l'Europe*, 143–78, and 2: 450–72; Halsall, *Barbarian Migrations*, 180–217; Stein, *Bas-Empire*, 191–267; Heather, *Goths and Romans*, 147–224, reworked in *Goths*, 135–51, *CAH* 13: 507–15, and *Fall*, 182–250; Alan Cameron, *Claudian: Poetry and Propaganda at the Court of Honorius* (Oxford, 1970), 63–188;

and Alan Cameron and Jacqueline Long, *Barbarians and Politics at the Court of Arcadius*, (Berkeley, Calif., 1993), 301–36. The best account of the political impact of Stilicho and Alaric on the court at Ravenna is John Matthews, *Western Aristocracies and Imperial Court, A.D. 364–425* (Oxford, 1975), 253–306. Maenchen-Helfen, *Huns*, 29, doubts the Huns' involvement at the Battle of Adrianople. See Ammianus 31.15.2–15 for the failed attack on the city of Adrianople and 31.16.3–7 for the bloody defense of Constantinople. Themistius' artful misrepresentation of Theodosius' peace settlement in 382 is *Oration* 16.211a–b. Odotheus' failed attempt to cross the Rhine is reported in Zosimus 4.35.1 and 4.38–39. The Hun raids across the Danube in 395 are mentioned in Philostorgius 11.8 with Wolfram, *Goths*, 139–40, and Demougeot, *La formation de l'Europe* 1: 389–90. Heather, *Goths and Romans*, 201, and *CAH* 13: 502 (following Maenchen-Helfen, *Huns*, 53), doubts that these raids took place: Philostorgius was only making a general point (not referring to a specific incident), and it is unlikely that the Huns would have been able to cross the Danube and the Caucasus in the same year. But if the Huns in the late fourth century were not a solid mass moving slowly westward under a unified leadership, then it is possible to envisage war bands moving independently east and west, particularly if the main concentration of Huns was still north of the Black Sea. For the Huns' eastern campaign, see Maenchen-Helfen, *Huns*, 51–59; Eutropius' military successes are sneered at by Claudian, *Against Eutropius* 1: 234–86 (ed. John Hall [Leipzig, 1985]; trans. Maurice Platnauer, Loeb Classical Library [Cambridge, Mass., 1922]); see Cameron, *Claudian*, 125. Jerome's lament in *Letter* 60.16 quoting *Aeneid* 6.625–27 (ed. Isidore Hilberg [Vienna, 1910]; trans. Frederick Wright, Loeb Classical Library [Cambridge, Mass., 1933]). The late seventh-century apocalyptic sermon—attributed to the fourth-century poet and preacher Ephrem—survives in Syriac, the language of Christians in Syria and northern Mesopotamia: Edmund Beck, ed., *Des Heiligen Ephraem des Syrers: Sermones III*, Corpus Scriptorum Christianorum Orientalium, Scriptores Syri 138/39, *Sermon* 5.281–88. Uldin's activities in the East are reported in Zosimus 5.22.1–3; his alliance with Stilicho and the defeat of Radagaisus, in Zosimus 5.26.3–5, Marcellinus 406.2–3, *Chron. Gall. 452* 50–52, and Jordanes, *Rom.* 321; the Rhine crossing of the Vandals and Alans, in Prosper 1230; the devastation in France, in *Chron. Gall. 452* 55 and 63. None of these brief ancient accounts offers any indication of the motivation of Radagaisus' Goths or the Vandals and Alans in entering the empire. It is important to emphasize that both are more than invading armies; they were accompanied by large numbers of women and children—at a rough estimate, the Vandals and Alans may have totaled 100,000 people. These are entire societies on the move. The suggestion that the Rhine crossings can be linked to the disruption caused by the westward advance of the Huns has been most fully argued by Peter Heather, "The Huns and the End of the Roman Empire in Western Europe," *English Historical Review* 110 (1995): 4–41, at 11–19. Walter Goffart, *Barbarian Tides: The Migration Age and the Later Roman Empire* (Philadelphia, 2006), 73–118, especially 75–78, makes the minimalist case: because the Huns are not mentioned by any ancient author, they cannot fairly be regarded as a factor. I am not persuaded. Goffart offers two alternative motives: the failure of the Roman empire to maintain its frontier defenses and the success of Alaric's Goths. The first is more a consequence than a cause of the Rhine crossings. In any case, weak defenses might explain an invasion force (such as the Huns in the 440s), but the movement of people is a more substantial event. The Goths might have looked successful in the decade after Adrianople; but given that they were shunted from East to West in 401 and held to a stalemate by Stilicho, it is not clear that Alaric's experience would have seemed worthy of imitation. The reasons suggested by Goffart were certainly important: but to my mind they are not sufficient to explain the highly risky movement of large numbers across the Rhine frontier. The Vandals were successful (see above, chap. 7, pp. 88–90), but Radagaisus and his followers, in part thanks to Uldin's Huns, were wiped out. Jerome's lament on the fall of Rome is from the prologue to his commentary on the Old Testament prophet Ezekiel; the biblical quotation is Psalm 39.2 (ed. François Glorie, Corpus Christianorum Series, Latina 75 [Turnhout, 1964]). For the Goths in France, see Thomas Burns, "The Settlement of 418," in John Drinkwater and Hugh Elton, eds., *Fifth-Century Gaul: A Crisis of Identity?* (Cambridge, 1992), 53–63, and Michael Kulikowski, "The Visigothic Settlement in Aquitania: The Imperial Perspective," in Ralph Mathisen and Danuta Shanzer, eds., *Society and Culture in Late Antique Gaul: Revisiting the Sources* (Aldershot, 2001), 26–38. The defensive advantages of Ravenna are surveyed in Neil Christie and Sheila Gibson, "The City Walls of Ravenna," *Papers of the British School at Rome* 56 (1988): 156–97. For the cultivation of asparagus, see Pliny, *Natural History* 19.54.

CHAPTER FIVE: HOW THE WEST WAS WON

The political transformation of Hun society on the Great Hungarian Plain is thoughtfully discussed in Thompson, *Huns*, 177–95; Demougeot, *La for-*

mation de l'Europe, 2: 530–53; Heather, *Goths*, 109–10, and *CAH* 13: 506–7, reprised in *Fall*, 326–29; and from a defiantly Marxist standpoint by János Harmatta, "The Dissolution of the Hun Empire I," *Acta Archaeologica Academiae Scientiarum Hungaricae* 2 (1952): 277–304, at 288–96. The economic constraints (and advantages) of the Great Hungarian Plain, and its limited grazing capacity, are explored in Rudi Lindner, "Nomadism, Horses and Huns," *Past and Present* 92 (1981): 3–19, and Denis Sinor, "Horse and Pasture in Inner Asian History," *Oriens extremus* 19 (1972): 171–83 (= *Inner Asia and Its Contacts with Medieval Europe*, Variorum reprints 57 [London, 1977], no. 2). For "steppe" diadems, see Anke, *Reiternomadischen Kultur*, 1: 31–41; Bóna, *Hunnenreich*, 147–49; and Ilona Kovrig, "Das Diadem von Csorna," *Folia Archaeologica* 36 (1985): 107–45. The finds from Pannonhalma are described in detail by Peter Tomka, "Der Hunnische Fürstenfund von Pannonhalma," *Acta Archaeologica Academiae Scientiarum Hungaricae* 38 (1986): 423–88. On the archaeological difficulty of locating the Huns, see Bóna, *Hunnenreich*, 134–39, and the (at times rather optimistic) discussions in Michel Kazanski, "Les Goths et les Huns: À propos des relations entre les barbares sédentaires et les nomades," *Archéologie médiévale* 22 (1992): 191–221, and Mark Ščukin, Michel Kazanski, and Oleg Sharov, *Des les Goths aux Huns: Le nord de la mer noire au Bas-Empire et à l'epoque des grandes migrations* (Oxford, 2006), 105–97. The clearest introductions to the complexities of Gothic archaeology are Michel Kazanski, *Les Goths (Iᵉʳ–VIIᵉ après J.-C.)* (Paris, 1991), especially 66–87; Heather, *Goths*, 18–25 and 68–93; and Kulikowski, *Rome's Gothic Wars*, 60–70. *Anda* and the *nöker* system are explained by David Morgan, *The Mongols*, 2nd ed. (Oxford, 2007), 34–35. Uldin's failed attack on the eastern empire in 408 is reported in Sozomen 9.5. Roger Blockley, *The Fragmentary Classicising Historians of the Later Roman Empire*, 2 vols. (Leeds, 1981–83), 1: 27–47, and John Matthews, "Olympiodorus of Thebes and the History of the West (A.D. 407–425)," *Journal of Roman Studies* 60 (1970): 79–97 (= *Political Life and Culture in Late Roman Society*, Variorum reprints 217 [London, 1983], no. 3), both offer sympathetic appreciations of Olympiodorus and his project. His history survives only in the précis of the ninth-century Byzantine bishop and bibliophile Photius. Given Photius' low estimate of Olympiodorus' intellectual merits, it is not clear why he bothered to summarize the text; see Photius, *Bibliotheca* 80 (ed. René Henry [Paris, 1959]; trans. Nigel Wilson [London, 1994]). See Olympiodorus 19 for the eight-line note on his embassy to the Huns, with Maenchen-Helfen, *Huns*, 73–74. See Olympiodorus 35 for the praise of his performing parakeet. The bird was perhaps *psittacula eupatria* (the Alexandrine parakeet) or *psittacula cyanocephala* (the plum-headed parakeet), both brought back to the Mediterranean from India by Alexander the Great.

CHAPTER SIX: A TALE OF TWO CITIES

Arcadius' death is noted briefly in Marcellinus 408.3, Theophanes 5901, Socrates 6.23.7, and Sozomen 9.1.1. There is no mention of his funeral. In imagining the ceremonies, I have drawn on two accounts: the funeral of Constantine in 337 as reported in Eusebius, *Life of Constantine* 4.66 and 70–71, Socrates 1.40.1–2, and Sozomen 2.34.5–6; and the funeral of Justinian in 565 as celebrated by the poet Corippus writing in honor of the new emperor Justin II (*In laudem Iustini Augusti Minoris* 3.1–61, ed. and trans. Averil Cameron [London, 1976]), with the helpful discussion in Sabine MacCormack, *Art and Ceremony in Late Antiquity* (Berkeley, Calif., 1981), 116–21 and 150–58. For Anthemius' career, see Martindale, *Prosopography*, 93–95; he is praised by Socrates 7.1.3. The involvement of Yazdgard in securing the succession is reported (among other competing versions) in Procopius, *Persian Wars* 1.2.1–10, and Theophanes 5900. I follow Roger Blockley, *East Roman Foreign Policy: Formation and Conduct from Diocletian to Anastasius* (Leeds, 1992), 48–52, in understanding it as part of a series of diplomatic exchanges between Constantinople and Ctesiphon initiated by Arcadius—who, according to Procopius, made his last request of Yazdgard from his deathbed. Geoffrey Greatrex and Jonathan Bardill, "Antiochus the Praepositus: A Persian Eunuch at the Court of Theodosius II," *Dumbarton Oaks Papers* 50 (1996): 171–97, at 172–80, suggest that, given the inconsistencies in the various accounts, it is plausible that the request might have been made as early as January 402, when the nine-month-old Theodosius was formally made co-emperor. *Theodosian Code* 7.17.1 preserves the authorization for the refitting of the Danube fleet. The most important survey of the Theodosian Walls remains Bruno Meyer-Plath and Alfons Schneider, *Die Landmauer von Konstantinopel* (Berlin, 1943), usefully supplemented by Janin, *Constantinople byzantine*, 265–83. It is unlikely that the moat could be flooded, although some sections were designed to catch and retain rainwater. The leaseback arrangement is set out in *Theodosian Code* 15.1.51. The best guide for walking the walls is Jane Taylor, *Imperial Istanbul: A Traveller's Guide*, rev. ed., (London, 1998), 27–38. Honorius' death is recorded in Olympiodorus 39.1 and Philostorgius 12.13. Stewart Oost, *Galla Placidia Augusta: A Biographical Essay* (Chicago, 1968), provides a detailed and well-judged account of its important subject; see 142–68 (marriage to Constantius) and 169–93 (exile and restoration). Events in Constantinople and Ravenna are related in Olympiodorus 33, 38, 39, and 43, Socrates 7.23–24 (for the shepherd), Hydatius 73–75, Prosper 1280–89, Procopius, *Vandal Wars* 3.3.8–9, and Philostorgius 12.12–14. Aetius' support of John is discussed in detail by Giuseppe Zecchini, *Aezio: L'ultima difesa dell'occidente romano* (Rome, 1983), 125–40, and Timo Stickler, *Aëtius: Gestalungsspielräume eines Heermeisters im ausgehenden Weströmischen Reich* (Munich, 2002), 25–35. His mission to the Huns and late arrival in Italy is reported in Philostorgius 12.14, Prosper 1288, and Gregory of Tours 2.8, quoting the now lost fifth-century historian Renatus Frigeridus (see Martindale, *Prosopography*, 485–86). Gregory's information on Aetius' family and his early life as well as the description of his appearance and character are all based on Renatus. Aetius was born sometime around 390, see Martindale, *Prosopography*, 21, and Zecchini, *Aezio*, 116. For Gaudentius' career, see Martindale, *Prosopography*, 493–94; his death is noted in *Chron. Gall. 452* 100. The dating of Aetius' time with the Huns is uncertain. According to Renatus, Aetius also spent three years as a hostage with Alaric. I follow the careful discussion in Zecchini, *Aezio*, 120–24, arguing that Aetius is most likely to have spent 405–7 with the Goths and to have been sent to the Huns at some point between 409 and 416. Honorius' levy of Hun mercenaries in summer 409 seems to offer a suitable context for the sending of hostages. How long Aetius spent beyond the Danube is unknown.

CHAPTER SEVEN: WAR ON THREE FRONTS

Abdaas' incendiary activities are related in Theophanes 5906 and Theodoret 5.39.1–5. The Persian War of 421–22 is discussed in detail in Blockley, *Foreign Policy*, 56–58; Omert Schrier, "Syriac Evidence for the Roman-Persian War of 421–422," *Greek, Roman and Byzantine Studies* 33 (1992): 75–86; Kenneth Holum, "Pulcheria's Crusade A.D. 421–22 and the Ideology of Imperial Victory," ibid. 18 (1977): 153–72, and *Theodosian Empresses: Women and Imperial Dominion in Late Antiquity*, (Berkeley, Calif., 1982), 102–11 and 121–23. The requisition order for the towers in the Theodosian Walls is at *Theodosian Code* 7.8.13. Robert Demangel, *Contribution à la topographie de l'Hebdomon* (Paris, 1945), 33–40, includes a detailed study of the remains of Theodosius' victory column and its inscription. The laconic notice on the Hun incursion is quoted from Marcellinus 422.3. The sequence and dating of the Hun attacks on the eastern Roman empire in the 420s and 430s are uncertain. I follow the elegant solution to a number of difficult problems proposed by Constantin Zuckerman, "L'empire d'Orient et les Huns: Notes sur Priscus," *Travaux et Mémoires byzantines* 12 (1994): 159–82, at 159–63. Zuckerman clearly distinguishes three episodes: 422, 434 (Rua's death), and 439 (peace talks at Margum; see above, chap. 9, pp. 117–18). For a radically different reconstruction, see Brian Croke, "Evidence for the Hun Invasion of Thrace in A.D. 422," *Greek, Roman and Byzantine Studies* 18 (1977): 347–67 (= *Christian Chronicles and Byzantine History, 5th–6th Centuries*, Variorum reprints 386 [Aldershot, 1992], no. 12). I agree with Croke, 351–52, that the previous treaty provisions mentioned in Priscus 2, including the payment of 350 pounds of gold, relate to the peace settlement in 422. Given the circumstances of the Hun withdrawal after Rua's unexpected death in 434, it seems unlikely that there were any formal negotiations at that point, and not until Margum in 439. The order of events for the 420s and 430s presented in this chapter and following leads to a different understanding of the relationship between Huns and Romans—and the strategic connections with North Africa and France—to that advanced (for example) in Thompson, *Huns*, 69–86, Maenchen-Helfen, *Huns*, 76–94, and Bóna, *Hunnenreich*, 46–56. For the Vandal push into North Africa, see the discussions in Walter Pohl, "The Vandals: Fragments of a Narrative," in Andrew Merrills, ed., *Vandals, Romans and Berbers: New Perspectives on Late Antique North Africa* (Aldershot, 2004), 31–47, at 38–41; Stein, *Bas-Empire*, 319–21, and Christian Courtois, *Les Vandales et l'Afrique* (Paris, 1955), 155–71. The Hun invasion of 434 is reported in *Chron. Gall. 452* 112, Theodoret 5.37.4, and Socrates 7.43, citing Proclus' sermon on Ezekiel 38–39.

CHAPTER EIGHT: BROTHERS IN ARMS

The accession of Attila and Bleda following Rua's death is noted in Jordanes, *Getica* 180. The expansion of the Hun empire under Rua and Bleda is helpfully discussed in Maenchen-Helfen, *Huns*, 81–85. The tribes pressured by Rua are listed in Priscus 2; Jordanes, *Getica* 126, associates them with the Huns' earlier westward progress from the steppes. Octar's defeat by the Burgundians is piously reported in Socrates 7.30. The extent of the Hun empire under Attila and Bleda is discussed in Thompson, *Huns*, 83–85, with doubts in Maenchen-Helfen, *Huns*, 125–26. The archaeological evidence—which may suggest transcontinental trading contacts rather than conquest—is surveyed in Jan Bemman, "Hinweise auf Kontakte zwischen dem hunnischen Herrschaftsbereich in Südosteuropa und dem Norden," in *Attila und die Hunnen*, 176–83. The Pietroasa treasure is now on display in the National Museum of Romanian History in Bucharest. The objects were described in detail in a magnificent three-volume work by the Romanian historian and politician Alexandru Odobescu, *Le trésor de Pétrossa, historique, description: Étude sur l'orfèverie antique* (Paris, 1889–1900; reprinted as *Opere IV: Tezaurul de la Pietroasa*, Bucharest, 1976, 44–735). Odobescu 3: 15–26 argued that the treasure had been buried by the Tervingi leader Athanaric sometime before his death in 381. Recent studies have suggested that on stylistic grounds the treasure dates to the fifth century and was probably buried sometime around 450, perhaps as a response to the breakup of the Hun empire (see above, chap. 24, pp. 267–70); see Radu Harhoiu, *The Fifth-Century A.D. Treasure from Pietroasa, Romania, in the Light of Recent Research* (Oxford, 1977), especially 7–18 (descriptions) and 31–35 (historical context). Ecaterina Dunăreanu-Vulpe, *Le trésor de Pietroasa* (Bucharest, 1967), is useful for its descriptions (15–44) and especially for the account of the modern history of the treasure (7–13), following Odobescu, *Le trésor*, 1: 1–68. The patera (shallow bowl) and its iconography are treated in detail by Madeleine von Heland, *The Golden Bowl from Pietroasa* (Stockholm, 1973), identifying (at 71–74) Antioch as a possible place of manufacture, and Gerda Schwarz, "Der Götterfries auf der spätantiken Goldschale von Pietroasa," *Jahrbuch für Antike und Christentum* 35 (1992): 168–84, proposing Alexandria. The treasure has been extensively restored. The great eagle brooch, when recovered from the dealer Anastase Vérussi, was in at least two pieces, with its precious stones removed. Major restoration was carried out in Paris before the treasure was displayed at the Universal Exhibition of 1867; before then, Odobescu, *Le trésor*, 1: 41, specifically notes, the head and body were separate. Immediately after the Paris exhibition, the treasure was put on public view for six months at the South Kensington (now Victoria and Albert) Museum in London. The Arundel Society for Promoting the Knowledge of Art commissioned a portfolio of photographs of the objects "for the use of Schools of Art and Amateurs": Richard Soden Smith, *The Treasure of Petrossa* (London, 1869). The photograph (plate 8) of the eagle brooch shows three significant differences from its current state: the head is turned slightly to the left (it now looks straight ahead); there is no "collar" extending from the last row of heart-shaped perforations on the neck to the breast; and there are two (not four) rock-crystal pendants hanging from the tail (see figures 14 [p. 98] and 35). These changes were made following damage to the brooch in the robbery of December 1875. The treasure was shown January–March 1971 in London at the British Museum's special exhibition "Treasures from Romania."

Following that exhibition, David Brown, "The Brooches in the Pietroasa Treasure," *Antiquity* 46 (1972): 111–16, suggested that in the repairs carried out during the nineteenth century the eagle brooch had been incorrectly restored. If the brooch was worn on the shoulder, as seems likely given its size, the curve of the body, and the pendants at the tail, then, as currently positioned, the eagle's head is arguably the wrong way around—its beak points straight up in the air rather than out across the wearer's shoulder. Harhoiu 18 accepts that the brooch is to be worn on the shoulder, registers Brown's suggestion, but offers no comment. The restoration has not been altered. For the site of Pietroasa, see Gheorghe Diaconu, "L'ensemble archéologique de Pietroasele," *Dacia* 21 (1977): 199–220, at 199–206. Maenchen-Helfen, *Huns*, 267–96, offers a fascinating—and unapologetically speculative—discussion of Hun religion.

figure 35
Nineteenth-century restoration of the eagle brooch from the Pietroasa treasure.

Thompson, *Huns*, 42–45, and Maenchen-Helfen, *Huns*, 260–67, for the Huns' hostile attitude to Christianity. Nestorius' challenge to Theodosius is quoted in Socrates 7.29.5; the story of the invisible bishop of Tomi is told in Sozomen 7.26.6–8. The finding of the war god's sword is recounted in Jordanes, *Getica* 183, explicitly citing Priscus as the source. For literary parallels, see Herodotus, *Histories* 4.62, and Ammianus 31.2.23. The sword from Pannonhalma is described in Tomka, "Der Hunnische Fürstenfund," 433–43, and Bóna, *Hunnenreich*, 279. The story of Zercon survives in the tenth-century encyclopaedia, the *Souda* Z 29 (ed. Ada Adler [Leipzig, 1928–38]). The information most probably derives from Priscus; see Blockley, *Fragmentary Classicising Historians*, 1: 118.

CHAPTER NINE: FIGHTING FOR ROME

The story of Aetius' plot to discredit Boniface is related in Procopius, *Vandal Wars* 3.3.14–30, followed by Theophanes 5931. There are other versions (Prosper 1294 does not mention Aetius), but no sure way of selecting between them. Rather than attempt a compromise—which might, of course, turn out to be the least accurate version—I have followed

Procopius. For discussion see John O'Flynn, *Generalissimos of the Western Roman Empire* (Edmonton, 1983), 77–81; Martindale, *Prosopography*, 23; Oost, *Galla Placidia*, 220–24; Heather, *CAH* 14: 5–6; Zecchini, *Aezio*, 146–50; and Stickler, *Aëtius*, 44–48. Galla's attempts to exploit the rivalry between Aetius and Boniface are noted in Hydatius 89 and *Chron. Gall. 452* 109 with Oost, *Galla Placidia*, 227–35; Zecchini, *Aezio*, 159–65; Stickler, *Aëtius*, 54–58; and Martindale, *Prosopography*, 22–24 and 239–40. The allegation that Aetius lengthened his lance before the battle at Ariminum is made in Marcellinus 432.3. Both Prosper 1310 and *Chron. Gall. 452* 112 note Aetius' appeal to Rua and his offer of help. The number of Hun troops that accompanied Aetius back to Italy is unknown. There is no record that any battle was ever fought. I follow the suggestion in Oost, *Galla Placidia*, 234, and Maenchen-Helfen, *Huns*, 87, that what really mattered was Aetius' threat of an invasion. There is no clear-cut solution to the problem of when part of Pannonia and Valeria were ceded to the Huns. I follow the carefully argued conclusion of Maenchen-Helfen, *Huns*, 87–90 (applauded by Stickler, *Aëtius*, 108), that the deal was made not with Rua but with Attila (for an opposing view, see Zecchini, *Aezio*, 161–63). Priscus 11, who reports the exchange with the Huns without mentioning either Rua or Attila, affirms that it was the result "of a treaty concluded with Aetius." I suggest that such an arrangement makes good sense in the context of Aetius' success in persuading Attila and Bleda to support Roman interests in France. There is no straightforward account of the campaigns of the Romans and their Hun allies in the 430s, only a series of scattered and often frustratingly brief notices in the chronicles. The most important are Hydatius 102, *Chron. Gall. 452* 118, and Prosper 1322 on the Burgundians; *Chron. Gall. 452* 117 and 119 on the Bagaudae (see above, chap. 22, pp. 245–46); Hydatius 108 and Prosper 1324 and 1335, on Litorius before Narbonne and Toulouse. The most useful modern discussions are Stein, *Bas-Empire*, 322–24; Maenchen-Helfen, *Huns*, 95–107; Thompson, *Huns*, 72–79; Heather, *CAH* 14: 7–10; Halsall, *Barbarian Migrations*, 242–47; Wolfram, *Goths*, 175–76, and Zecchini, *Aezio*, 212–22. The ritual of scapulimancy is described in Jordanes, *Getica* 196, and discussed in Maenchen-Helfen, *Huns*, 269–70. The warnings of Salvian of Marseille are taken from his polemical social critique *On the Governance of God* (*de Gubernatione Dei* 7.39, ed. Georges Lagarrigue [Paris, 1975]; trans. Jeremiah O'Sullivan [Washington, D.C., 1947]), quoting the Gospel of Luke 14.11.

CHAPTER TEN: SHOCK AND AWE

The fall of Carthage is lamented in Prosper 1339; see Stein, *Bas-Empire*, 1: 324–25. See *Chron. Pasch.* 439 with Dagron, *Naissance d'une capitale*, 270, and Janin, *Constantinople byzantine*, 294, for the extension of the sea walls in Constantinople; the regulations for the improved defense of Rome issued in March 440 are set out in an imperial law collected in the *New Laws of Valentinian* (Valentinian III, *Novellae* 5.2–4; ed. Theodor Mommsen and Paul Meyer [Berlin, 1905]; trans. Clyde Pharr, *The Theodosian Code and Sirmondian Constitutions* [Princeton, 1952], 515–50); the announcement of the sailing of the Vandal fleet is *Novellae* 9. Theodosius' armada and the expedition to Sicily are noted in Prosper 1344 and Theophanes 5941–42. As with Aetius' campaigns in France in the 430s, there is no surviving narrative history of the Huns' attacks on the eastern empire in the 440s. The sequence of events must be jigsawed together from the notices in the chronicles and the fragmentary text of Priscus (see above, chap. 13, pp. 151–52. I have followed the chronology suggested in Zuckerman, "L'empire Orient," 164–68, building on Maenchen-Helfen, *Huns*, 112–16; Blockley, *Fragmentary Classicising Historians*, 1: 168–69 n. 48 (but see *Foreign Policy*, 62); Brian Croke, "Anatolius and Nomus: Envoys to Attila," *Byzantinoslavica* 42 (1981): 159–70, at 159–63 (= *Christian Chronicles*, no. 13), and "The Context and Date of Priscus Fragment 6," *Classical Philology* 78 (1983): 297–308 (= *Christian Chronicles*, no. 14). There are four propositions on which this reconstruction rests. First, that Priscus 9.3, which deals with Anatolius and Nomus' negotiations with Attila, should be dated to 447 and not 443; second, that there were no peace negotiations in either 442 or 443; third, that the first Hun invasion should be dated to 441–42; and, fourth, that Theophanes 5942 telescopes into his summary of 449 events that occurred across the preceding eight years. For examples of alternative readings, see William Bayless, "The Treaty with the Huns of 443," *American Journal of Philology* 97 (1976): 176–79, and Croke, "Anatolius and Nomus," 164–70, arguing for an embassy led by Nomus in 442. None of the standard, and in other respects extremely helpful, accounts of the Hun invasion of 440s take fully into account the revisions consolidated in Zuckerman; see, for example, Demougeot, *La formation de l'Europe*, 2: 534–40; Thompson, *Huns*, 86–95; Bóna, *Hunnenreich*, 61–72; Stephen Williams and Gerard Friell, *The Rome That Did Not Fall: The Survival of the East in the Fifth Century* (London, 1999), 63–81; and Heather, *Fall*, 300–12; but *CAH* 14: 41 (Doug Lee) and 704 (Michael Whitby). As with the campaigns in France in the 430s, any shift in the basic sequence of events has an impact on understandings of the broader pattern of strategic, political, and diplomatic considerations confronting both Romans and Huns. The most important ancient account is Priscus 2 (location of Constantia), 6.1 (attack on Constantia and tomb-raiding bishop of Margum), 6.2 (siege of Naissus), and 11.2 (the later visit to Naissus; see above, chap. 14, p. 166). Priscus does not name the Roman envoy at Margum in 441. I have speculated that it might have been Aspar on the basis of the brief notice in Marcellinus 441.1 that indicates he commanded troops in the Balkans in that year; see Martindale, *Prosopography*, 166, and Maenchen-Helfen, *Huns*, 116. I understand the one-year peace of 441–42 mentioned in Marcellinus to refer to the eastern frontier and not to Aspar's campaign. The suggestion that it refers to both (Brian Croke, *The Chronicle of Marcellinus* [Sydney, 1995], 85; Blockley, *Foreign Policy*, 61–62; and Martindale, *Prosopography*, 84–85 and 166), stretches Marcellinus' already ambiguous text too far. Priscus' description of the siege of Naissus is another fine example of the problematic representation of events by a self-consciously literary author eager to demonstrate his knowledge of the classics. Edward Thompson, "Priscus of Panium, Fragment 1b," *Classical Quarterly* 39 (1945): 92–94, doubts the historical value of Priscus' account of the siege; in Priscus' defense, Roger Blockley, "Dexippus and Priscus and the Thucydidean Account of the Siege of Plataea," *Phoenix* 26 (1972): 18–27, and Barry Baldwin, "Priscus of Panium," *Byzantion* 50 (1980): 18–61, at 53–56. The Huns' ability to take cities by siege is usefully discussed in Hugh Elton, *Warfare in Roman Europe, AD 350–425* (Oxford, 1996), 82–86. Only the main cities attacked are listed: Priscus 6.1 records Margum and Viminacium, 6.2 Naissus; Marcellinus 441.3 Singidunum and Naissus (thus establishing a context and date for Priscus 6.2). Following Maenchen-Helfen, *Huns*, 116, and Thompson, *Huns*, 89, the sacking of Sirmium, noted in Priscus 11.2 (see above, chap. 19, p. 220), can reasonably be added, since it lies at the head of the same marching route along the Sava River and through the Morava River valley. Marcellinus 442.2 reports that the Huns reached as far as Thrace; hence (as it also lies on the same route) I have followed Thompson, *Huns*, 92, and included Serdica mentioned in Priscus 11.2 (see above, chap. 14, p. 164). For the cruel impact of war on urban and rural communities, see the excellent discussion in Doug Lee, *War in Late Antiquity: A Social History* (Oxford, 2007), 133–41. The murder of Bleda is reported in Marcellinus 445.1; see also Jordanes, *Getica* 181, Prosper 1353, and *Chron. Gall. 452* 131.

CHAPTER ELEVEN: BARBARIANS AT THE GATES

The earthquake in 447 is reported in Marcellinus 447.1 (fifty-seven towers destroyed), Malalas 14.22, and *Chron. Pasch.* 450. Theophanes 5930 explains the origin of the Trisagion. I follow the understanding of these sometimes contradictory versions as worked out in an elegant essay by Brian Croke, "Two Byzantine Earthquakes and their Liturgical Commemoration," *Byzantion* 51 (1981): 122–47 (= *Christian Chronicles*, no. 9). Aristotle's understanding of earthquakes is set out in his *Meteorology* (*Meteorologica* 2.7–8; trans. Jonathan Barnes, ed., 2 vols. [Princeton, 1984], 1: 591–96). The sporting and political activities of the "circus factions" are discussed by Dagron, *Naissance d'une capitale*, 348–64, and in detail by Alan Cameron, *Circus Factions: Blues and Greens at Rome and Byzantium* (Oxford, 1976). Constantinus' achievement is noted by Marcellinus 447.3; the commemorative inscription is recorded in Janin, *Constantinople byzantine*, 278, and Meyer-Plath and Schneider, *Die Landmauer*, 133, no. 35. The notices in the chronicles for the invasion of 447 are disappointingly brief: Marcellinus 447.2 and 4–5 (no cities listed); *Chron. Gall. 452* 132 (no fewer than seventy cities, but none named) and Theophanes 5942 (compressing the Hun invasions of the 440s into a single entry). I have aimed to make the best of the ten cities and forts listed in Theophanes, who notes that these are just a selection from "very many others." I have excepted Naissus and Constantia as belonging to the campaign of 441–42. The remainder—Ratiaria (also mentioned in Priscus 9), Philippopolis, Arcadiopolis, Callipolis, Sestus, Athyras, Adrianople, and Heraclea—make coherent strategic sense in terms of an advance on Constantinople and the Roman army's attempts to impede it. For the walls of Adrianople, see Ammianus 31.15 (see above, chap. 4, p. 47); for Philippopolis, Ammianus 26.10.4. The Balkan landscape and its numerous fortified settlements are surveyed in a fascinating study by Ventzislav Dinchev, "The Fortresses of Thrace and Dacia in the Early Byzantine Period," in Andrew Poulter, ed., *The Transition to Late Antiquity: On the Danube and Beyond* (= *Proceedings of the British Academy* 141) (Oxford, 2007), 479–546.

CHAPTER TWELVE: THE PRICE OF PEACE

The terms of the peace negotiated by Anatolius are outlined in Priscus 9.3 and 11.1 (the evacuation of territory), along with the harsh criticism of Theodosius and the impact of his policy of appeasement. Zuckerman, "L'empire d'Orient," 168, suggests that the lump sum quoted by Priscus may have included the cost of ransoming POWs. The master of the offices, Nomus, may have been part of the delegation. This is no more than an inference. Croke, "Anatolius and Nomus," 166–67, makes the attractive suggestion that those senior courtiers declared acceptable as envoys by Attila in 449 (Priscus 13.1; see above, chap. 15, p. 182) were already known to him from previous embassies. Attila's list included Nomus, who certainly joined Anatolius in negotiations with Attila in 450 (Priscus 15.3; see above, chap. 18, p. 210); this was perhaps a reprise of their partnership three years earlier. For attempts to estimate the purchasing power of the solidus, see the examples collected in Jones, *Later Roman Empire*, 1: 445–48, and Evelyne Patlagean, *Pauvreté économique et pauvreté sociale à Byzance 4ᵉ–7ᵉ siècles* (Paris, 1977), 341–421. The costs for a fourth-century recruit are set out in *Theodosian Code* 7.13.7.2; the prices from Nessana, in Caspar Kraemer, *Excavations at Nessana III: Non-literary Papyri* (Princeton, 1958), no. 89. There are insufficient hard data to allow any certain reconstruction of the revenue of the Roman empire; using these fragile figures, I offer no more than a sighting shot following Jones, *Later Roman Empire*, 1: 462–65; Michael Hendy, *Studies in the Byzantine Monetary Economy c. 300–1450* (Cambridge, 1985), 157–60 and 164–78; and Elton, *Warfare in Roman Europe*, 119–20. If anything, the figure of 66,000 pounds of gold is likely to be low; Jones (at 1: 463) estimated the annual revenue from Egypt—the empire's wealthiest province—at 20,000 pounds. The taxation settlement in Numidia is set out in Valentinian III, *Novellae* 13. Senatorial wealth is helpfully estimated in Jones, *Later Roman Empire*, 2: 554–57 and 782–84; the figures quoted are from Olympiodorus 41.2. For the costs of war, see Elton, *Warfare in Roman Europe*, 120–27, and Lee, *War in Late Antiquity*, 105–6. Positive assessments of Theodosius' foreign policy are offered by Edward Thompson, "The Foreign Policies of Theodosius II and Marcian," *Hermathena* 76 (1950): 58–75, and *Huns*, 211–24; Blockley, *Foreign Policy*, 59–67, and Lee, *CAH* 14: 39–42. The use of subsidies in Roman diplomacy is helpfully discussed in C. D. Gordon, "Subsidies in Roman Imperial Defence," *Phoenix* 3 (1949): 60–69; Roger Blockley, "Subsidies and Diplomacy: Rome and Persia in Late Antiquity," *Phoenix* 39 (1985): 62–74; Hendy, *Byzantine Monetary Economy*, 257–64, and especially in the levelheaded analysis of Lee, *War in Late Antiquity*, 119–22. Zuckerman, "L'empire d'Orient," 169–72, suggests that Theodosius relieved both Aspar and Ariobindus of their posts in 447. Priscus 6.1 reports the designation of trading posts at Constantia, across the

river from Margum, and 11.1 at Naissus. Priscus 9.3 notes the execution of
Hun exiles by the Romans.

CHAPTER THIRTEEN: MISSION IMPOSSIBLE

For Constantine VII Porphyrogenitus' editorial projects, see Arnold Toyn-
bee, *Constantine Porphyrogenitus and His World* (London, 1973), 575–82; Paul
Lemerle, *Le premier humanisme byzantin: Notes et remarques sur enseignement
et culture à Byzance des origins au 10ᵉ siècle* (Paris, 1971), 274–88; and Carl de
Boor, "Die Excerptensammlungen des Konstantin Porphyrogennetos,"
Hermes 19 (1884): 123–48. The selection of excerpts on embassies is edited by
de Boor, *Excerpta de Legationibus* (Berlin, 1903). Together with three further
anthologies collecting examples of virtues and vices (*de Virtutibus et Vitiis*),
wise remarks (*de Sententiis*), and conspiracies (*de Insidiis*), roughly 3 percent
of Constantine's original project has survived. The most important discussion of Priscus of Panium is Blockley, *Fragmentary Classicising Historians*, 1:
48–70; see, too, Baldwin, "Priscus of Panium"; Thompson, *Huns*, 12–16;
Warren Treadgold, *The Early Byzantine Historians* (Basingstoke, Eng., 2007),
96–102; and Martindale, *Prosopography*, 906. On the exact title of Priscus'
history, its publication date, and contents, see Baldwin, "Priscus," 25–29,
and Blockley, *Fragmentary Classicising Historians*, 1: 49–52. For sophisticated
and sympathetic accounts of the Roman education system, see Raffaella
Cribiore, *Gymnastics of the Mind: Greek Education in Hellenistic and Roman
Egypt* (Princeton, 2001), and Teresa Morgan, *Literate Education in the Hellenistic and Roman Worlds* (Cambridge, 1995), with a discussion at 105–16 on
the popularity of Homer and Euripides. On Maximinus' career, see usefully
Martindale, *Prosopography*, 743. From Priscus' description (especially at 20),
I have presented Maximinus as a well-connected army officer; there is no
persuasive reason to follow Thompson, *Huns*, 113, or Baldwin, "Priscus,"
20–21, and conflate this military Maximinus with any of the legally trained
Maximini known to have worked in the 430s on the compilation of the
Theodosian Code. The account of Edeco's experiences in Constantinople is
based on Priscus 11.1; the preceding four Hun embassies are noted at 10.
The intricate formalities of court etiquette and their ideological importance
are discussed by Christopher Kelly, *CAH* 13: 139–50, and *Ruling the Later
Roman Empire*, 19–26, and Michael McCormick, *CAH* 14: 156–60; trousers
and garments made from animal skins are prohibited in *Theodosian Code*
14.10. For the ceremony of "adoring the purple" (*adoratio purpurae*), see
Theodosian Code 8.7.8, 9 and 16; W. T. Avery, "The *Adoratio Purpurae* and the

Importance of the Imperial Purple in the Fourth Century of the Christian Era," *Memoirs of the American Academy in Rome* 17 (1940): 66–80. For eunuchs at the Roman imperial court, the splendid essay by Keith Hopkins has not been bettered, *Conquerors and Slaves* (Cambridge, 1978), 172–96; see, too, Jacqueline Long, *Claudian's "In Eutropium," or How, When, and Why to Slander a Eunuch* (Chapel Hill, 1996), 107–46, and Shaun Tougher, *The Eunuch in Byzantine History and Society* (London, 2008).

CHAPTER FOURTEEN: CLOSE ENCOUNTERS

The most important treatment of Priscus' journey beyond the Danube by any modern scholar is Thompson, *Huns*, 108–36. Priscus' narrative is retold in Wolfram, *Germanic Peoples*, 130–36, and Heather, *Fall*, 313–24. The carelessness of Constantine's editorial team means that Priscus' now fragmentary text is not always coherent; sometimes the narrative stumbles, and the links between incidents are difficult to explain. In the reconstruction offered in this chapter, I have assumed that the dispute between Vigilas and Edeco at Serdica was staged. The alternative might be, as suggested by Thompson, *Huns*, 114, sheer tactlessness on Vigilas' part, perhaps the result of drunkenness. I have given Vigilas more credit. Nor is it clear (as assumed by Thompson, *Huns*, 115) that Edeco had already revealed the details of the assassination plot to Orestes. Orestes' remark to Priscus and Maximinus could equally well be the result of a well-judged suspicion. In the surviving text, Priscus never explains (or speculates on) how Attila came to know the contents of Theodosius' letter before it had been handed over by Maximinus. It seems consistent with the careful preparations made in Constantinople to imagine that the letter was shown to Edeco before he left—not least, if he were ever challenged, to give him a plausible justification for his private meetings with Chrysaphius. The narrative in this chapter is based on Priscus 11.2 with the exception of the description of Attila from Jordanes, *Getica* 182. Jordanes specifically notes (at 178) that this information comes from Priscus. Priscus' route after Naissus is difficult to follow; however, at 11.1 he clearly states that Naissus is a five-day journey from the Danube frontier. Thompson, *Huns*, 116, and Robert Browning, "Where was Attila's Camp?" *Journal of Hellenic Studies* 73 (1953): 143–45 (= *Studies on Byzantine History, Literature and Education*, Variorum reprints 59, [London, 1977], no. 2) both only allow a day's journey from Naissus to the frontier. On the basis of Priscus' journey time, I assume he traveled northwest from Naissus, remaining for five days within territory once part of the

Roman empire, and crossing the Danube near Margum or Viminacium; see, too, Blockley, *Fragmentary Classicising Historians*, 2: 382 n. 29.

CHAPTER FIFTEEN: EATING WITH THE ENEMY

The narrative is based on Priscus 11.2 and 13. Scottas' embassy to Constantinople in 447 is noted at 9.3. Priscus' vague geography makes it impossible to locate Attila's main residence; detailed discussions in Blockley, *Fragmentary Classicising Historians*, 2: 384 n. 43, and Thompson, *Huns*, 276–77. For a careful review of Priscus' descriptions of Attila's compound and the surrounding village, Edward Thompson, "The Camp of Attila," *Journal of Hellenic Studies* 65 (1945): 112–15. For Priscus' confusion about the seating plan and the ceremonies at Attila's feast, see Blockley, *Fragmentary Classicising Historians*, 2: 387–88 nn. 78–80. The evidence for the brewing of barley beer in the northern provinces of the Roman empire is surveyed in Max Nelson, *The Barbarian's Beverage: A History of Beer in Ancient Europe* (London, 2005), 1–3, 41–44, and 55–63. The beads found in the graves at Singidunum are catalogued, illustrated, and described in superb detail in Vujadin Ivanišević, Michel Kazanski, and Anna Mastykova, *Les necropoles de Viminacium à l'époque des grandes migrations* (Paris, 2006), 51–117. The excavation of the graves is reported in Vujadin Ivanišević and Michel Kazanski, "La nécropole de l'époque des grandes migrations à Singidunum," in Marko Popović, ed., *Singidunum* 3 (Belgrade, 2002): 101–57. The Şimleu Silvaniei treasure is presented in a magnificently illustrated catalogue published by the Kunsthistorisches Museum in Vienna for an exhibition in 1999: Wilfried Seipel, ed., *Barbarenschmuck und Römergold: Der Schatz von Szilágysomlyó*. For the fourth-century material as evidence of high-level contacts across the Danube, see Radu Harhoiu, "Die Medaillone aus dem Schatzfund von Şimleul Silvaniei," *Dacia* 37 (1993): 221–36, and Lenski, *Failure of Empire*, 347–48. For the dating of the concealment of the finds, see the discussion in the exhibition catalogue by Attila Kiss, "Historische Auswertung," 163–68, substantially revising his earlier views in "Der Zeitpunkt der Verbergung der Schatzfunde I und II von Szilágysomlyó," *Acta Antiqua Academiae Scientiarum Hungaricae* 30 (1982–84): 401–16. Kiss now argues for a date in the 440s, as a response by a local ruler to the expansion of the Hun empire; but as the latest objects in the treasure cannot be dated on stylistic grounds with any more precision than to the mid–fifth century, it is equally plausible—as has been suggested for the Pietroasa treasure—that the Şimleu Silvaniei treasure was buried in the 450s during the Hun empire's collapse (see above, chap. 24, pp. 267–70). If so, then some of the magnificent items manufactured in the Roman empire in the fifth century might represent the profitable results of cooperation with the Huns. The large silver plate (29 inches in diameter) known as the Missorium of Theodosius is discussed in MacCormack, *Art and Ceremony*, 214–21, and described in detail in Martín Almagro-Gorbea, ed., *El disco de Teodosio* (Madrid, 2000).

CHAPTER SIXTEEN: WHAT THE HISTORIAN SAW

Onegesius' bath building is described at Priscus 11.2. For a comprehensive introduction to Roman baths and bathing culture, see Fikret Yegül, *Baths and Bathing in Classical Antiquity* (New York, 1992), 30–47 and 314–49. The excavation of the private bath building in Sirmium is briefly reported in Noël Duval and Vladislav Popović, *Sirmium VII: Horrea et thermes aux abords du rempart sud* (Rome, 1977), 75–78. For excellent surveys of Roman dining practices in the fourth and fifth centuries, see Jeremy Rossiter, "Convivium and Villa in Late Antiquity," and Katherine Dunbabin, "Triclinium and Stibadium," in William Slater, ed., *Dining in a Classical Context* (Ann Arbor, Mich., 1991), 121–48 and 199–214. For an elegant exploration of the dining habits of the Roman elite, see Matthew Roller, *Dining Posture in Ancient Rome: Bodies, Values, and Status* (Princeton, 2006), with discussion at 84–95 on sitting and standing at dinner as expressions of an inferior social status. The use of chairs was common in cheap restaurants and pubs; see Tönnes Kleberg, *Hôtels, restaurants et cabarets dans l'antiquité romaine: Études historiques et philologiques* (Uppsala, 1957), 114–15. The grand luncheon at the villa of Tonantius Ferreolus is described in Sidonius, *Letters* 2.9. Priscus relates his meeting with the renegade Roman trader at 11.2; the staged nature of the debate and its philosophical and literary pretensions are noted in Blockley, *Fragmentary Classicising Historians*, 1: 55–59 and Baldwin, "Priscus," 40–41. In his account of the feast, Priscus uses a rare word, *kissybion*, for Attila's wooden cup. Some readers may have recognized its origin: it was used by Homer, *Odyssey* 9.346, for the Cyclops' drinking cup. Priscus delighted in such knowing literary games. His deliberate use of Homeric vocabulary recalled one of the powerful evocations of *nomades* in classical literature. It reminded readers of the stereotype that this description of Attila was intended to undercut. The virtues that well-educated Romans expected their emperors to exemplify included moderation, clemency, frugality, accessibility, self-control, and a willingness to uphold the rule of law; a tendency to tyranny (or barbarity) was indicated by telltale vices such as cruelty, self-indulgence, capriciousness, unpredictability, and excess; see Andrew Wallace-Hadrill, "The Emperor and His Virtues," *Historia* 30 (1981): 298–323, and Christopher Kelly, *CAH* 13: 145–50. One of the best guides to contemporary attitudes is the *Panegyrici Latini*, a collection of twelve speeches given before (always virtuous) emperors, often celebrating their victories over (always vicious) usurpers; for an excellent introduction and translation, see Ted Nixon and Barbara Rodgers, *In Praise of Later Roman Emperors: The Panegyrici Latini* (Berkeley, Calif., 1994). The vilification of Magnus Maximus is quoted from *Pan. Lat.* 2.25–28. For first-rate discussions of dining habits as an index of morality, see Justin Goddard, "The Tyrant at Table," in Jaś Elsner and Jamie Masters, eds., *Reflections of Nero: Culture, History and Representation* (London, 1994), 67–82, and Emily Gowers, *The Loaded Table: Representations of Food in Roman Literature* (Oxford, 1993), 1–49.

CHAPTER SEVENTEEN: TRUTH AND DARE

The narrative follows Priscus 14–15.2. Attila was right to single out Flavius Zeno as a potential threat to Theodosius; see above, chap. 21, p. 233, with Thompson, *Huns*, 133–34, and Zuckerman, "L'empire orient," 172–73.

CHAPTER EIGHTEEN: END GAME

The surviving text of Priscus jumps straight from Attila's instructions to Orestes and Eslas (15.2) to an account of Anatolius and Nomus' embassy (15.3–4). I have filled some of the gap with a passage from John of Antioch. The evidence for the close relationship between John and Priscus is set out in Blockley, *Fragmentary Classicising Historians*, 1: 114, and Umberto Roberto, *Ioannis Antiocheni Fragmenta ex Historia chronica* (Berlin, 2005), CXLIV–VI. Like Priscus' *History*, much of the surviving text of John is preserved in Constantine's *Excerpta* (see the important discussion in Treadgold, *Byzantine Historians*, 311–29). John's remarks on Theodosius and the baleful influence of Chrysaphius were included in the collection on virtues and vices (ed. Theodor Büttner-Wobst [Berlin, 1906], *Excerpta de Virtutibus et Vitiis* 72 = Priscus 3 = ed. Roberto, John of Antioch 291). Priscus does not indicate when he was able to interview Vigilas; but at 11.2 (quoted above, chap. 14, p. 172) he mentions that sometime later he and Maximinus learned the truth from Vigilas about the assassination plot. I have placed that meeting in Constantinople after Chrysaphius' execution when Vigilas might have felt it safe to return. Priscus mentions his further missions with Maximinus and his death at 20.3 and 27; the complex chronology of these events is discussed in Zuckerman, "L'empire orient," 176–79. Priscus' other works (none survive) are mentioned in the brief entry on the historian in the tenth-century encyclopaedia, the *Souda* ∏ 2301. Praise for Priscus' *History* is quoted from Evagrius, *Ecclesiastical History* 1.27 (ed. Joseph Bidez and Léon Parmentier [London, 1898]; trans. Michael Whitby [Liverpool, 2000]), and *Chron. Pasch.* 450.

CHAPTER NINETEEN: HEARTS AND MINDS

See Jordanes, *Getica* 184, for the cruel story of Theodoric's daughter and Geiseric's gifts to Attila; for the rebellion, Prosper 1348. For the dating of Huneric and Eudocia's engagement, see Frank Clover, "Flavius Merobaudes: A Translation and Historical Commentary," *Transactions of the American Philosophical Society* 61 (1971): 1–78, at 23–24; for its implications, Oost, *Galla Placidia*, 260–64. Jordanes, *Getica* 168, for his uncompromising assessment of Geiseric. Attila's honorary rank is noted by Priscus 11.2 (as part of his account of his conversation with the envoys from Valentinian and Aetius); see Martindale, *Prosopography*, 182–83. As Stickler, *Aëtius*, 110–14, advises, the "friendship" between Attila and Aetius should again be seen firmly within a diplomatic context. The Bagaudae have long been favorites of historians seeking to find evidence of class struggle in the ancient world, or at least the uprising of an exploited peasantry against the oppressions of imperial rule. The classic account is by Edward Thompson, "Peasant Revolts in Late Roman Gaul and Spain," *Past & Present* 2 (1952): 11–23 (= Moses Finley, ed., *Studies in Ancient Society* [London, 1974], 304–20). By contrast, recent studies have stressed the involvement of local landowners and the well educated. Eupraxius, the Bagaudae leader who sought asylum with Attila, was a doctor: *Chron. Gall. 452* 133. The best-argued response to Thompson is Raymond van Dam, *Leadership and Community in Late Antique Gaul* (Berkeley, Calif., 1985), 25–56. The role of displaced landowners is explored in John Drinkwater, "The Bacaudae of Fifth-Century Gaul," in Drinkwater and Elton, eds., *Fifth-Century Gaul*, 208–17. Priscus 11.2 reports his meeting with Romulus, the story of Constantius and the silver bowls, and Romulus' claims that Attila was thinking of a Persian expedition.

CHAPTER TWENTY: THE BRIDE OF ATTILA

The core of the narrative is preserved in a fragment of John of Antioch included in Constantine's collection of extracts on conspiracies and based on John's reading of Priscus (ed. Carl ed Boor [Berlin, 1905] *Excerpta de Insidiis* 84 = Priscus 17 = John of Antioch 292). Jordanes, *Getica* 224, briefly notes his disapproval of Honoria's passions. Marcellinus 434 dates Honoria's affair with Eugenius to that year and combines it with her appeal to Attila. John also combines both incidents, but places them in 449. I follow the arguments of Croke, *Marcellinus*, 80–81, for separating the two events and dating the liaison with Eugenius to 434. For an alternative reconstruction (disregarding Marcellinus), see Martindale, *Prosopography*, 416 and 568–69, Oost, *Galla Placidia*, 282–84, and J. B. Bury, "Justa Grata Honoria," *Journal of Roman Studies* 9 (1919): 1–13. Honoria's story is curtly dismissed by Maenchen-Helfen, *Huns*, 130, as having "all the earmarks of Byzantine court gossip." For the minimum legal age for marriage, see Susan Treggiari, *Roman Marriage: Iusti Coniuges from the Time of Cicero to the Time of Ulpian* (Oxford, 1991), 39–42. Galla's time in Constantinople in the mid-420s is discussed above, chap. 6, p. 81. The saintliness of Pulcheria and her sisters is described in Theophanes 5901 and Sozomen 9.3.1–2; their vow of virginity and Pulcheria's outstanding intellectual ability at 9.1.5; for the strict regime of holiness in the Great Palace, see Socrates 7.22.1–5 with Holum, *Theodosian Empresses*, 91–93 and 143–46. Jordanes, *Rom.* 328, records the confinement of Honoria in the sisters' palace in Constantinople; for its location near the Hebdomon, see Janin, *Constantinople byzantine*, 139–40, and Demangel, *L'Hebdomon*, 43–47. Only Marcellinus 434 reports that Honoria was pregnant. For Galla Placidia's piety, see Oost, *Galla Placidia*, 264–78; her encounter with Germanus is related in the saint's life written around 480 by Constantius of Lyon (*Vita Germani* 35; ed. René Borius [Paris, 1965]; trans. Frederick Hoare, *The Western Fathers* [London, 1954], 283–320). For Herculanus' consulship in 452, see Martindale, *Prosopography*, 544–45. The date of Honoria's death is unrecorded; Oost, *Galla Placidia*, 285, argues for sometime before 455.

CHAPTER TWENTY-ONE: TAKING SIDES

Priscus 20.1 recounts the diplomatic confrontation between Attila and Valentinian over Honoria. My understanding of the complex set of political alliances behind Marcian's sudden advancement follows Zuckerman, "L'empire orient," 169–76, in making Aspar and Zeno the prime movers, but acting in close concert with Pulcheria; see Holum, *Theodosian Empresses*, 206–9, and Jones, *Later Roman Empire*, 1: 218. Richard Burgess deprives Pulcheria of any leading role in determining the succession: "The Accession of Marcian in the Light of Chalcedonian Apologetic and Monophysite Polemic," *Byzantinische Zeitschrift* 86/87 (1993–94): 47–68, at 61–68. Aspar's claim of Theodosius' approval for Marcian is reported in John Malalas 14.27 and *Chron. Pasch.* 450. The emperor's planned military strike against Zeno is noted by John of Antioch 292 = Priscus 16 = *de Insidiis* 84. The unflattering description of Marcian is quoted from John Malalas 14.28. On his marriage and coronation, the brief notices in the chronicles disagree: *Chron. Pasch.* 450 (no detail), Theophanes 5942 (proclaimed by Pulcheria), John Malalas 14.28 (crowned by the Senate). Pulcheria's role in the coronation is strenuously defended by Wilhelm Ensslin, "Zur Frage nach der ersten Kaiserkrönung durch den Patriarchen und zur Bedeutung dieses Aktes im Wahlzeremoniell," *Byzantinische Zeitschrift* 42 (1943–49): 101–15, 369–72, and denied with equal vigor by Burgess, "The Accession," 65–67. The details of the ceremony are not known; I have followed the description of the coronation of Leo I seven years later, in February 457. These were included in Constantine Porphyrogenitus' handbook on imperial ceremonial (*de Ceremoniis* 410–12 [1.91], ed. Johann Reiske [Bonn, 1829]); see, too, the helpful discussion in MacCormack, *Art and Ceremony*, 242–45. Thompson, "Foreign Policy," 69–72, and *Huns*, 147–48, views Marcian's "blunt refusal of the tribute" as a "display of audacity" that "brought the East Romans to the edge of the abyss." By contrast, Robert Hohlfelder, "Marcian's Gamble: A Reassessment of Eastern Imperial Policy toward Attila AD 450–453," *American Journal of Ancient History* 9 (1984): 54–69, at 60, suggests that Marcian's response was an "opening move" in a more complex strategy. Hohlfelder's view is strengthened if Priscus can be assumed to be reflecting the precise diplomatic language central to the Roman agreement with the Huns. The three embassies sent by Attila to Valentinian in late 450/early 451 are reported in Priscus 20.3 (Honoria's signet ring), Jordanes, *Getica* 185 (disagreement with Theodoric), and *Chron. Pasch.* 450 (demand to prepare the palace). Jordanes, *Getica* 186, notes Attila's diplomatic skill. Valentinian's communiqué to Theodoric is quoted from Jordanes, *Getica* 187–88.

CHAPTER TWENTY-TWO: THE FOG OF WAR

The most helpful introductions to the complex web of miracle stories associated with the Hun invasion of France are Jean-Yves Marin, "La campagne des Gaules dans l'hagiographie," in *Attila, les influences danubiennes*, 135–39, and Émilienne Demougeot, "Attila et les Gaules," *Mémoires de la Société d'Agriculture, Commerce, Sciences et Arts du département de la Marne* 73 (1958): 7–42, at 25–34 (= *L'Empire romain et les barbares d'Occident (IVe–VIIe siècle): Scripta Varia*, 2nd ed. [Paris, 1988], 215–50, at 233–42). The accounts of Servatius of Tongeren and the destruction of Metz follow Gregory of Tours 1.5–6. Nicasius' defiant Bible reading is related by the tenth-century historian Flodoard of Reims in his *History of the Church at Reims (Historia Remensis Ecclesiae* 1.6, ed. Johann Heller and Georg Waitz, *Monumenta Germaniae Historica, Scriptores*, vol. 13 [Hannover, 1881], 405–599). By contrast with this much later account, the *Life of St. Geneviève* probably dates back to the early sixth century; see Martin Heinzelmann and Joseph-Claude Poulin, *Les vies anciennes de sainte Geneviève de Paris: Études critiques* (Paris, 1986). The story of Geneviève's rallying the people of Paris is from *Vita Genovesae* 12 (ed. Bruno Krusch, *Monumenta Germaniae Historica, Scriptores rerum Merovingicarum*, vol. 3 [Hannover, 1896], 204–38). The tradition of Lupus' confrontation with Attila (and the phrase *flagellum dei*) is by far the latest of all these miracle stories: it is part of the *Life of Germanus of Auxerre* as told in the thirteenth-century *Legenda Aurea* by Jacobus de Voragine, one of the most popular books in the Middle Ages. An English translation was published by William Caxton in 1483; for a modern version, see William Ryan, *Jacobus de Voragine, The Golden Legend: Readings on the Saints*, 2 vols. (Princeton, 1993) with the *Life of Germanus*, at 2: 27–30. Isidore of Seville's understanding of the Huns' role as agents of God's anger is set out in his *History of the Goths, Vandals, and Sueves (Historia Gothorum Wandalorum Sueborum* 29, ed. Theodor Mommsen, *Monumenta Germaniae Historica, Auctores Antiquissimi*, vol. 11 [Berlin, 1894], 241–303; trans. Guido Donini and Gordon Ford, 2nd ed. [Leiden, 1970]). The biblical reference is to the *flagellum iundans* (the "overwhelming whip") of Isaiah 28.15 and 18. For the contrasting versions of the Hun attack on Orléans, see Jordanes, *Getica* 194–95, and Gregory of Tours 1.7. Aside from brief notices in the chronicles, the only detailed account of the clash on the Catalaunian Plains is Jordanes, *Getica* 197–218 (with praise of the Gothic brothers at 199–200, Attila's speech at 202–6, and Aetius' advice to Thorismud at 215–17). Ulf Täckholm,

"Aetius and the Battle on the Catalaunian Fields," *Opuscula Romana* 7 (1969): 259–76, offers a meticulous reconstruction of events. The substantial local literature and speculation on the precise location of the battlefield on the Catalaunian Plains is sympathetically reviewed by Demougeot, "Attila et les Gaules," 34–37, and summarily rejected by Maenchen-Helfen, *Huns* 131. Suspicions of Aetius' motives are insinuated by Jordanes, *Getica* 216–17, and less subtly elaborated by medieval writers such as Fredegar, *Chronicle* 2.53 (ed. Bruno Krusch, *Monumenta Germaniae Historica, Scriptores rerum Merovingicarum*, vol. 2 [Hannover, 1888], 1–168). A distrust of Aetius still lies behind many modern accounts. Recent reassessments are more sympathetic; for example, Stickler, *Aëtius*, 143–44; Täckholm, "Aetius and the Battle," 268–71; Williams and Friell, *The Rome That Did Not Fall*, 87–88; Heather, *Fall*, 339; and particularly Zecchini, *Aezio*, 273, suggesting that it was Thorismud's decision to leave for Toulouse that compromised the safety of Aetius' remaining troops. Thorismud's assassination in 453 is reported in Jordanes, *Getica* 228, Hydatius 148, and Prosper 1371.

CHAPTER TWENTY-THREE: THE LAST RETREAT

Apollonius' adventures across the Danube are recounted in Priscus 23.3. Marcian's three letters to the bishops at Nicaea were included in the official record of the Council of Chalcedon, ed. Eduard Schwartz, *Acta Consiliorum Oecumenicorum* II.3 (Berlin, 1935), 20–21 (*Letter* 32), and II.1 (Berlin, 1933), 28–30 (*Letters* 14 and 16), translated with an excellent introduction by Richard Price and Michael Gaddis, 3 vols. (Liverpool, 2007), 1: 107–10, nos. 12, 14, and 15. Jordanes' assessment of Attila's tactics is at *Getica* 225; Attila's fury at his defeat in France is reported in *Chron. Gall. 452* 141. The Christian community in Aquileia is thoughtfully illuminated in a superb study by Claire Sotinel, *Identité civique et christianisme: Aquilée du IIIe au VIe siècle* (Rome, 2005). Giovanni Brusin and Paolo Zovatto, *Monumenti paleocristiani di Aquileia e di Grado* (Udine, 1957), 20–140, offer a fascinating and detailed description of the mosaics in the basilica. The siege of Aquileia and the flight of the stork is reported in Jordanes, *Getica* 219–21, and Procopius, *Vandal Wars* 3.4.30–35; the story may derive from Priscus; see Blockley, *Fragmentary Classicising Historians*, 1: 115. The fortified landscape threatened by the Huns is surveyed by Neil Christie, "From the Danube to the Po: The Defence of Pannonia and Italy in the Fourth and Fifth Centuries AD," in Poulter, ed., *The Transition to Late Antiquity*, 547–78. For the short sermon associated with Maximinus of Turin, see *Patrologia*

Latina 57: 469–72, and Maenchen-Helfen, *Huns*, 138–39. Little remains of fourth- and fifth-century Milan apart from its churches; the best introduction is Krautheimer, *Three Christian Capitals*, 68–92. The few, uninspiring archaeological traces of what may be the imperial palace are surveyed in the exhibition catalogue *Milano capitale dell'impero romano, 286–402 d.C.* (Milan, 1990), 99–100 and 201. The immense, and at times frustratingly idiosyncratic, editorial project that resulted in the *Souda* is outlined in Lemerle, *Le premier humanisme*, 297–300. The entry on Milan is at M 405; its possible connection with Priscus' account is explored by Blockley, *Fragmentary Classicising Historians*, 1: 118. The Barbarini Ivory is described in detail in Richard Delbrueck, *Die Consulardiptychen und verwandte Denkmäler*, 2 vols. (Berlin, 1929), 1: 188–96, no. 48, and usefully discussed in MacCormack, *Art and Ceremony*, 71–72. The meeting between Leo and Attila is piously reported in Prosper 1367; the saintly detail of the old man appears in the *Roman History* of the eighth-century monk Paul the Deacon (*Historia Romana* 14.12, ed. Amedeo Crivellucci [Rome, 1914]). Raphael's *L'incontro di Leone Magno e Attila* is one of the frescoes in the Stanza di Eliodoro originally commissioned by Pope Julius II, but completed—with suitable alterations in the design—under his successor Leo X. Raphael's shrewd diplomatic and artistic maneuvering between these two powerful patrons is explored in Jörg Traeger, "Die Begegnung Leos des Grossen mit Attila: Planungsphasen und Bedeutungsgenese," in Christoph Frommel and Matthias Winne, eds., *Raffaello a Roma: Il convegno del 1983* (Rome, 1986), 97–116. For the plague in Italy, see Hydatius 146 with Maenchen-Helfen, *Huns*, 139–40. Marcian's military activity across the Danube is mentioned in a confused notice in Hydatius 146 explained by Zecchini, *Aezio*, 277 n. 65, and Richard Burgess, "A New Reading for Hydatius *Chronicle* 177 and the Defeat of the Huns in Italy," *Phoenix* 42 (1988): 357–63, at 360–62. Attila's threatening embassy to Marcian in 452 is reported in Jordanes, *Getica* 225. For Attila's death, *Getica* 254 (information Jordanes explicitly notes is derived from Priscus), Theophanes 5946 (an accident), Marcellinus 454.1 (Ildico or an accident), and Malalas 14.10 (accident or Ildico or the result of Aetius' bribery). For Marcian's angelic visitation, see Jordanes, *Getica* 255, again explicitly attributed to Priscus.

CHAPTER TWENTY-FOUR: ENDINGS

The most important discussions of the collapse of the Hun empire are Thompson, *Huns*, 167–75, and Maenchen-Helfen, *Huns*, 144–68. Jordanes,

Getica 259–63, briefly comments on the rivalry between the sons of Attila and the Battle of the River Nedao; the subsequent clashes between the Huns and the Goths are noted at 268–69 and 272–73. The consolidation of Gothic control over Pannonia under Valamer, Thuidimer, and Vidimer is explored by Heather, *Goths and Romans*, 242–46, and Wolfram, *Goths*, 258–68. Heather (251–63) also discusses the settlement of Goths in Thrace. Priscus 46 reports Leo's response to Dengizich and Ernac's embassy and at 48.1 Dengizich's demands the following year. For Dengizich's defeat and decapitation, see Marcellinus 468 and *Chron. Pasch.* 468. For the identification of the Xylokerkos, see Janin, *Constantinople Byzantine*, 274 and 440–41, and Dagron, *Naissance d'une capitale*, 305. By far the best discussion of the movement of the Goths, conventionally known as the Ostrogoths or "eastern Goths," into the eastern empire in the 470s and their consolidation under Theodoric is Heather, *Goths and Romans*, 264–308, condensed in *Goths*, 154–65 and 216–18. The assassination of Aetius in September 454 is reported in John of Antioch 293.1 = *de Insidiis* 85 = Priscus 30.1, Hydatius 152, Prosper 1373, Marcellinus 454.2, and Theophanes 5946. The courtier's acid quip (surely never said to Valentinian's face) is quoted in Procopius, *Vandal Wars* 3.4.28. For the Vandal sack of Rome, see Procopius, *Vandal Wars* 3.5.1–6, Prosper 1375 (emphasizing Leo's role), and Theophanes 5947 (the treasures from Jerusalem). For excellent studies of the transition from imperial to local rule in France, see Wolfram, *Goths*, 181–246; Jill Harries, *Sidonius Apollinaris and the Fall of Rome, AD 407–485* (Oxford, 1994); Ian Wood, *The Merovingian Kingdoms, 450–751* (London, 1994) and *CAH* 14: 506–24; and Edward James, *The Franks* (Oxford, 1988). The best account of the Vandal kingdom in North Africa remains Courtois, *Les Vandales*, pts. 2 and 3, and see, too, Averil Cameron, *CAH* 14: 553–59. For the failed expeditions against Geiseric, see Hydatius 195, Procopius, *Vandal Wars* 3.6, and Theophanes 5961 = Priscus 53. The collapse of imperial rule in Italy and the rise of Theodoric is thoughtfully discussed in Stein, *Bas-Empire*, 365–99; Heather, "The Huns and the End of the Roman Empire," 29–41, and *CAH* 14: 18–30; O'Flynn, *Generalissimos*, 104–49; Penny MacGeorge, *Late Roman Warlords* (Oxford, 2002), 165–293; Mark Humphries, *CAH* 14: 525–51; John Moorhead, *Theodoric in Italy*, (Oxford, 1992); and Patrick Amory, *People and Identity in Ostrogothic Italy, 489–554* (Cambridge, 1997). Theodoric's comment after murdering Odoacer is reported in John of Antioch 307 = *de Insidiis* 99. See Sidonius, *Letters* 1.2, for his description of a day in the courtly life of Theodoric II, with Marc Reydellet, *La royauté dans la littérature latine de Sidoine Apollinaire à Isidore de Séville* (Rome, 1981),

69–80, and Harries, *Sidonius*, 127–29, for the date. In Ravenna, Theodoric (the Ostrogoth) was praised by the aristocrat and bishop Ennodius around 507 (*Panegyric* 88, ed. with an Italian translation by Simona Rota [Rome, 2002]); see MacCormack, *Art and Ceremony*, 229–35, and Reydellet, *La royauté*, 164–82. For Theodoric's Roman-ness and local aristocratic responses, see Moorhead, *Theodoric*, 39–51, and Sam Barnish, "Transformation and Survival in the Western Senatorial Aristocracy, *c.* A.D. 400–700," *Papers of the British School at Rome* 56 (1988): 120–55. More generally, Julia Smith, *Europe after Rome, 500–1000: A New Cultural History* (Oxford, 2005), and Peter Brown, *The Rise of Western Christendom: Triumph and Diversity, A.D. 200–1000*, 2nd ed. (Oxford, 2003), both offer brilliant and humane expositions of the cultural and religious transformation of classical antiquity in the formation of medieval Europe. For a broad perspective on the complexities of this transition, see the sophisticated and wide-ranging discussion in Chris Wickham, *Framing the Middle Ages: Europe and the Mediterranean, 400–800* (Oxford, 2005). For a superb introduction to Byzantium, see Averil Cameron, *The Byzantines* (Oxford, 2006).

EPILOGUE: REPUTATIONS

For useful guides to the afterlife of Attila, see Franz Bäuml and Marianna Birnbaum, *Attila: The Man and His Image* (Budapest, 1993); *Attila, les influences danubiennes*, 143–201; and Herbert Pahl, "Attila und die Hunnen im Spiegel von Kunst und Literatur," in *Attila und die Hunnen*, 368–73. The circumstances of Wilhelm II's speech are usefully set out in Robert Massie, *Dreadnought: Britain, Germany and the Coming of the Great War* (London, 1991), 282–83; Thomas Kohut, *Wilhelm II and the Germans: A Study in Leadership* (Oxford, 1991), 143–48; and the detailed study by Bernd Sösemann, "Die sog. Hunnenrede Wilhelms II: Textkritische und interpretatorische Bemerkungen zur Ansprache des Kaisers vom 27. Juli 1900 in Bremerhaven," *Historische Zeitschrift* 222 (1976): 342–58 (with the full text of the speech at 349–50). The transformation of Attila into good king Etzel is thoughtfully discussed in Jennifer Williams, *Etzel der rîche* (Berne, 1981), 177–98; Ursula Schulze, "Der weinende König und sein Verschwinden im Dunkel des Vergessens: König Etzel im Nibelungenlied und in der Klage," in *Attila und die Hunnen*, 336–45, and Teresa Pàroli, "Attila nelle letterature germaniche antiche," in *Popoli delle Steppe*, 2: 559–619, at 600–13. The fight in King Etzel's hall is told in *Nibelungenlied* Aventiure 33 (ed. Ursula Schulze [Düsseldorf, 2005]; trans. Arthur Hatto, rev. ed. [London,

1969]; and into modern verse, Burton Raffel [New Haven, 2006]). Edward Gibbon's matchless account of Attila and the Huns occupies most of chapters 34–35 of *The History of the Decline and Fall of the Roman Empire*, vol. 3, (London, 1781). Thomas Hodgkin's version—freighted with Victorian morality—in *Italy and Her Invaders,* vol. 2, *The Hunnish and Vandal Invasion* (Oxford, 1880; reprint, London, 1996), bk. 1, chap. 1–4 (comparison of Attila with Napoleon at 180–81; the dangers faced by twentieth-century democracy at 612–13). Matthias Corvinus' re-presentation of Attila as a Hungarian nation builder is explored in Marianna Birnbaum, "Attila's Renaissance in the Fifteenth and Sixteenth Centuries," in *Attila: The Man and His Image,* 99–105, and *The Orb and the Pen: Janus Pannonius, Matthias Corvinus and the Buda Court* (Budapest, 1996), 121–29. Corvinus' new image was (unsurprisingly) easily turned against him by his Italian critics; see Birnbaum, "Attila's Renaissance," 84–86, and the fascinating discussion by Lajos Elekes, "La politica estera di re Mattia e gli Stati italiani nella seconda metà del secolo XV," in Tibor Klaniczay, ed., *Rapporti veneto-ungheresi all'epoca del Rinascimento* (Budapest, 1975), 243–55. *Sign of the Pagan* was directed by Douglas Sirk for Universal Pictures. According to the film's studio publicity, "Against the ravaging hordes of Attila stood a warrior's might and a people's faith. Against his ruthless pagan lusts the power of a woman's love." In this epic revision of Roman history, the mighty warrior is the future emperor Marcian (Jeff Chandler), and his bride (the ballerina Ludmilla Tchérina) is Pulcheria. This is—of course—a passionate love match, and once Attila is defeated, the couple go on to rescue the West from a feckless Valentinian and reunite the Roman empire.

ANCIENT TEXTS

I have included editions of ancient texts. I hope this helps to resolve any confusion in the numbering of sections/paragraphs that sometimes, and tediously, varies between modern editions and translations.

AMMIANUS MARCELLINUS
Ammianus Marcellinus, the most important Latin historian of the fourth century; the surviving part of his *Res Gestae* deals with the period 353–78; ed. Wolfgang Seyfarth (Leipzig, 1978); trans. John Rolfe, Loeb Classical Library, 3 vols. (Cambridge, Mass., 1935–39); Walter Hamilton, Penguin Classics (Harmondsworth, 1986).

CHRON. GALL. 452
Chronica Gallica ad annum CCCCLII = *The Gallic Chronicle of 452*; an anonymous Latin chronicle written in France around the year 452; ed. Theodor Mommsen, *Monumenta Germaniae Historica, Auctores Antiquissimi* vol. 9 (Berlin, 1892), 646–62; Richard Burgess, "The Gallic Chronicle of 452: A New Critical Edition with a Brief Introduction," in Ralph Mathisen and Danuta Shanzer, eds., *Society and Culture in Late Antique Gaul: Revisiting the Sources* (Aldershot, 2001), 52–84; trans. Alexander Murray, *From Roman to Merovingian Gaul: A Reader* (Peterborough, Ont., 2000), 76–85.

CHRON. PASCH.
Chronicon Paschale = *Easter Chronicle*; an anonymous Greek chronicle written in Constantinople in the early seventh century; ed. Ludwig Dindorf (Bonn, 1832); trans. Michael and Mary Whitby (Liverpool, 1989).

EUSEBIUS
Bishop of Caesarea, contemporary and self-appointed biographer of the emperor Constantine. *Life of Constantine,* ed. Friedhelm Winkelmann, 2nd ed. (Berlin, 1991); trans. Averil Cameron and Stuart Hall (Oxford, 1999).

GREGORY OF TOURS
Sixth-century historian, bishop, and saint; *History of the Franks,* ed. Bruno Krusch and Wilhelm Levison, *Monumenta Germaniae Historica, Scriptores rerum Merovingicarum,* vol. 1, 2nd ed. (Hannover, 1951); trans. Ormonde Dalton (Oxford, 1927) and Lewis Thorpe, Penguin Classics (Harmondsworth, 1974).

HYDATIUS
Spanish bishop, his *Chronicle* completed around 470 concentrates on events in France and Spain; ed. and trans. Richard Burgess (Oxford, 1993); trans. Murray, *Roman to Merovingian Gaul,* 85–98.

JORDANES
Getica = *de origine actibusque Getarum* = *The Origins and Deeds of the Goths*; written around 550 in Constantinople. The most important early history of the Goths; ed. Theodor Mommsen, *Monumenta Germaniae Historica, Auctores Antiquissimi,* vol. 5 (Berlin, 1882), 53–200; trans. Charles Mierow, 2nd ed. (Princeton, 1915).

Rom. = *Romana* = *de origine actibusque gentis Romanorum* = *The Origins and Deeds of the Roman People*; a brief summary of all of Roman history; ed. Theodor Mommsen, *Monumenta Germaniae Historica, Auctores Antiquissimi,* vol. 5, (Berlin, 1882), 1–52.

MALALAS
John Malalas, an imperial bureaucrat from Antioch, in Syria, completed his *General History* around 565; a world history in 18 books, the last five of which concentrate on the East after Constantine; ed. Hans Thurn (Berlin, 2000); trans. Elizabeth and Michael Jeffreys and Roger Scott (Melbourne, 1986).

MARCELLINUS
Count Marcellinus (no relation of Ammianus), an army officer from the Balkans who wrote his *Chronicle* in Latin covering the period 379–534 for readers in the East; ed. Theodor Mommsen, *Monumenta Germaniae Historica, Auctores Antiquissimi,* vol. 11 (Berlin, 1894), 37–108; trans. Brian Croke (Sydney, 1995).

OLYMPIODORUS

Early fifth-century historian, diplomat, and bird fancier; part of his *History* survives in the summary by the ninth-century bibliophile Photius; ed. and trans. Roger Blockley, *The Fragmentary Classicising Historians of the Later Roman Empire*, 2 vols. (Leeds, 1981–83), 2: 151–220.

PHILOSTORGIUS

Church historian, writing in the early fifth century and, unlike Socrates, Sozomen, and Theodoret, from a heretical viewpoint. As a result, his work survives only in fragments. *Ecclesiastical History*, ed. Joseph Bidez and Friedhelm Winkelmann, 3rd ed. (Berlin, 1981); trans. Philip Amidon (Atlanta, 2007).

PRISCUS

Most important historian of Attila and the Huns; ed. and trans. Roger Blockley, *The Fragmentary Classicising Historians of the Later Roman Empire*, 2 vols. (Leeds, 1981–83), 11: 221–400.

PROCOPIUS

Most important Greek historian of the sixth century, especially of the emperor Justinian. *The Wars*, Books 1 and 2 = *The Persian Wars*; *The Wars*, Books 3 and 4 = *The Vandal Wars*; ed. Jakob Haury (Leipzig, 1962); trans. Henry Dewing, Loeb Classical Library (Cambridge, Mass., 1914–16).

PROSPER

Prosper of Aquitaine, a French monk at the papal court in Rome; his *Chronicle* runs from 379 to 455; ed. Theodor Mommsen, *Monumenta Germaniae Historica, Auctores Antiquissimi*, vol. 9 (Berlin, 1892), 341–499; trans. Murray, *Roman to Merovingian Gaul*, 62–76.

SIDONIUS

Sidonius Apollinaris, fifth-century French aristocrat, poet, politician, and bishop; his *Letters* ed. and trans. William Anderson, Loeb Classical Library (Cambridge, Mass., 1936–65).

SOCRATES

Church historian, lived in Constantinople 380–440. *Ecclesiastical History*, ed. Günther Hansen (Berlin, 1995); trans. Andrew Zenos, *A Select Library of Nicene and Post-Nicene Fathers of the Christian Church*, 2nd ser., vol. 2 (Oxford, 1891).

SOZOMEN

Church historian, lawyer in Constantinople in the fifth century. *Ecclesiastical History*, ed. Joseph Bidez, 2nd ed. (Berlin, 1995); trans. Chester Hartranft, *A Select Library of Nicene and Post-Nicene Fathers of the Christian Church*, 2nd ser., vol. 2 (Oxford, 1891).

THEMISTIUS

Fourth-century court orator. *Orations*, ed. Heinrich Schenkl, Glanville Downey, and Albert Norman, 3 vols. (Leipzig, 1965–74); trans. Peter Heather and John Matthews, *The Goths in the Fourth Century* (Liverpool, 1991) (*Orations* 8 and 10), Peter Heather and David Moncur (Liverpool, 2001) (*Orations* 1, 3, 5, 6, 14–17, 34).

THEODORET

Church historian, bishop of Cyrrhus, in Syria, in the fifth century. *Ecclesiastical History*, ed. Léon Parmentier and Günther Hansen, 3rd ed. (Berlin, 1998); trans. Blomfield Jackson, *A Select Library of Nicene and Post-Nicene Fathers of the Christian Church*, 2nd ser., vol. 3 (Oxford, 1892).

THEODOSIAN CODE

Collection of imperial laws compiled and edited on the orders of Theodosius II; contains 2,500 imperial rulings issued since 312, ordered by topic; ed. Theodor Mommsen, Paul Krüger, and Paul Meyer (Berlin, 1904); trans. Clyde Pharr (Princeton, 1952).

THEOPHANES

Theophanes the Confessor, monk from a wealthy family; *Chronicle* written in the early ninth century covering the period 284–813; ed. Carl de Boor (Leipzig, 1883); trans. Cyril Mango and Roger Scott (Oxford, 1997).

ZOSIMUS

New History written in Greek at turn of the fifth century; valuable perspective on contemporary events from an ardent anti-Christian; ed. François Paschoud (Paris, 1971–89); trans. Ronald Ridley (Sydney, 1984).

CHRONOLOGY, AD 375–455

364–78	**Valens** (eastern Roman emperor)
375–83	**Gratian** (western Roman emperor)
375	Huns attack Athanaric's Goths west of Black Sea
376	Tervingi under Fritigern cross Danube
378	Battle of Adrianople (9 August); attacks on city of Adrianople and Constantinople
379–95	**Theodosius I** (eastern Roman emperor, and from 392 of a reunited empire)
382	Goths and Hun allies settled south of Danube
386	failed crossing of Danube by Greuthungi under Odotheus
388	Theodosius defeats western usurper Magnus Maximus
394	Theodosius defeats western usurper Eugenius at Battle of the River Frigidus
395–423	**Honorius** (western Roman emperor)
395–408	**Arcadius** (eastern Roman emperor)
395	Goths under Alaric rebel
398	Huns in Armenia defeated by Eutropius
399–420	Yazdgard I (King of Persia)
401	Arcadius' alliance with Uldin; Alaric's Goths move west and attempt to enter Italy
406	Radagaisus' Goths defeated by Stilicho and Hun mercenaries under Uldin; Vandals and Alans cross Rhine (December)
407–11	Constantine III, usurper in France
408	arrest and execution of Stilicho; Uldin's attack across the Danube; Alaric's Goths invade Italy
408–50	**Theodosius II** (eastern Roman emperor)

409	Honorius levies 10,000 Hun mercenaries; Aetius sent as hostage
410	Alaric's Goths sack Rome (24 August)
412	construction of Theodosian Walls in Constantinople
413	Olympiodorus' embassy to Charaton and Donatus
418	Goths settled by Constantius in southwestern France
418–51	Theodoric rules Goths in France
420	Abdaas burns Zoroastrian temple in Khuzistan
421	**Constantius** (western Roman co-emperor with Honorius)
421–22	Theodosius' failed crusade in Mesopotamia
422	Hun attack on Thrace
423	Galla Placidia flees to Constantinople with her children
425	western usurper John defeated in Ravenna; Hun army under Aetius arrives too late
425–55	**Valentinian III** (western Roman emperor)
427	alleged conspiracy of Boniface
429	Vandal invasion of North Africa
430	death of Octar on campaign against Burgundians
432	Boniface promoted and made patrician; killed by Aetius at Ariminum
433	Aetius claims a Hun army is marching on Italy
434	Hun attack on Thrace and sudden death of Rua; Honoria sent to Constantinople in disgrace
434–40	Attila and Bleda joint rulers of Huns
435	treaty with Geiseric and Vandals in North Africa; agreement between Aetius and Huns; surrender of parts of Pannonia and Valeria
437	Huns and Romans wipe out Burgundians and suppress Bagaudae
439	Romans and Huns defeated by Goths at Toulouse; at Margum, Attila agrees to a treaty with the eastern empire; Geiseric takes Carthage (19 October)
441	Roman expeditionary force sails to Sicily; Attila and Bleda open Balkan offensive
442	expeditionary force recalled; Huns withdraw; new treaty with Geiseric, who returns Theodoric's mutilated daughter to Toulouse; engagement of Huneric and Eudocia
445	Bleda murdered
445–53	Attila sole ruler of Huns

446   Hun ambassadors in Constantinople demand enforcement of the treaty agreed to at Margum

447   earthquake in Constantinople (26 January); Theodosian Walls rebuilt by Constantinus; Attila's major and most destructive Balkan offensive; narrow defeat of Arnegisclus at Utus River; peace negotiated by Anatolius and Nomus

448   Aetius suppresses Bagaudae in France

449   Priscus, Maximinus, and Romulus (western ambassador) at the court of Attila

450   further negotiations by Anatolius and Nomus; appeal of Honoria to Attila; death of Theodosius (28 July); death of Galla Placidia (November)

450–57   **Marcian** (eastern Roman emperor)

451   Attila's offensive in France, ends with Battle of the Catalaunian Plains (June); Apollonius' failed embassy; Marcian commands troops in the Balkans (September); Priscus and Maximinus travel from Constantinople to Alexandria

451–53   Thorismud rules Goths in France

452   Attila's offensive in Italy; Marcian leads only Roman attack across Danube; death of Maximinus in Egypt

453   death and *strava* of Attila

453–66   Theodoric II rules Goths in France

454   defeat of Huns at the Battle of the River Nedao; murder of Aetius in Rome

455   murder of Valentinian; murder of Petronius Maximus; Vandals sack Rome (June)

ILLUSTRATION ACKNOWLEDGMENTS

1. Kunsthistorisches Museum, Vienna.
2. Kunsthistorisches Museum, Vienna.
3. Author's collection.
4. Hungarian National Museum, Budapest.
5. From M. A. Dévlet, *Sovetskaia Arkeologiia* 3 (1965), 129, fig. 5. Reproduced by kind permission of the Syndics of Cambridge University Library.
6. Département des Monnaies, Médailles et Antiques, Bibliothèque Nationale de France, Paris.
7. Galleria Nazionale d'Arte Moderna, Rome / akg-images.
8. Hungarian National Museum, Budapest.
9. Xantos János Museum, Györ, Hungary / Tanai Csaba Taca.
10. The Art Archive / Musée du Louvre / Gianni Dagli Orti.
11. Chris Hellier / Corbis.
12. Département des Monnaies, Médailles et Antiques, Bibliothèque Nationale de France, Paris / The Art Archive / Jan Vinchon Numismatist, Paris / Gianni Dagli Orti.
13. Département des Monnaies, Médailles et Antiques, Bibliothèque Nationale de France, Paris / Bridgeman Art Library.
14. National Museum of Romanian History, Bucharest.
15. National Museum of Romanian History, Bucharest.
16. National Museum of Romanian History, Bucharest.
17. Hungarian National Gallery, Budapest.
18. Xantos János Museum, Györ, Hungary / Tanai Csaba Taca.
19. Nicolas M. Salgo Collection, USA / Bridgeman Art Library.
20. Author's collection.
21. Author's collection.
22. Kunsthistorisches Museum, Vienna.

23. Hungarian National Gallery, Budapest.

24. Hungarian National Museum, Budapest.

25. Real Academia de la Historia, Madrid / Werner Forman / Corbis.

26. Glenn Woods.

27. Hunterian Museum and Art Gallery, Glasgow.

28. AISA.

29. Treasury, Troyes Cathedral / Photo Monsallier, Troyes.

30. akg-images / Cameraphoto.

31. Musée du Louvre / Giraudon / Bridgeman Art Library.

32. Vatican Museum and Galleries, Vatican City / Bridgeman Art Library.

33. akg-images.

34. Tiroler Landesmuseum Ferdinandeum, Innsbruck / akg-images.

35. Richard Soden Smith, *The Treasure of Petrossa*, London, 1869, plate 8. Reproduced by kind permission of the Syndics of Cambridge University Library.

INDEX

Page numbers in *italics* refer to illustrations.